D1610890

# A Trenchard 'Brat'

# A Trenchard 'Brat'

F. A. B. Tams

Roy + Aud
Kind regards + best wishes
Frank Tams

The Pentland Press Limited
Edinburgh • Cambridge • Durham • USA

First published in 2000 by
The Pentland Press Ltd.
1 Hutton Close
South Church
Bishop Auckland
Durham



British Library Cataloguing in Publication Data.
A Catalogue record for this book is available
from the British Library.

ISBN 1 85821 747 4

Typeset by CBS, Martlesham Heath, Ipswich, Suffolk
Printed and bound by Bookcraft (Bath) Ltd.

*Contents*

## *List of Illustrations*

# *Acknowledgements*

My gratitude to Stewart Andrews, not only for persuading me to write these memoirs but in ensuring that I did by lending me a tape recorder and supplying the necessary tapes. He took me flying in his Piper Navajo and later let me fly it. In his crew room later his chief pilot and some of his pilots asked me about my career and Stewart then said, 'You have a story to tell.' I would also like to thank the air historian Roy Nesbit for his advice and help in putting me in touch with the Photographic Department of the MoD from whom I obtained photographs of some of the aircraft shown and for putting me in touch with the French Resistance section who witnessed our raid and discovered the crashed Beauforts and the graves of the crews. My thanks go to J. Illias for providing the information and to Mrs Sylvie Richardson for translating the letters. Reference has been made to *My Secret Journal* by Squadron Leader B. Arct and *Wire Bound World* by H.P. Clarke. I am also grateful to Mrs Judy Lusty for the loan of a computer on which I have spent many hours recording and altering this project; to Eric Weir for his technical assistance in scanning the original before the editing of the document; and my great nephew Stephen Fisher for his assistance in producing Adobe copies of the photographs and help generally. Last but by no means least, my thanks to my son Jonathan for his comments, proof reading and many hours devoted to correcting the typed script and to my daughter Jacci Singer for her unswerving support.

## *Foreword*

Throughout its eighty year history, the Royal Air Force has relied very heavily on engineers and others who joined the Service as boys. Most of these boys were trained as Aircraft Apprentices at the technical schools of Halton and Cranwell. Frank Tams was one such entrant, but like many others of his pre-war vintage he went on to gain his pilot's 'wings', and fly on active service.

His book tells of his early days as a garrison 'brat' in Ireland and in India, before describing his time at Halton as an Apprentice and later on operational RAF stations as an aircraft fitter. After his flying training, he flew on operations over France in aircraft such as the Anson and the Beaufort, neither of them in the least suitable for the missions they were expected to undertake. Losses were heavy, and Frank was lucky to survive being shot down over Brest in early 1941. He spent the rest of the war as a POW, but returned to duty in 1945 and served on at home and abroad, notably in Malaya during the Emergency there, until his retirement in 1959.

The whole book is a tribute to a generation that accepted hardship in peace and war in a way that today would be beyond the imagination of many people. Frank Tams's account of those times, their trials and tribulations, their humour and the dedication of those who served, forms a most worthy record.

Air Chief Marshal Sir Michael Armitage KCB CBE RAF (Rtd)
(A Halton Apprentice from 1947 to 1950)

# *INTRODUCTION*

It was due in the main to the persistence of Hugh Trenchard that, in 1918, a separate air service received the Royal Assent and on 1 April the Royal Air Force was born. Air Marshal Trenchard became Chief of the Air Staff and set about the enormous task necessary to form the new Service. First and foremost was the need to form a technical arm: to this end he set up schools to accept youths of ages between fifteen and a half and sixteen and a half to be trained for three years under rigid discipline and high class instruction in both technical and academic spheres.

The generosity of the Rothschild family had made their Estate available to the Services as early as 1913. The school of Technical Training, started at Cranwell, was moved to Halton, as originally planned, on the completion of the special barrack blocks required to accommodate three thousand apprentices. The Trenchard Scheme really came into being when No. 1 School for Technical Training, comprising three wings at Halton, started.

Lord Trenchard, as he now was, aimed at producing the finest technical service in the world from the young men trained at Halton. Over thirty five thousand apprentices were trained, producing one Chief of the Air Staff, eighty officers of Air Rank and many officers of senior rank both in the Technical and in the General Duties (Flying) Branches. It was Lord Trenchard's wish that an ex 'Brat' would become Chief of the Air Staff and this was fulfilled when Marshal of the Royal Air Force Sir Keith Williamson, one of the early apprentices, achieved this distinction. Two others should be mentioned: Air Chief Marshal Sir Michael Armitage who is the Chairman of the Halton Aircraft Apprentices Association which, based at Halton, keeps the ex 'Brat' tradition alive; and Air Commodore Sir Frank Whittle, the inventor of the jet engine, who was an apprentice 1924–1927 and a Cranwell Cadet 1927–1928, proving, if proof were necessary, that the training designed by Lord Trenchard was justified and his desire to produce the best technical exponents vindicated. On leaving the service many have become prominent in civilian life.

To provide officers for the new Service a college at Cranwell, in Lincolnshire, was established. Entry was by examination and selection; Trenchard intended to provide the right type of commissioned personnel to command the NCOs and airmen of this highly trained technical Service. Entry was normally from the public schools. Two or three outstanding aircraft apprentices from each Entry were selected for cadetships at Cranwell and as an indication of the high standards of the apprentice scheme the Sword of Honour was won on a number of occasions by an ex apprentice.

The many administrative requirements of the new Service required training in this sphere and a school to fulfil this demand was set up at Ruislip to train apprentice clerks. Youths of similar ages to the Aircraft Apprentices were trained for a period of two years under the same rigid discipline as the Halton apprentices. Like the aircraft apprentices many became Sergeant Pilots; some were later commissioned and served with distinction.

The step taken by Lord Trenchard in forming a separate air arm under the control of its own senior officers was to prove a major factor in reducing the cost of controlling tribes in isolated areas such as Mesopotamia, Somalia and the North West frontier of India simply by dropping leaflets ordering them to behave or their village would receive punishment. If this had no effect a further leaflet would be dropped advising them to evacuate their village as aircraft were about to attack. In most cases it worked, saving large numbers of troops from being deployed, possibly involving casualties and certainly much hardship. These were the days of recalcitrant tribesmen and the methods are possibly not applicable today, but the advantages of the use of air power were at least demonstrated.

The value of air power under separate control was proved beyond all doubt during the Second World War. Used in conjunction with the other two Services, but not in subordination to them, it was of paramount importance. Having been shown to work, the three Services now function in the closest co-operation and harmony. 'Boom' Trenchard's (the nickname coming from his deep voice that boomed around the corridors of the Air Ministry leaving no one in any doubt about his wishes) persistence has been more than justified.

This then was the separate Service set up by Lord Trenchard who inevitably became known as the Father of the Royal Air Force and his

Apprentices as Trenchard 'Brats', a title which they are proud to bear. This rather derogatory tag resulted from Lord Trenchard's sobriquet and to us at Halton, joining as young boys, being brought up in his ways, the name stuck. The Halton Apprentice Scheme ceased in 1993 after seventy-one years of excellence and Halton's worldwide recognition as the premier technical college. Nearing publication of these memoirs, I understand that apprentices are again to be trained in the Royal Air Force.

It was to become part of this scheme that I took the entrance exam in early 1930 and was informed of my selection for the entry reporting to Halton in September of that year.

# *CHAPTER 1*

## *Early days*

I was born on 19th February 1914, at an Army garrison where my father was serving with his regiment, the North Staffordshires, at Buttevant in County Cork at the time when the whole of Ireland was part of the United Kingdom. My birth certificate records my birth as a female on 13th February 1914. My mother is adamant that the date was the 19th and that the child was male. I was delivered at home by an Irish midwife and it seems possible that she made two deliveries during the same week and confused the dates and sexes when registering the births. Some four years later my birth certificate was changed by the midwife in the presence of the Registrar. I can only assume that the parents of the other child, presumably a girl, had made enquiries and the midwife, Anna Lanahan, realised her error and had it corrected officially but why it took four years is beyond me.

The regiment remained at Buttevant until the outbreak of the 1914–18 war when my father went to France and my mother and I returned to England to stay with family friends near Littlehampton. I remember very little of this period except for one small incident which made an impression; I was sitting at the window and the aunt we were staying with pointed out a number of German planes flying towards the coast. Later in the war when the United States joined the conflict, we were in rather poor lodgings which also accommodated a party of actors and I remember them constantly singing, 'The Yanks are coming', a song prominent in their show and being practised non stop. Peculiar how certain things, even at that young age, make an impression and stay in the memory.

At the end of hostilities the regiment were stationed at Wallsend, near Newcastle upon Tyne. It was the time of the great 'flu epidemic to which I fell victim. We were living in the customary poor accommodation, a flat on the third floor of a terraced house in a fairly heavily populated area of the town. During my convalescence I used to sit at a window overlooking a street watching funeral processions, two or three a day, mainly victims of the epidemic: a strange and morbid memory for a small boy. My first outing was with my father who took me for a short walk in the shopping area of the town and, passing a greengrocer's, he asked if I would like anything special. Some bananas were on display and not having seen this fruit before I asked for one: it cost threepence, just over one penny in modern terms, but a considerable sum in those days. Little did I realise that in later life when serving in Malaya, now Malaysia, I would be able to pick them fresh from the tree in my own garden.

The North Staffs were again sent to Ireland in 1919, this time to the large garrison at the Curragh, of racecourse fame. My father used to visit the races occasionally on his motorbike. It was on the pillion of this bike that I recall going with him to Dublin and being stopped at road blocks by the nationalist political party, Sinn Fein, already active but a very different animal from the present party. The Irish air obviously had an effect on my parents for on 1st April 1921 my sister was born at the Curragh. No mix-up this time and her birth certificate entry was made correctly. My only strong recollection from this period is the crossings on leave to England over the turbulent Irish Sea, no air passages in those days. Fortunately we were all good sailors and were not affected, unlike many of our fellow travellers, who often had a very distressing crossing.

I started school some three miles away from the army garrison and had to walk both ways each day which was quite an ordeal for a small boy. The school was so dirty that I would not use the lavatories and on one occasion was unable to contain myself and reached home in a state of great embarrassment. My parents considered the daily trek and the dirty school too much for me and for the last twelve months of their stay in Ireland I stayed in England with relatives. I particularly remember staying with an uncle in Chorlton-cum-Hardy near Manchester. He had lost two fingers in an explosion, which was particularly noticeable to a small boy. His house was considerably larger and more comfortable than I had been accustomed to, as he was employed as Managing Director of John Lewis's in Manchester. Our paths were to cross again several years later when he had bought a nursery near Lymington in Hampshire which my father managed after leaving the army.

This was the first of a number of repetitions during my life: Gibraltar with my father in 1921 and then in 1949, Commanding 224 Squadron on my own posting to the Rock, as it is universally known in Services life. A meeting with the Duke of Cornwall's Light Infantry in India when my father commanded the Chota Nagpur Horse and a detachment came to help train the unit and again when stationed in Cornwall during the fifties. 217 Squadron opened RAF St Eval in 1939 and I returned there as Wing Commander Admin. in 1956 with the sad duty of closing the station down in 1959. At No. 1 School of Technical Training Halton in 1930 and again after I had retired and joined the Halton Aircraft Apprentices Association, I returned in 1997 for the unveiling of the 'Tribute' to the Aircraft Apprentice scheme by Her Majesty. On this occasion I stayed the night in my old Barrack block, although it was very much altered by that time. At this 'Tribute' Ceremony, it was a great thrill for me to see Lord Trenchard's grandson at the unveiling. Another memorable event was marching down the hill from the parade ground, reliving the daily march I had made as an Apprentice to the workshops some seventy years before. This followed the parade at which Her Majesty presented The Colour to Royal Air Force Halton, the only RAF Station to receive this honour. The next year at a Triennial meeting of the Association I marched up the hill to the parade ground. We marched in order of Entry; my Entry, the 22nd, now in our mid-eighties, were thin on the ground, but still occupied the second rank with only three earlier Entry members ahead of us. My first return to Halton had been in much less happy circumstances when I spent some considerable time in the RAF hospital there.

Early 1921 the regiment was posted to Gibraltar. We lived in a married quarter at Europa Point on the western side of the Rock where the regimental barracks were. It was an excellent site which had a view overlooking the coast of Africa that was enjoyed by very few people; indeed very few people had any view at all to speak of, on this very cramped garrison. In those days the harbour was usually occupied by several ships of the Royal Navy, both from the Mediterranean Fleet and also from other fleets on passage out or home to England. I remember particularly well the battle cruisers *Hood* and *Repulse* with their escorting destroyers occupying the whole harbour on the occasion of the Prince of Wales', later Edward VIII's, world tour. In those days the Royal Navy normally held 'Open House' on these 'show the flag' visits and so we went aboard *Repulse*. She was dressed overall, immaculate and spotless throughout; decks brought to brilliant whiteness with pumice stone, brasses highly polished and in the galley the preparation tables also scrubbed to a brilliant white. This prompted my father to say that he must get his chaps to see how tables should be scrubbed. In later years as a mess orderly when an Aircraft Apprentice at Halton, I too had to scrub tables to this degree of whiteness and learned to appreciate the effort required. The most memorable part of the trip however was the party which was traditionally given by the sailors for the children of the garrison which included all kinds of games and entertainment.

Gibraltar was a happy time for me; the weather was warm and we could swim all year round. I attended a school in the town and my holidays were spent on a small beach facing Algeceras, generally speaking with one of my friends. When I was learning to swim I lacked confidence in my ability and went through the motions, but was careful to keep one foot on the bottom. How long this would have continued I don't know, but one day I was fooling around on a groyne when I slipped and ended up in deep water. I was naturally very frightened and went through my customary motions; I am not quite sure when I realised that I was staying afloat, but realise it I did when it suddenly dawned on me that I was swimming. I rushed home to boast to my father who came down to see his proud son demonstrate his new found skill. From then on I spent many hours on this beach which had a fig tree just back from the shoreline that produced gorgeous ripe fruit. I had up until this time only seen the dried variety and found these so delicious that I overindulged with the inevitable embarrassing consequences. Nevertheless, figs straight from the tree are undoubtedly delicious.

We embarked on a troopship bound for India, a voyage that was to take some three weeks. One Company of the Regiment had been sent to quell a disturbance in Turkey and we called in to pick them up *en route*. I recall sailing up the Bosphorus, which was full of jellyfish, a quite amazing sight. Travel by troopship is far from comfortable at the best of times, but getting into tropical temperatures it is pretty horrendous; for the families it was unpleasant, but for troops, unaccustomed to sleeping in hammocks, in the bowels of the ship with no stabilisers to counter rough seas and in tropical heat to boot, with up to a thousand men in a confined space, really ghastly. They suffered nearly three weeks of discomfort and time wasting, a far cry from the movement of troops today, with the same journey taking less than twenty-four hours. Air travel may be more expensive, but units are away from their normal duties for a very short time and the real costs must be greatly reduced.

Eventually arriving in India, we were taken to Secunderabad in the Deccan by train, again rather uncomfortable due to the heat. Secunderabad was a large, widely spaced Garrison, at that time accommodating four or five regiments covering an area with a radius of about five miles. The North Staffordshire barracks were furthest away from the Garrison entertainments and schools. There was no electricity and transport was by bullock cart;

even the ambulance was a canvas covered wagon with steel rimmed wheels drawn by two bullocks, so 'don't get wounded' was the watchword. We later went the five miles to school in one of these horrors. Secunderabad has a hot dry climate and although it had little effect on me, my mother found it very oppressive and could not wait for the arrival of the monsoon. The heavy rain which this brings, at least reduced the heat to some extent, although just to make sure that life does not become too pleasant, the humidity is increased. I remember her dashing out into this downpour, revelling in the pleasure of the rain.

There was no electricity in Secunderabad and lighting was therefore, of necessity, by oil lamps and with no electric fans punkahs were used to stir up the hot air, giving an illusion of heat reduction although, in fact, the effect was minimal. At night the punkah was operated by an unfortunate Indian who sat in a small shelter at the end of the bungalow, his toe wrapped round the end of a rope which operated the punkah through a pulley system. Inevitably he would fall asleep and the lack of air movement would awaken the sleepers. On one occasion, to keep the punkah wallah awake, some wag spread sugar in the shelter, which attracted ants who had little difficulty in livening the poor chap up. A punkah comprises a strip of wood about the width of the room in which it is used; attached to it is a pelmet about two feet deep; the rope is attached to this to allow it to be moved backwards and forwards to disturb the air, rather like the effect of running a spoon across the surface of a cup of tea. During the evenings we would sit out on the veranda to enjoy any breeze there might be. All manner of flying insects filled the air and in an endeavour to reduce their number and the annoyance they caused, the lamps were placed in bowls of water. The light from the lamps attracted the flying hordes which hit them and fell into the water. Even though the basins were inches deep in insects by the morning, those that escaped still gave plenty of irritation.

When we arrived at the bungalow in which we were to live, as we had not yet engaged servants, my mother sent me to get butter from the dairy about half a mile away. Returning with the butter on the plate she had given me I was aware of a sudden 'Whoosh', the feeling of a wing brushing my face and the butter disappearing. It was only then that I discovered that it had been grabbed in the claws of a kite hawk. These birds are scavengers who soar to about a thousand feet, have keen eyesight and swoop, as this one did, on any food visible. I had not seen this bird and was both frightened and annoyed at being made to look such a fool, so I decided to try to turn the tables. I attached a small piece of meat to the tail of a kite, child's variety, not hawk, measuring some fifty feet in length. The bird took the meat and although a little laboured to begin with, managed to stay airborne until the meat had been consumed; rounds one and two to the hawk. I next attached my meat to a large stone; the hawk swooped, took it but this time almost capsized and lost the meat as well. A Pyrrhic victory perhaps, but at least my pride was restored.

The heat of the afternoon was siesta time, but a young boy with lots of energy found this a waste and cast around for better things to do. My father had a pushbike on which he went to work. I borrowed this and although it was too big for me, managed to ride with one leg under the crossbar. Having mastered the pushbike I decided to borrow his Harley Davidson. The noise of the motor awoke my father and this escapade was short lived. Some other way of passing the afternoons was required. A Garrison swimming bath, situated at the barracks of the Scottish Regiment five miles away, was my next afternoon venture; unfortunately for me, I had no means of telling the time and enjoying myself in the pool had no idea how long I had been away from home. Suddenly, one of the boys I was with shouted, 'Your father's here.' I dived under the water in fright, with all the innocence of youth, foolishly thinking he would not know I was there. On coming to the surface I realised I was again in trouble. He was very angry and told me to get on the pillion of his Harley Davidson. A quaking little boy prepared for a good hiding was taken home. My mother was so relieved to see me. I had been away hours and both parents had been so worried that even my father had calmed down by the time we were home and a severe admonishment was the extent of my punishment. But I had learned my lesson and always let them know where I was going from then on. It was not until my own son disappeared one afternoon when we were on a family holiday and was not found until several hours later, some miles from where we were staying, happily wandering along a road, amusing himself by collecting the different cigarette packets that he found by the roadside and completely oblivious to the time and worry he had caused, that I really appreciated how my parents had felt.

It was not long before I encountered a more vicious insect than the flying variety that drowned in the bowls round the lamps, a scorpion. In those days topees, the large cork hats covered with cotton that became commonplace in films about India and Africa, had to be worn to ward off sunstroke or so it was thought, although it was later found to be quite unnecessary. However, I had a topee complete with puggeree, a kind of miniature turban wound round the topee, and this had become detached; in trying to fix it back on, I felt a distinct prick on my finger which I thought was the pin which normally holds the puggeree in place, but on trying again felt another prick and on investigation saw a small khaki coloured object with a long tail. I called our bearer who panicked and rapidly took me to the sickbay. There they showed little concern, merely bathing the pricks with chloroform. They did advise me to be more careful as the older darker coloured scorpions were quite dangerous and I should refer to a medical centre immediately if stung by one of them.

The Army controlled the school I attended, as they did everything of note. It was situated in the barracks occupied by a Scottish Regiment, five miles away from home. As I described earlier, we used to travel in an ambulance, a cart drawn by a couple of bullocks. It was covered, and displayed a large red cross, but any wounded being conveyed in this vehicle must have suffered hell. Going to school was uncomfortable, especially if we were late and the driver had to make the bullocks improve their leisurely meandering; to achieve this he would twist their tails to produce a jog trot which caused us great amusement even though it increased the discomfort. A Scottish teacher ran the small school and so not surprisingly we had Scottish dancing lessons. I must admit they were quite fun. In my second term I volunteered to write for the school magazine. I decided on a serial and would produce a couple of pages for each monthly issue all about boys' adventures. It was written piecemeal; I had no idea what the next contribution would be about until I wrote it. How I attained any story continuity was amazing. It seemed to be accepted and each article appeared to be looked forward to.

The Regiment moved to Calcutta where, although the temperature was lower than that in the Deccan, the humidity was excessive and caused permanent perspiration which in turn produced a particularly irritating prickly heat rash which made life very uncomfortable. We were housed in a lodge on one side of the gate guarding the Garrison. Here at least we had electricity which allowed us to escape from oil lamps and had electric fans to replace the punkah, which at least in that respect, made life a little more comfortable than Secunderabad. Our nearest neighbours were two families who lived in private houses opposite the lodge. Three boys and two rather attractive girls of about my age lived there when on holidays from the boarding schools they all attended. A little later, I too went as a boarder, to Bishop Westcotts School, and my three months' holiday coincided with theirs.

The boys organised a sports meeting in the large field adjacent to their houses during our first holiday. They were keen athletes and had won a number of prizes at their school sports, which they donated as prizes for these sports. The intention was to have a formal prize giving by one of the boys' mothers and the sports were so organised that the donor won the prize he had donated. Unfortunately, the plan did not work, events were won not by those expected to win them, so afterwards the prize giving trophies had to be returned to their rightful owners. It was also arranged that any prize that I won did not belong to either of the boys. In fact, I won only one, for the three miles, run in the heat of the afternoon, which the mother who was to present the prizes wanted to call off after two miles. Since I was leading, big-headedly I would have none of it and kept going. After the prize giving, a party was held in their house to which the girls and their friends were invited. I was specially attracted to one of the girls, an attraction that seemed to be reciprocated and this was helped by a game of Postman's Knock which stands out in my memory. If the game is known at all today it would be regarded as much too formal; the basis of today's parties seems to be, grab a girl, or vice versa, and get down to some heavy petting at the drop of a hat. I prefer the old way.

It is traditional in the Services for officers and senior NCOs to serve Christmas dinner to their men. On one particular Christmas my father had gone to do this duty, my mother to attend a wives' party while I went out to visit friends. I returned early and was sitting in a chair awaiting their return when my eye was attracted to a bottle on the sideboard: Crabbie's ginger wine with its distinctive green label. I decided to try it; it tasted good, so I tried it again, and again, until the bottle was empty – luckily it had been only half full at the outset – and fell asleep in the chair. I was awakened by a loudish plop beside my chair. Looking down I saw a small snake, which I promptly hit on the head and killed. Proud of myself, I put the corpse on display, in much the same way that a cat proudly displays its kills for the approval of its owners, next to the Crabbie's bottle on the sideboard. Expecting praise when my father returned, I was very put out when I was severely chastised instead. Apparently the 'small snake' was a krait, one of the most poisonous species, which lives in the rafters, hence the plop as it fell next to my chair. He was furious because it was likely that the mate, which was probably also in the rafters, might have come looking for the dead snake and could have dropped down too. I might not have been as fortunate the second time.

For a time I went to school in Calcutta. Not only was I behind in a number of subjects, but I had not even started one or two. Latin in particular, I remember, was one. The Master was Eurasian, as were the majority of the pupils, and he took great pleasure in ridiculing me on every possible occasion. I was most unhappy and my father soon realised that I would learn little in this state of mind. He arranged for me to be accepted as a boarder in a school run by the army at Mussoorie in the Himalayas. It was a mixed school and the normal age limit for boys was twelve. An exception was made in my case as I was just on the limit. The journey to Mussoorie was by train as far as Dehra Dun; but the remainder of the journey had to be either by pony or by dandy, a small chair carried by porters, which my mother used while my father and I took the ponies. This was the first time I had ridden, but thankfully they were very docile. This trek took the best part of a day; the train had taken over two days, which together made the journey to school a lengthy process. I liked Mussoorie, especially since I was allowed special privileges as a favourite of the Matron and got away with murder because I was the oldest boy. What was then called a Wolf Cub Pack, which would now be known as Cub Scouts, was started by a sergeant major who had a daughter at the school; he had lost his wife and made frequent visits to see his daughter, giving much of his time during his visits to the Cub Pack, giving drill lectures and generally training both girls and boys alike. The discipline he instilled in me at that tender age has remained with me all my life and was particularly useful when I joined the RAF as an Aircraft Apprentice.

The Inspector of Army Schools came to see us on a routine visit, the school being operated at Army expense. One of our favourite pastimes, when the weather permitted, was to fly the paper aeroplanes we made, launching them into the wind caused by the updraught on the hill. These simple, easily made, little planes would soar for quite an appreciable time and the Inspector became fascinated and spent more time watching the soaring planes than listening to the Headmaster who was with him. So interested, in fact, that he produced a piece of foolscap and had one made for him to launch. I'm sure he had seen enough of the school to realise that the teaching was sound and the school was well run and this small recreation enhanced his opinion of it. On two occasions during my time at Mussoorie locust swarms invaded us, a sight which has to be seen to be believed: quite an experience. Quite quickly the whole sky is darkened by thousands of these marauders who settle on anything green, leaving complete barrenness in their wake. The school boasted a small number of apricot trees which provided large quantities of fruit, so much so in fact, that apricot puddings and apricot jam filled so much of the Matron's menu that I still hate apricots in any form. I did succumb many years later when, as a PoW I used dried apricots in some of my 'hooch', our term for moonshine, to provide 'apricot brandy' for our Christmas dinner. To return to the locusts and preserving the apricots, the arrival of the locust swarm heralded the beating of saucepans, blowing of bugles, shouting, indeed anything to make as much noise as possible to frighten and distract the invasion. It was successful provided the noisemakers arrived in sufficient strength and early enough. To the pupils it was all good fun, relieving the monotony of the daily routine of a boarding school.

Sport at the school was very limited, in fact virtually non existent, owing to the lack of facilities; we played hockey on the only piece of hard ground, our little parade ground in fact. Since all the boys were younger than me and half of the ten or fifteen there were, in any event, not athletic, there was very little scope for team games. Our only exercise was on the walks in the surrounding wooded areas: very educational, but not sufficiently energetic for me. The sort of sport which appealed to me was only available during the long holidays, a good example being the sports meeting with the boys in the house opposite that I mentioned earlier. However, my father decided that a little toughening up was required and arranged boxing matches against some of the Regiment's bandboys, lads slightly older than me, but of roughly the same size and weight. Some were quite good, but after a few contests I started to win and my father, not wanting me to become big-headed, decided to find better opponents. This led to a boy from a school in Calcutta being invited to oppose me. This chap, an Armenian, was well skilled in ringcraft and gave me a good hiding. I certainly discovered that seeing stars and a ringing sound in the ears following a solid punch was no myth, and eventually I went down for the count. Later this stood me in good stead when we all had to go into the ring at Halton.

Shortly after this my father decided to leave the North Staffordshire Regiment. He joined the Chota Nagpur Horse (in spite of the name there were no signs of horses), an Indian Regiment based at Dacca, now the capital of Bangladesh. I was placed as a boarder at Bishop Westcott's School at Ranchi in the Bihar State. The school was attended by both boys and girls who were separated by about a mile of open ground; my sister was at the girls' section. We remained in school for nine months and returned home for the remaining three months of the year. During the three months' holiday my father enlisted me as a bugler in the Chota Nagpur Regiment which he now commanded. Then attending summer camp I shared a tent with my father and paraded with the unit in the normal way. During this time one of the flying circuses visited, I believe it was Alan Cobham's, and I was given my first experience of flying in his Tiger Moth, for the princely sum of five rupees. It was a wide circuit of the field lasting about ten minutes which I found very thrilling.

The summer camp was visited by a section of the Duke of Cornwall's Light Infantry, to provide training to this Territorial Unit. Two DCLI Buglers took me some half a mile away, up a hill to practise bugle calls. No sooner had we arrived at the top of the hill than one of them shouted, 'There's a fire,' and insisted that I ran down to the camp and sounded the fire call. They fell about laughing when I returned very much out of breath to say it was a false alarm. Having had their bit of fun, we got on well and I learnt a lot from them as did the Chota Nagpur Regiment in general, but drilling and marching at the Light Infantry pace of 160 paces to the minute, they found quite startling. I find it a great delight particularly watching the Gurkhas who seem to increase this pace even more, almost breaking into a run. Rather better to watch than perform as I discovered many years later, when I took a small party of airmen from RAF St Eval, where I was Wing Cdr. Admin. in 1956, to a Church Parade at the DCLI depot at Bodmin. We marched behind them and I am convinced they increased the pace up the hill for our benefit; I certainly needed the drink in their mess afterwards.

Back at Bishop Westcott's the food was not acceptable to a few of us and I decided to do something about it – I discovered that, for some reason, people followed my lead – and it was decided to leave school and spend a few days in the local villages. Pocket money that was received weekly from a Master was saved, dried food was also stored and when I considered sufficient cash and food had been put aside five of us departed with the object of making the Headmaster investigate our complaint. We planned to be absent for about a week. After spending the day walking round the local villages, having spent all our money, and eaten the food we had saved and feeling very tired, we decided to return. We sent one of our number to explain why we had played truant. The Headmaster had been upset and anxious at having five boys roaming round the villages and relieved that we had returned fit and well, so our only punishment was to catch up on the lessons we had missed. It is a sad reflection on the teaching at the school that all the lessons scheduled for that day were completed in one hour. We were given the food we had missed and were sent to bed. However, the outing had the desired effect; there was a marked improvement in the food from then on.

Sport at Bishop Westcott's was devoted to hockey and cricket, neither a particular favourite of mine. Later in life I played hockey in Gibraltar, the hard ground of the Rock making soccer and rugby impossible; I only played cricket once, soon after joining 217 Squadron at Tangmere when my ability was summed up concisely by my CO, 'Tams, you would do better with a shovel,' and I decided it was not for me. Boxing was part of the sporting scene, but I took part against my will, since the games master felt himself rather adept at it and at the slightest pretence would use it as a punishment.

He justified it by first giving a punishment of a quantity of lines, to be written in an impossibly short space of time. This meant that the boxing became a punishment for the non-completion of the lines rather than for the original misdemeanour. It was beautifully engineered to satisfy his sadistic tendencies and impossible to complain about. As he was bigger and stronger than any boy there, we had to suffer his tantrums. The headmaster was obviously too uninterested to enquire into this treatment of his charges. That he was a very weak character anyway was instanced by his lack of discipline when we played truant and roamed the countryside for a day. It was at Bishop Westcott's that I was awarded the only school prize I ever won, the prize for the best VI Form pupil. It was a leather bound volume of *Westward Ho!* by Charles Kingsley. My only thought is that the competition was so poor that the name must have been drawn out of a hat.

Our house at Dacca was fairly large and the servants included a little Tamil boy who was given the responsibility of looking after me during my school holidays. My parents trusted him implicitly and he accompanied the family on their several moves. He was a small, solidly built, fit young man from what was then called Ceylon, now Sri Lanka, with whom I formed a strong bond. He was adept at football and during the afternoons when my parents were having the customary rest from the heat, I would escape to play football with him using a tennis ball in bare feet. This was followed by a meal of the very hot Madras curry he made, eating with our fingers, as they do, making small bite sized balls of rice mixed with the curry. I have enjoyed hot curry ever since, even though now more conventional eating habits have to be observed. On one of my holidays at Dacca we experienced one of those violent storms which occur fairly frequently in India and on occasions cause considerable damage. The one in particular that I recall reached tornado proportions, lifting roofs off the native buildings, as well as any building not constructed of brick; it simply lifted them into the whirlwind as it progressed on its path. Small whirlwinds are frequent at certain times of the year but this one was frightening.

Frequent moves and changes of school left me somewhat behind academically, a problem from which I have suffered ever since. On the other hand I have seen quite a lot of the world. How many people in the West have seen a swarm of locusts, let alone driven them off, or survived a tropical storm; met and associated with people spread over a wide social background and of varying communities and cultures and felt comfortable with them all? These experiences stood me in good stead when I became an Aircraft Apprentice living in close contact with boys of a similar age but from a variety of backgrounds and regions of the British Isles; and much later as a PoW living in cramped and trying conditions. In spite of what one is led to believe, education is not just about academic achievement.

The family returned to England when I was about fourteen years old, staying with relations in Ramsgate. I was accepted at St George's School, as the headmaster at Chatham House School, the premier school in the local area with Edward Heath, but far more importantly, the girl who would later become my wife, as alumni, had refused to accept me as a result of my varied education. Perhaps my guardian angel was looking after me in my non acceptance at Chatham House, as it was the St George's headmaster who recommended the Aircraft Apprentice Scheme to me and put me forward for the entrance examination. I doubt if the Chatham House Head would have done so and I might have been deprived of the definitive experience of my life.

I liked St George's, was soon accepted and made good friends. A particular friend was keen on cross-country running and persuaded me to join him on Saturday afternoons. Wet and plastered in mud we would return to the pub owned by his parents to shower and change. I also started boxing at school. We used the central assembly hall that divided the boys' and girls' parts of the school in the evenings; all was well until a small spot of blood from a nose bleed was discovered by the girls' games mistress, who disapproved of boxing anyway, and used this to complain to our head and had boxing stopped. However, another friend of my size wanted to continue and we would meet in the pub where his father held the licence. I think it is only coincidence that both my friends' fathers were publicans. Summer arrived and having decided to substitute cross-country running for sprinting I joined another friend in early morning training before school. We became quite good and our training was rewarded with success at the one hundred and two hundred and twenty yard events in the school sports. Winter brought my return to a wet and muddy Saturday afternoon, but on the soccer field rather than slithering round the countryside. My parents had returned to India and I stayed with relations of my mother in Ramsgate. I made use of my swimming ability by entering the Kent junior swimming championship. With only a few entrants and the only race being across Ramsgate harbour I managed to win the cup.

Although I managed to catch up in most subjects, I found that some had never been covered at my previous schools and inevitably my colleagues were well advanced; French and drawing especially come to mind. The headmaster had convinced me that I should take the entrance examination for the Halton Apprentices Scheme, and as a result I was given additional tuition in subjects that were applicable to this when my form were taking the lessons that were inappropriate. I was also given additional homework in them. Examination papers were sent to the school that the candidate was attending, papers were returned to the examiners to be marked and candidates were informed of the result later, based on the position attained. Some two thousand boys sat the papers in 1930 of which some six hundred were selected to attend Halton for medical examination and acceptance. Those successful were enlisted as aircraft apprentices for three years and would be trained in the technical trades required by the Royal Air Force. Entries were at six monthly intervals and the number required for each entry was decided by the 'powers that be' on the likely requirement three years hence, that is at the end of their training. This guessology could be very wrong as was demonstrated by my junior entry which started training eighteen months after us, that is in 1932 and which would graduate in 1935, just as the major expansion of the Air Force started; regrettably this intake had been reduced to one hundred boys. My own entry had about a hundred partially trained apprentices discarded, purely on the grounds that too many had been enlisted initially. These chaps would have been worth their weight in gold six years later.

I had taken the Aircraft Apprentices Entrance Examination and was awaiting the result. My parents had returned from India and my father was managing the small nursery my uncle had bought as a hobby where he could relax from the stresses of being the Managing Director of Lewis's in Manchester. I joined them there in a small bungalow next to the nursery in the little village of Pennington near Sway, a few miles from Lymington, in Hampshire. I worked on the nursery, my uncle's intention being for me to take over when my father retired, but my plans by this time were obviously very different.

# *CHAPTER 2*

## *Aircraft Apprentice*

## *Halton – Trenchard Brat*

As I have said, Entries to Halton were at six monthly intervals, each wing accepting an entry every six months in rotation; thus, my entry, the 22nd, replaced the 16th and we became the junior entry to the 19th. Our junior entry became the 25th. Each wing worked to the same sequence. This then was the life that I was to join; I was informed of my acceptance, received a railway warrant and instructions to reach Marylebone Station by 1100 hours on 9th September 1930. Arriving in good time I soon noticed many other youths of about my age, most looking very apprehensive. As 1100 hours approached a formidable looking warrant officer appeared who immediately made his presence felt by telling us that he was now in charge. We were to board the special train waiting at the station, eight to a compartment, no smoking, and we were to obey the two sergeants with him. The train was bound for Wendover station where we would disembark and be taken to No. 4 Wing Halton. We disembarked and were told to get into ranks of four to march to Halton. In those days all troops formed up in fours, that is in four ranks, an arm's length apart when in close order and three paces apart in open order. This was later changed to ranks of three with the same spacing. Some of us had learned how to march, but most had not and it was rather a motley assembly that managed to get into fours with the help of the two sergeants to set off for Halton Camp some three miles away.

Arriving at the bottom of the hill leading to 4 Wing barracks we were greeted with a variety of catcalls: cries of 'Rookies,' 'Get some in,' 'Cough,' referring to one of the indignities facing us on the morrow, and similar calls, as we shambled up the hill; all this from boys who had arrived on the previous Tuesday and had been accepted as Apprentices. Our Entry, the

22nd, was a large one and it had been decided to have two intakes. We were the second; the first, regarding themselves as 'old sweats' as a result of their few extra days, were the ones yelling from the barrack block windows. We were taken to the Wing dining hall and given a very welcome supper of sausage and mash and a mug of tea. Called to attention during this repast, we were informed of the routine for next day, starting at 0800 hours after breakfast in this dining hall. Divided into groups of twenty, we were taken to a barrack room and allocated a bed, the good old Macdonald in which the frame fits together to enable it to push up into half its length, three bedding biscuits to form a mattress, two sheets and four blankets. All very tired and apprehensive, we settled down for the night. Some had never been away from home before and there were a few sniffles during the night from the homesick boys who were finding the harsh bedding and rough sheets difficult after the soft beds at home.

At 6.30 a bugler sounding Reveille which startled most of us; a Sergeant told us to wash and dress and go to the dining hall for breakfast and we would be given the itinerary for the day. This amounted to reporting to the medical centre immediately after breakfast for our medical examination; those who passed would be enrolled and kitted out; those who did not would be given railway warrants to return home. The medical centre had been divided into a number of booths and we progressed from one booth to the next clad in underpants and a blanket. Each booth was occupied by a doctor or medical orderly, who carried out an examination of various parts of the body, including an eyesight test and a dental check, not forgetting the ubiquitous 'cough', with all the results carefully recorded. Those passed as fit were sworn in, in groups followed by each one being given a service number. My entry, the 22nd, were mainly 564s, but as everything is done in alphabetical order in the services, I was at the end of the queue and mine was 565013. The thirteen at the end caused the Sergeant awarding the numbers to comment, 'With a number like that, lad, you could be unlucky.' Later events show that he could not have been more wrong.

Next, we were shepherded to the clothing stores where we were issued with uniforms, boots and PT shoes and kit, and three each of the following: towels, shirts, socks, vests and underpants, in fact all the bare necessities required for a young apprentice. The issue in threes, like most things in service life, had a purpose and a logic to it, even if it were not immediately apparent: one on, one in the wash, and one in the locker on the wall above the bed or in the large kit-box under the bed. Knife, fork and spoon and a mug were issued and these items had to be displayed on the top of the bedside locker which each of us had on the left hand side of the bed; the two shelves in this locker provided space for toothbrush, toothpaste, soap, hairbrush and comb, which had to be placed on the first shelf, and boot brushes and polish on the bottom as well as a button stick, a strip of hardened card split up the centre which was inserted behind the buttons on the uniform when they were being cleaned to stop the liquid cleaner staining the material, and Brasso, all laid out in a special way. The official order was, 'Kit will be laid up as laid down.' Every item of kit had to be marked with the Service number we had been given. This was achieved with a stamp made up with the number dipped into marker ink and pressed onto the item. Boots and 'irons' were stamped with metal stamps, each number being done separately, as was the button stick. I don't think toothbrush, soap or toothpaste had to be marked, but by then I wouldn't have been surprised by anything. Obviously we were kept busy for the rest of the day.

Uniform at the time was of rough worsted slacks and a tunic which was buttoned up to the neck and could be quite uncomfortable. 'Best Blue' comprised a second tunic similar to the first but which was worn only on special occasions when the slacks were replaced by breeches (pantaloons) and puttees. Puttees were lengths of blue material similar to horse bandages which started at the top of the boots and were wound round the legs to end just below the knee so that the seam of the puttee coincided with the seam of the pantaloons; a narrow tape held them in position and was neatly tucked in facing downwards. This was the dress for ranks up to and including corporal. Senior noncommissioned officers and warrant officers wore blue shirts and black ties instead of buttoned up tunics. Dress for all ranks has been changed frequently over the years and is now designed for comfort in working conditions. Ceremonial dress is still 'Best Blue' but no longer breeches and puttees, I am pleased to record. Aircraft Apprentices wore a brass four blade propeller inside a wheel on the left sleeve of both uniforms. The black cap band on airmen's caps was replaced with different colours for the different wings of the college: red (Four Wing), blue (Two Wing) and green (One Wing). Within each Wing Squadrons were recognised by coloured discs behind the cap badge, yellow, white or black. Forage caps and berets were not yet part of the uniform.

Commissioned ranks up to and including Flight Lieutenant also wore breeches and puttees; Squadron Leaders and above wore riding boots but no spurs, a relic of the cavalry. There is a story that one of the Atcherly brothers amused the crowd at a Hendon Air Display by flying an Avro Tutor sitting perched up in the cockpit with reins attached to the controls. This same officer reputedly flew under one of the London bridges in a Gladiator; I believe it was 'Batchy' Atcherly who gained Air rank later in his service, as did his brother. Rings on their lower sleeves, similar to those in the Royal Navy, but in braid not gold, denoted officers' ranks. Having stolen the Navy's method of denoting ranks for the officers, the Army method of chevrons was used for other ranks. Aircraft Apprentices led to Leading Aircraft Apprentices (LAA) and later Corporal and Sergeant Apprentices, the rank denoted by miniature chevrons worn just under the Apprentices' wheel.

A visit to the tailor for minor adjustments to the uniform having been executed, a visit to the camp barber was next on the list: short back and sides with emphasis on short with no option. These final details having been carried out we were now ready for drill instruction, known throughout the services as 'square bashing'. There were two Sergeant Drill instructors under the eagle eye of the Station Warrant Officer, Sammy Marshal, service number 41, the smartest man I have ever met, always immaculate, to the extent of having his hair trimmed daily. The two Drill Sergeants, one an ex-guardsman, instructed us first. We were initially in small groups to master the basic drill movements, proceeding to Flight drill and eventually progressing to Wing drill under Sammy Marshal himself. The instruction was designed to include much of the drill which would be required during our three years of apprenticeship including the advance in review order, the basic requirement for the passing out parade. Inspection by Sammy Marshal was quite an ordeal. He could pick out the smallest fault, a mark on a boot or a button not polished to his satisfaction, a tunic or slacks not pressed correctly and so on. But Sammy appreciated that some boys were naturally a bit untidy, although trying hard to meet his very high standards; to these he would have a quiet word of encouragement which usually did the trick. At the end of the two weeks of square bashing, there was little resemblance to the motley arrivals of two weeks earlier. A mob had been moulded into a smart and efficient unit working to a word of command as one man and the pride in this achievement was very evident in every one of the Entry. Sammy Marshal was also the envy of 4 Wing Apprentices because he owned a beautiful MG, which he would drive out of camp at weekends. Flight Sergeant Barnard, one of the workshop engineer instructors, had an Austin Swallow which also caused interest and envy. In those days it was unlikely that we would own a car for some years; even motorbikes were out of the question for some time to come.

After the fortnight of square bashing we were considered fit to march down the hill, an exercise which would become well known to us over the next three years as we attended either workshop or school instruction. The fortnight of square bashing flew by; we had been fully occupied not only in drill, physical training, kit inspections and sport, but were learning to live together, an absolutely critical factor in any close knit and disciplined environment. Our little circle came from all parts of the UK, and from a variety of backgrounds; at this early stage in our training we were a little tight group. In addition to the drill we were put in the hands of the men in dark blue trousers and wasplike jerseys. Each day began with an hour at the hands of these PTIs and soon we were in good physical shape. They were also responsible for the early cross-country runs and for arranging for each of us to oppose someone of equal size and weight in the boxing ring.

Air Commodore Bonham-Carter, who commanded RAF Halton, had lost a leg in the First World War and rode his horse when visiting drill sessions or on camp inspections. He took a keen interest in our progress on the square and would often ask the ex-guardsmen Sergeant drill instructors how to order complicated movements. Bonham-Carter was often seen in the Apprentices' Wings on his horse, seldom his staff car. On one occasion, a weekend I think, I saw him in a furious temper. A number of us were on the hill overlooking the valley adjacent to Princess Mary's RAF Hospital when a aeroplane circled and then dived over the hospital in our direction. Unfortunately the pilot had not reckoned on the eddies caused by the wind over the hill behind us and the ensuing down draught made it impossible to pull out of his dive. The aeroplane crashed and the sight of this was the reason for the Air Commodore's temper. He shouted at us, ordering us to return to our barracks when he saw us running towards the crash. The two officers in the machine were killed instantly; the pilot we learned later had been impaled on his joystick. Apparently they had just been discharged from the hospital and had decided to impress the nursing sisters by putting on this show.

With the exception of Saturdays and Sundays we paraded on the Square, were inspected and the Colour was hoisted. From this time onwards, crossing the Drill Square was prohibited and punishable when not on parade. When I returned many years later for the unveiling of the Tribute to the Apprentices, it was strange to see servicemen crossing the square with impunity, while we, the old lags, still felt a sense of reverence and almost expected to be pulled up for our error. On the other hand it was remarkable to see the existing recruits at Halton marching and very smartly I might add, wherever they were going, something which we had never been required to do.

The workshops occupied a large area on the left of the road leading to Halton village and the school building, Kermode Hall, named after the chief academic instructor, was on the right of this road almost opposite the workshops. Beyond the workshops a large area of open ground was, and still is, available for all the sports activities of the station personnel. A full size swimming bath and gymnasium were housed in the workshop area. For the next three years almost seventy per cent of our time would be spent in this area learning our trade. But first we had to learn how to use the tools of that trade and we were introduced to a piece of round mild steel three inches in diameter, a cold chisel and a hammer. These were the only tools which could be used to chisel a hexagon from the steel bar. The new entry could always be recognised by the large numbers of apprentices with bandaged fingers and thumbs, damaged through their inefficient use of the hammer and chisel. Later, this male hexagon was fitted to a cast iron female hexagon, but at least for this we were permitted to make use of a variety of files, ranging from rough, for the initial enlarging, down to the smooth to obtain the final result. After eight weeks we had a fair knowledge of the basic tools, their names and uses, and were able to produce accurate results, no longer damaging fingers and thumbs when chiselling. A cartoon in the Halton magazine of October 1930 showed an Aircraft Apprentice of the 22nd Entry with hands bandaged under the caption, 'Dancing with tears in my eyes', a popular tune at the time.

During this period about a quarter of our time was spent at school. The subjects covered were allied to the particular trade the apprentice was training for, in my case FAE (Fitter Aero Engines). I started in F5; the groups were streamed ranging from Fl to F9 for fitters and for riggers R1 to R9. The armourers went with the fitters. Written examinations each term resulted in re-grading and I slipped back slightly on the first exam result to F6 but was able to stay in this group for the remainder of my school training. Groups at school were different from those in workshops and friends and acquaintances were widened as a result. Similarly groups in the workshops tended to change which also extended the number of friends. Rugby and athletics provided an even greater variety, extending the initially very small group to fifty or sixty close acquaintances and produced a very happy atmosphere.

The rate of pay for Apprentices in the first year was one shilling a day, five pence in modern terms, but we received only three shillings at the end of each week, the remainder being retained in individual accounts against stoppages incurred through barrack damages or replacement of clothing and so on. Most of the money retained was paid on the parade prior to leave. In the third year pay was increased to one and sixpence a day, ten and six a week, and the Apprentice receiving five shillings. These princely sums were dispensed on the pay parade each Friday. We were lined up in alphabetical order, names were called by a sergeant and each boy in turn marched to the pay desk, halted, saluted said, 'Sir,' and gave his last three service numbers; the paying officer placed the three shillings on the blanket covered table and the recipient scooped the money with his right hand into his left, saluted, turned about and marched away. With my initial 'T' I had to wait for most of the Entry to be paid before it was my turn. What a waste of time for all concerned and thank God the system no longer exists.

Youths of sixteen and seventeen had to be different and in spite of the rigid discipline, or perhaps because of it, Apprentices in their second year had to show they were different from those who had not been initiated or blooded. Making alterations to uniform is, of course, an offence but caps were made to look more rakish and pantaloons were altered to make the wings more pronounced. The caps were fitted with a piece of metal in the front to force up the front of the cap behind the badge; the top was dampened and stretched on the back of the bed by clamping the opposite side of the badge and stretching it overnight. Provided this was not overdone even Sammy Marshal turned a blind eye as he also did to the pantaloons which had been tightened at the knee and the wing squared by a little judicious sewing. If either of these alterations was overdone the culprit was charged and awarded a punishment of CC (Confined to Camp) and made to pay for replacements.

Church Parade every Sunday morning was quite an ordeal. We had been prepared for the parade part in the two weeks of drill, but it was the dress for this parade which caused considerable difficulty on the first occasion. Getting puttees to sit with spacing regular and to end with the seam in the right place proved more difficult than it seemed; the puttee ended up too tight or too slack and I remember the occupants of our room, after numerous attempts, at last getting the desired result and rather than go through it all again next morning, many sleeping in their pantaloons and puttees that night. Next morning on parade with legs throbbing and aching we decided not to repeat this stupidity. In fact once the knack is mastered it is difficult to understand why one had been so stupid, but on that first parade in 'Best Blue', we could not let Sammy Marshal down either in turn out or drill and I don't think we did, however uncomfortable it may have been.

Before the daily Colour Hoisting Parade at 0800 every morning barrack rooms had to be left clean and tidy. The three bedding biscuits were stacked on the front of the Macdonald bed which had been reduced in length by pushing together the top and bottom halves, thus providing more space in the room. Blankets and sheets were folded and arranged in the order: blanket, sheet, blanket, sheet, blanket and the assembly encircled with the remaining blanket, to provide a neat and square display. The floor-space on the left of each bed was the responsibility of the occupant; it contained his personal bedside locker. Attached to the wall behind each bed was a tin locker; into these were fitted in precise order all the items of kit and clothing that had been issued. Our civilian clothes had been sent home when we enlisted.

This then was the Monday to Friday routine. Sunday was Church Parade and Saturdays were inspection days. Two room members were detailed by the LAA each week as room orderlies. They were responsible for the linoleum in the centre of the room, scrubbing the six-foot table and benches to pristine whiteness and for the cleaning of the bath, wash basins, taps, and so on. Each of the occupants was responsible for his bed, his floor-space and the bedside locker which had to be scrubbed to the same pristine whiteness. Ronuk, a liquid wax based polish, was splashed on the floor, scrubbed in, buffed up using a bumper which was a large flat brush about twelve inches by nine which could be covered with rags and was attached to a broom type handle by a hinge that allowed it to be swung backwards and forwards to develop a shine, and finally polished. After all this effort not a mark was allowed to appear on the floor, so all the occupants walked on floor pads until the inspection was over. Friday nights were HELL! One of these Friday evenings, the LAA (Leading Aircraft Apprentice) in charge of our room called me over and asked if he could have a word in private. One of the privileges of being an LAA was to have the luxury of a private room; when I got into his he said he had noticed that the other Apprentices seemed to follow my lead and asked me to assist him in getting them on his side. I was somewhat taken aback and did not know what to say, particularly when, as a devout member of the Plymouth Brethren, he asked me to join him in prayer. He went down on his knees and closed his eyes and I quietly left the room. The subject was never mentioned again. I did not realise it at the time but the episode would have a profound effect on my RAF career.

Once a month the Saturday inspection became a kit inspection to ensure that each Apprentice had a complete kit that was in good repair. For kit inspections the Macdonald bed was left at its full length and the three bed biscuits left in place. All the items from the tin locker were laid out on the bed with numbers showing, boots were displayed with soles uppermost which had been blackened and studs and blakeys polished, spare laces were coiled and shown on the soles. Any item missing had to be replaced at the expense of the individual and items in need of repair, shirt, buttons, socks and so on, were noted by the NCO who would arrange a 'Make and Mend' Saturday after the morning inspection.

The occupants of each barrack room messed together in the dining room. Each week two of us were detailed as mess orderlies. We drew from the kitchen a tray of food which we divided into the required number of portions, one for each member of the room, but hungry boys could be forgiven if the two orderlies kept a little extra for themselves; anyway it evened out in the end since we all had our turn. On the downside the table had to be scrubbed until it was white and a corporal ensured that it was. 'Turn it over and scrub it again,' was a frequent cry. The food was not particularly good, but as growing boys taking lots of exercise we could always have managed more. Our three shillings a week pay lasted from Friday, payday, until Tuesday if we were careful; a cup of tea and a wad, a cake of the Bath bun variety, each break-time at school and workshops, soon eroded the pay.

On 31st October 1997, Her Majesty the Queen presented her Colour to RAF Halton, the only RAF Station to be so honoured. Later that day she was to honour the Halton Aircraft Apprentices Association by unveiling their 'Tribute'. I was privileged to be accommodated in a barrack block which I had inhabited some sixty-four years earlier when I was an Aircraft Apprentice in the early thirties and the comparison between my life as an Apprentice and the life of a modern recruit was interesting. In 1930 we were accommodated in the same barrack blocks which still provide the accommodation for today's recruits. We were in a dormitory of twenty, with a linoleum floor and the small amount of furniture that I have already described. At the time of my visit the dormitories had been subdivided and I had a room which I shared with three others; the floor was carpeted and a large wardrobe provided for each occupant. The Macdonald bed and three biscuits had been replaced with a single bed and mattress with blankets far superior to the brown blankets of the 1930s. The wardrobes were positioned to give a fair degree of privacy for each occupant. A writing table and chair was available in each half of the room. Strip lighting provided adequate light for reading and writing and could be controlled in each half of the room. In addition, reading in bed was possible without disturbing roommates by use of an overhead bedside light. Lights in the thirties were either 'On' or 'Off' for the whole room and provided by electric light bulbs with white shades hanging from the ceiling. Ablutions now were very similar to those in the thirties, but obviously catered for a smaller number.

Messing arrangements were very different. Catering is no longer the preserve of RAF cooks, but provided by outside caterers, Granada in this case I believe, who are responsible for the preparation, cooking and serving, which is done on a cafeteria system. Tables are for four, covered in Formica and cleaned by the catering staff, as is the floor. Cutlery is provided and washed up, no more stamping your individual number on 'irons' and paying for losses. There is plenty of choice and seemingly unlimited rations available from the serveries, so no need for orderlies to award themselves extra rations, indeed no need for orderlies. Tea, coffee and a variety of soft drinks are always available on a self-service basis. Cereals are available in the same way for breakfast. The airman of today has a great variety to choose from and in greater quantity. The days of the lino polishing are over and no doubt vacuum cleaners are available for the carpet cleaning. I was grateful for my nostalgic experience and envy the modern airman; but wonder if he, or more correctly these days he or she, is being treated too softly.

And so to our first leave, Christmas 1930. I collected sufficient back pay for my rail fare to Lymington, as my parents were still at the nursery near Sway, and I enjoyed a very happy Christmas with them, proudly arriving in my uniform. On our return from this leave, we continued our education in the use of tools; in addition to files, using scrapers and lathes, until we were able to produce test pieces to prove our proficiency in the use of tools. During the second and third years, a number of courses relating to our trade were introduced into the syllabus: metallurgy, the properties of metals, the Brinell hardness tests, magnetos, coppersmithing and so on, which kept us fully stretched. One of the final tests was to make a small vice, which entailed the use of many of the tools, not least the cutting of the screw thread using the lathe. I was able to keep my vice which is still in use today, a tribute to the materials, the tools and the teaching and just a little, I hope, to my skill in putting them all into practice.

Summer leave arrived. I had completed my first year and on my return would be instructed in aero engines and the ancillary parts of those engines. Now I was getting down to the nitty gritty of my chosen trade and my three years at Calshot in the Engine Repair Shop, after I had graduated from Halton, proved how good that instruction had been. It was this formidable two years of instruction that faced me after a very pleasant fortnight at Christchurch near Bournemouth, where my parents now lived. I spent the time swimming, fishing and generally having a lazy time. I had completed my first year as a 'Trenchard Brat', and enjoyed the fellowship, the discipline and above all the sport. The routine did not bother me. The morning parade took place at 0800 hours with the colour hoisting ceremony, before marching down the hill behind the band of Halton Pipers or the bugles, fifes and drums bound for school or workshops according to the itinerary. Then we marched up the hill again for the midday meal, which was never sufficient for growing youths so if any money was left over from the three shillings pay, a cup of tea and a 'wad' (cake) would be enjoyed in the NAAFI canteen before parading again for the return to school or workshops.

I accepted all of this with some pride; some of the others found it hard. In fact, I remember after my first night at Halton praying that I would be accepted into this unique body. My granddaughter had a similar reaction when she attended an open day at the University of Durham: she was desperate to achieve the required qualifications. Like me her wish was granted. Somehow I think you know when you are in the right environment.

Participation in sport is of paramount importance in the services and certainly the facilities available to the Apprentices were excellent. Having been a keen sportsman all my life, played soccer, hockey and cricket at the various schools I attended, boxed against Army bandboys of my father's Regiment and run cross-country, I found Halton very satisfying indeed. In the first few weeks each boy of the new entry was matched against a boy of similar weight, height and build in the boxing ring. Since I had had some experience I did rather well and was soon representing my squadron at welterweight. Inevitably and possibly unfortunately my weight increased, which put me in the next division in which I met a very heavy puncher and decided to give up this sport. The Flight Sergeant in charge of the squadron team tried to persuade me to continue, but I discovered that he regarded me as a good hustler and wanted to use me to bring out the best in his team, a sparring partner, in fact, which made me adamant that I would not continue.

The other compulsory occupation on Wednesday afternoons for the new entry was the cross-country run. Some boys found very soon that this form of exercise did not appeal to them and found ways of short circuiting the course and joining in to finish with those completing the whole distance. The PTIs (Physical Training Instructors) were experienced in the ways of Apprentices and arranged for date stamps to be applied to the wrists as the furthest point was reached; not to be outdone the Apprentices managed to transfer the stamp from one of the runners to a scrimshanker and a few got through, but the PTIs then stamped the back of the neck which made transfer impossible. All this was taken in good part on both sides and only lasted a short time, effectively until those with any talent were discovered. Certainly one of these with ability previously undiscovered, I think his name was Hennessy and I hope I'll be forgiven if it wasn't, went on to represent the RAF in distance running. Halton also boasted a first class swimming bath, but I found that the junior Kent champion was no match for the swimming talent in my squadron let alone the Wing or Station and I made use of it only for exercise.

As I have already mentioned, the playing fields were excellent and it was an annual event for both Oxford and Cambridge Universities to play the RAF on our ground, an event at which I was an avid spectator. It was thrilling to watch first class rugby; remember that this was in an age before television and the only way to see any top class sport was actually to attend. In those days the university teams would boast several internationals and be of a very high standard, as would each of the service teams. I will always remember George Beamish, then I think a wing commander and an Irish international, gathering the ball with three opposing forwards hanging on for grim death, but with little success as he crashed over the line for a try. He was one of three brothers serving in the RAF: one, a dentist, represented the RAF at golf and I think the other two had both been Irish rugby internationals. Later I served the then Air Marshal George Beamish as a Wing Commander Org. 1 when he was the Air Officer Commanding Technical Training Command at Brampton. He lived in his official residence and kindly had my wife and me to dinner. A kind man with a gentle manner except on the rugby field, this very large man had a quiet high pitched voice which came as shock the first time it was heard as one could hardly believe that such a tiny voice could come from such a huge frame.

Not caring very much for Church Parade on Sundays I volunteered to join the tug of war team which was excused this parade for training. The training concentrated on getting legs strong and building the strength of the arms and hands. To achieve leg strength we were taken on long hikes averaging twenty miles. This was done on Sunday mornings and was the principal reason for being excused Church Parade. After thirty minutes PT we set off on our hike which lasted about four hours before returning to camp for the midday meal.

The arms and hands were strengthened on a contraption we named 'The Killer'. A large builder's bucket was suspended from an overhead pulley some twelve feet above the ground; the tug of war rope passed through this and under another pulley about two feet above ground, which put it at the correct height, and the team pulled it. The bucket contained weights and the objective was to take it to the top pulley; this signalled the team manager, a warrant officer who had a dog revelling in the wonderful name of 'Yussof", to put more weights into the bucket and again it was pulled to the top. This routine continued until the bucket could no longer be taken up. After a few weeks of training with legs, arms and particularly hands, gaining strength, it was surprising how much more weight was being hoisted. The chosen team, in which I was not included, represented Halton at Olympia. They were opposed by teams from the Army and Navy who were equally well practised and although not winning, acquitted themselves honourably.

Those of us who were selected for the athletics team were permitted to train on the sports grounds before breakfast. One morning I was returning after one of these sessions and saw that a high jump bar had been left at a fairly low height; never a high jumper, I considered four feet just about within my poor capability. I ran up, slipped on take off on the damp grass and put my hand down as both feet shot forward. I landed very heavily on this hand which caused me considerable pain as it had been pushed back some distance towards the wrist. Not normally one to forego food at any time, on this occasion I could not face breakfast, an indication of the pain I was in. I reported to the sick bay to be told by a very irate corporal orderly to report on sick parade at 0830 hrs. and not to bother him at this early hour in the morning; it was all of 0730. When I was eventually allowed to be examined I was sent to Princess Mary's Royal Air Force Hospital Halton, where an X-ray showed that I had broken the wrist, which resulted in me spending ten days in plaster and ended my high jumping career. No mention was made by the doctor of the fact that I had not been seen earlier; in fact it seemed that my broken wrist was of secondary importance to the corporal medical orderly's sleep.

Very rigid restrictions were placed on Aircraft Apprentices. Camp bounds covered a radius roughly three miles from the Wings: not very far when one considers the school and workshops were about half that distance. To the north were the wooded Chiltern Hills, excellent for a walk or tobogganing in winter snow, but towards Wendover or Tring there was little to excite anyone. Close to the camp going towards Wendover was a small shop that sold stale cakes that had been soaked and compressed into squares, recycling was pretty basic in those days, at a price affordable to apprentices; or towards Tring, there was Uncle Tom's Cabin which offered cups of tea and soft drinks; these were the two main ports of call. A pass was required to go beyond this limit which could only be obtained once a month, signed by the Flight Commander, which entailed dressing in 'Best Blue' and being inspected at the guardroom to see that all was in order. Aylesbury was the popular port of call on these occasions, where a cup of tea and a sticky bun was all we could afford. Life was so much simpler then; it is difficult to imagine the seventeen-year-old of today accepting this as a satisfactory form of entertainment. It was on one of these visits that, very daringly, I had my first half-pint of beer. The licensee of the Hen and Chickens would oblige at the back door but with my red capband and brass wheel I felt very vulnerable; I didn't like the beer anyway: well, not then, but it's remarkable how it becomes an acquired taste. Once in each term a pass could be obtained from the Squadron Commander, in my case Squadron Leader Walker, to go further afield. The Wing Commander was 'Bill' Hicks who took office for the more serious offences but whom, except for disciplinary reasons, we rarely came into contact with and who, when we moved to 2 Wing, was replaced by Wing Commander Herring.

At that time my girlfriend from school days was attending Kerr Sanders secretarial college in London and we would arrange to meet at Whipsnade Zoo. She would bring a picnic lunch, which would be eaten sitting on the Downs watching the gliders from Dunstable Gliding Club. It was a most enjoyable break for both of us, but cycling nine miles each way in breeches and puttees made it a labour of love for me. Some seven or eight years later we married when I was a Sergeant Pilot at Tangmere so it was all well worth while, especially since two healthy children, a girl before the war and a boy after it, were the result.

Aircraft Apprentices were subject to Air Force Law in the same way as all members of the Royal Air Force but in addition, smoking was a punishable offence. It was prohibited at any time for AAs under the age of eighteen. On reaching that age a 'Smoking Pass' could be granted on application to the Flight Commander which entitled the holder to smoke but only when outside the Camp. An Apprentice caught smoking, or with smoking material in his possession, would be so charged and would appear before his Flight Commander. If found guilty, punishment would be three days confined to camp for a first offence , seven days for the second, ten days for the third, fourteen days for the fourth offence, and anyone foolish enough to be caught again would appear before the Officer Commanding the Wing who had the authority to award detention, and I don't mean being kept in after school, but rather the cells in the guardhouse. I knew of only one instance of this. When you consider that in those days as a matter of course, most people and in particular men, smoked, this now seems draconian, but we accepted it without question as a normal part of the discipline.

Inevitably many Apprentices were charged with a variety of minor offences, as discipline was very strict and rigidly applied. An award of confined to camp entailed being confined to Wing bounds, wearing an armband to show all concerned that the wearer was a 'Janker Wallah' (on cc) and having to report throughout the day to various places in a number of changes of uniform. For example: 0630 report to the guardroom in slacks and tunic, boots and buttons polished. 0800 parade for workshops, dressed in the same way. Return from school or workshops, have tea, change into breeches and puttees for an hour's drill with full pack, then change into fatigues for an hour of cleaning duty wherever the Orderly Sergeant decided, usually the cookhouse or the guardroom. This last chore was made easier during my time as an Apprentice as one of the acting corporals overseeing the punishment was studying for his promotion exams. He would get the defaulters to help him and as the poor chap lacked education he needed a lot of assistance. On one occasion he had a maths problem and the boy asked to help suggested using logs (logarithm tables). The corporal not having heard of these asked if matches would do. He didn't pass his promotion exams during my time at Halton and the poor chap was given little respect and had his leg pulled unmercifully. He wasn't bright enough to understand so it was all rather wasted. But perhaps he was brighter than we thought, as he got his own back by being especially meticulous about our dress when reporting to him at the guardroom before going out: boots and buttons polished to perfection and, if in 'Best Blue', the seams of the puttees and the breeches had to be exactly in line or you were ordered to go back and get it right.

In my second year a case of meningitis was diagnosed and all boys in the squadron were confined to their dormitories. We had to gargle an obnoxious mixture three times a day and I made it appear less offensive by getting a champagne bottle into which I put my mixture. At first we were highly delighted to be able to skive off from discipline and work, but the inactivity soon became boring and we longed for the time to pass and to be able to return to normal life. In an effort to reduce the boredom and to alleviate the inactivity which was relieved only by playing board games and reading, on one very hot afternoon four or five of us decided to plug all the outlets from the ablutions, including the door. We then turned on all the taps and soon had about three feet of water covering the room, in which we had a noisy and enjoyable time splashing and skylarking about. A Senior NCO, hearing the noise, demanded that the door be opened. After several demands from him while we got rid of some of the water, he was asked to stand clear and the door was opened. We were on the top floor and the water rushed out on to the landing and down the stairs, providing for a short time a very effective waterfall. The ensuing mess had to be cleared up and the Senior NCO, aware of our frustration and the effort required in cleaning three stairways and their surrounds, with greater understanding than was usual in those days, decided not to charge us. So thankfully I avoided 'Jankers' on this occasion.

A much more stupid piece of skylarking may well have ended my apprenticeship, and could have led to a trip to the 'Glasshouse' at Colchester. It occurred during the course on magnetos. One Friday afternoon we had completed the work and the instructor told us to revise our notes while he departed to another bay well away from us. The slow turning engine then in use did not provide a sufficiently strong spark to fire the mixture and as a result the hand starter magnetos were in general use to provide the spark while the engine was being turned, and were installed in every cockpit. It was operated quite independently of the engine and turned by a small handle which produced a large number of hefty sparks to the cylinders. One or more sparks would reach the mixture in the cylinder on the firing stroke and once having fired, the engine magnetos took over. There were occasions when the mixture became too rich and the engine had to be cleared. Everything 'Off' was the order, as the engine was turned to blow out the rich mixture. Only when it was clear could the whole starting process begin again.

A version of the hand starter magneto which we had been working on to learn its functions was available on the bench. Notes were soon revised and we started to investigate how far the spark could be made to jump. A number of steel 'Tommy' bars were aligned leaving a small gap which was gradually enlarged until the optimum gap was reached. It seemed amusing at the time so then I decided to dangle a petrol soaked rag in the gap, which immediately caught fire. In a panic I threw it down without looking, straight into a tray of petrol which was being used to clean the bench. My guardian angel was looking after me, for against all odds it fell into the petrol and did not catch fire. Had it done so, the whole bay could have caught fire and dousing this sort of conflagration would have been difficult; the instructor would certainly have noticed and the 22nd Entry would have been one AA less. I went ashen, so I'm told. I know I felt very sick, and went to a quiet corner and sat feeling very subdued for the rest of the afternoon. My larking about with things I did not fully understand ended there.

A political decision to reduce costs in the armed forces resulted in a reduction of one hundred Apprentices in the 22nd Entry after only a year of training. Furthermore, the three Entries following our junior Entry, the 25th, were reduced in number, only seven hundred Apprentices being accepted in place of the normal rate of about two thousand. The 25th Entry, in fact, was only one hundred in total, all of whom had matriculated which would be the equivalent to three 'A' levels today. It is probably worth making a comparison between the examination system that existed in the thirties and that which is in operation today. In those days the first qualification was the School Certificate. A fixed set of subjects had to be passed at the same time, and failure in one subject meant failure of the 'School Cert.', as it was known. Nowadays GCSEs are taken in any number of subjects of the candidate's choice and failure in any one does not detract from the passes in any of the others and in fact it is possible to retake the subject in which one failed and if a pass is obtained it is added to the number of those already attained. Therefore it is much easier to show an impressive education result and is, I think, a fairer system since in the old system one compulsory subject for which one had no aptitude could prevent a 'School Cert.' being obtained with the inevitable repercussions on the individual's future career prospects.

Similarly, the Matriculation examination required a pass in all subjects with no option to choose and pass separately. Of course re-sits are taken into account these days by Universities and employers, but at least one bad day will not ruin the rest of your life. The number of subjects available today is very much larger than in 'Matric' days and it is therefore necessary to select those subjects which qualify one for the career which it is wished to pursue. Three 'A' levels normally qualify for University, but the number of Universities has increased to such an extent that the standard has obviously been reduced except for entry to the top universities. All in all, I think the present system is better, allowing students more choice of subjects although getting good grades is no less difficult; and indeed grades are of particular relevance in determining which University will accept the candidate. In my day it was either pass or fail, with little regard being given to whether you achieved a good pass or just scraped through.

The reduced numbers in the 22nd and the low intakes in the 25th to 29th resulted in No. 4 Wing being closed and we in the 22nd were split between Nos. 1 and 2 Wings some distance away. Fitters went to 1 Wing and Riggers to 2 Wing. How much the Government regretted the decision to reduce the numbers of these young men who were being trained to such a high standard in aircraft engineering when war broke out so few years later, when their skills would have been invaluable, it is impossible to know, but they should have been thoroughly ashamed. It is sad to see that no lessons were learned and the short-term expedient over the long-term benefit is still the order of the day in Government terms.

It is worth commenting on the high educational standards of these reduced-sized Entries. In the late 1920s and early 1930s this country was in deep recession and even those with high qualifications were unable to obtain employment. There was no welfare state and men would accept almost any form of work. As an example I heard of men in the Merchant Navy who were holders of Master's Certificates, taking on deck-hand jobs because of the shortage of ships and an excess of qualified Captains. I select the Merchant Navy because of my first hand knowledge of their bravery in the Second World War. They braved the 'U' Boat and surface raider onslaught, the results of which I witnessed as an aircrew member of Coastal Command. Many lost their lives in the most awful conditions keeping this country supplied with its needs. Tankers bringing the very necessary oil were attacked and sunk, resulting in the sea being covered with oil which, bad enough in itself for survivors, was invariably ignited, a ghastly sight with little or nothing anyone could do from the air; in the Arctic convoys, there was no chance of survival if your ship was sunk in those frozen waters. All this required a very special courage which was given willingly by men who had been treated so badly in the very recent past.

The second year was devoted to aero engines and all their ancillary parts. Twelve of us were put in the charge of a rather unprepossessing little man of about forty years of age of whom I remember little apart from his evil smelling pipe. On the other hand the senior instructor, a well spoken, imposing man, an ex Naval Commander, I believe, had the overall responsibility for the efficient instruction in the engine bays. Both were very helpful. The radial engines were the first that we had to learn about; separate bays housed a seven cylinder Lynx, a nine cylinder Jupiter and a fourteen cylinder Jaguar. In the course of time each of these was stripped and reassembled and each non-mechanical ancillary area covered, broadly at this stage, and later separately in great detail. Dismantling and reassembling was fairly simple since they had received this treatment many times from Apprentices over the years. However it served its purpose, taught us about valve and ignition timing, lining up of cylinders, piston ring fitting and clearances, oil scraper rings and so on, and the many intricacies of these engines.

Later came the instruction on the liquid cooled engines, the Napier Lion and the Rolls Royce, both in two banks of six at a sixty-degree angle. These were more complicated; in particular the valve timing which was achieved through a mass of gearing at the rear end. As with the radials, ancillaries were touched on but dealt with in detail on separate courses. Our knowledge was tested at regular intervals and examinations seemed to occur almost weekly. At school, classes were allied to the instruction we were receiving in the workshops. Maths and engineering drawing were taught in small classes, normally in the group in which we had been assessed, allowing those in the higher groups not only to be given more advanced subjects, but also to move ahead at a faster rate; F1 for example were taught calculus whilst F9 were not. Lectures on general subjects, RAF history, geography, the theory of flight and similar matters, were given to the whole Entry in the large lecture hall now known as the Kermode Hall after the senior lecturer of the time. The lecturers had all served in the First World War as officers; one in particular had lost an arm in that conflict. The only name other than Kermode I remember is Whittaker, a friendly shy man who organised and took us on visits abroad during holidays.

A fortnight on the airfield was included as part of our training to give us experience in working on aircraft in the open, which was where we would be doing most of our routine work after graduation. Almost all of this instruction was relevant in the thirties but is no longer possible on modern aircraft. The airfield course included swinging the prop by hand, or for the larger engine, by using a bag with an attached rope over the tip of one of the blades of the propeller. The procedure in both cases was the same. The starter would shout, 'All switches off,' and the pilot would repeat, 'All switches off.' The starter would turn the prop through two or three turns sucking in fuel to charge the cylinders with a combustible mixture; he would say, 'Ready,' and the pilot would reply, 'Contact,' at which he would start to turn the hand starter magneto in the cockpit to produce sparks in the cylinders at the same time as the propeller was swung. The hope was that the combustible mixture would be fired as the piston reached the correct spot. The starter magneto produces a constant supply of powerful sparks and normally the engine would start after two or three attempts. The necessary engine revs would allow the two magnetos operated by the engine to take over. When the engine failed to start, the whole starting procedure was repeated; frustrating for the pilot and exhausting for the fitter. Starter motors are now used for starting the larger engines and, of course on jets, although light aircraft still use the prop swinging method on occasions.

Engines in airframes too high off the ground for hand or bag swinging were started by using a rather Heath Robinson arrangement known as the 'Hucks Starter'. Mounted on a model T Ford type of vehicle, an arm with a claw fitted to its end was engaged with a matching claw on the engine. The vehicle could be driven up to an aircraft and the claws engaged. The vehicle claw turned at a fairly high speed until the engine started, using its own magnetos; as soon as it fired the starter claw was thrown out of engagement, the same principal as that used in a starter motor on a car, at least until recently, just on a much bigger scale. Later some engines were started by using a type of gyro. An airman standing on the wing root would operate the gyro with a handle through the nacelle. The gyro would be engaged to turn the engine when a sufficient speed had been reached. Removal of an engine in the field using sheer legs was another, now obsolete, activity. Two large poles were positioned some six to eight feet apart and a third placed the same distance in front to form a firm triangular base. The three poles were secured near the top with a rope to which a pulley was attached. A further rope, attached to the engine being removed, was fed through the pulley to hoist the engine.

The aerodrome course was not all outside work; lectures in the classroom and examinations filled a fair amount of the time. One of our group, feeling the pressure of work, on seeing a group of cows lying in an adjacent field chewing the cud remarked, 'How I would like to be one of those cows.' Incidentally, this was the same chap who had the heavy punch which persuaded me to give up boxing. He got a cadetship to Cranwell so he must have been more than just a good boxer.

At the end of our two years at school we were given a set task to produce an essay of about ten thousand words on any subject of our own choosing. It was to be done in our own time and for me entailed a lot of evening work. I chose the Empire Flying Boat route from Poole to Cape Town. This was a leisurely and comfortable journey of some four to five days alighting several times after short flights with night stops at luxurious hotels, first along the Mediterranean to the Nile and then down various lakes on the African Continent in splendid luxury while in flight, in many ways similar to taking a cruise aboard ship. Compare this with the hustle and bustle of modern air travel, congestion at airports, cramped in-flight conditions and even though the time from departure to destination is but a fraction of the time taken in those days, comparison is surely unfavourable. I suppose the people taking the Flying Boat trip would all be travelling first class these days which would of course reduce the inconvenience. Researching and preparing this project taught me a lot about the route and the various alighting sites. A few Apprentices went to great trouble producing bound copies in book form, maybe to impress, but more likely because of their enthusiasm for their subject .

But we had another year of concentrated workshops before us on engines and their ancillaries: magnetos, propellers, generators, carburettors and so on. Examinations came thick and fast. We even had a course on the transport of the day, in particular the Leyland lorry with solid tyres. All very different from today.

At last our three years of hard work at school and in the workshops had come to an end and we were poised for the final parade at Halton. The green capband of 1 Wing Apprentices would soon be replaced by the black capband of an airman. The brass wheel of the Apprentice would no longer be worn on the sleeve above the left elbow; the lucky ones would replace it with a small cloth propeller (PROPS) indicating the grade of Leading Aircraftsman (LAC) with the pay of thirty-eight and sixpence (one pound ninety-three pence) a week. To attain this grade a mark of eighty per cent was required, but I missed it by one and a half per cent which gave me the grade of Aircraftsman First Class (AC1) and weekly pay of twenty-nine and ninepence (one pound forty-eight pence). Although my workshop results were slightly above average, my school results were only average. The effect was nearly nine shillings a week difference in my pay. Forty-five pence does not seem much now, but it was about a thirty per cent difference. Convert that into modern terms and you'll see what it meant.

It is claimed with some justification that the RAF combines the efficiency of the Sappers with the smartness of the Guards. Anyone in doubt should have seen a Passing Out Parade of the Halton Apprentices. The Queen's Colour Squadron of the RAF Regiment will give you some impression of the standard. As far as efficiency is concerned, Halton is recognised as the finest engineering college in the world. In the summer of 1933 graduation day for the 22nd Entry had arrived and we were on parade smart and proud, a credit, I hope, to Sammy Marshal. Our reviewing officer was none other than Air Chief Marshal Lord Trenchard with Air Commodore Bonham-Carter, the Air Officer Commanding Royal Air Force Halton, in attendance, on his horse as always. And so we were inspected, at least three times, marched past in fours, advanced in Review Order, marched off and dismissed. We rushed to our barracks, collected our kit, attended pay parade where I collected a handsome sum in back-pay and set off on fourteen days' leave to await posting instructions.

*Lord Trenchard inspecting a passing out of an early entry of his 'Brats'. The Leading Aircraft Apprentice chevron and the 'wheel' are shown on the shoulder of the 'marker' at the end.*

And so I ended my Halton training and took my place in the RAF proper. I may have ceased to be an Aircraft Apprentice, but I had not ceased to be a 'Brat' because that is something that is with you for life: once a 'Brat' always a 'Brat', I am pleased and proud to say.

# *CHAPTER 3*

## *Engine Repair Shop*

## *Calshot*

And so to fourteen days' leave with my parents at Sway. On a rate of pay of nearly thirty shillings a week, a substantial increase on my Apprentice days, I was feeling pretty well off. I was thrilled to be posted to RAF Calshot, a flying boat base situated opposite the Isle of Wight. It was not far away from my home which was probably the reason for my being posted there. Calshot was a Coastal Command Station, but had started life as a Royal Naval Air Service base and it was here that the first ever torpedo dropping trials from an aircraft took place in 1914. At the time of my posting Calshot was the base for two Southampton Flying Boat Squadrons, a Saro Cloud Squadron and a couple of Walrus amphibian aircraft. There were a number of floatplanes whose use was soon discontinued. This was fortunate, since the pilots were under flying training and had a habit of putting the aeroplane on its nose by hitting the water with the front tip of the floats on landing. As the engine, or most of it, was capable of being salvaged, this error usually entailed a twenty-four hour shift for the engine repair shop; the pilot just got a fright.

The High Speed Flight had just won the Schneider Trophy outright having been successful for the third time. This was the trophy awarded for an international air race for floatplanes, challenged for by various nations. Although the Flight had been disbanded, the buzz of their success was still part of the station's talk. It was won on this occasion in the Supermarine S6B. The power unit was a Rolls Royce Merlin, a twelve cylinder engine in two banks of six in a sixty degree 'V' which gave very little wind resistance. The aircraft was designed by Reginald Mitchell and was developed by discarding the floats and fitting a retractable undercarriage to become the

Supermarine Spitfire, probably the best known British aircraft of all time, which provided the RAF with one of the main fighter aircraft to oppose the Luftwaffe in the Battle of Britain. I can only assume that the S6B was a floatplane to allow the 'takeoff' length required for this high speed aircraft, since long runways were not then in existence and had to be built with the introduction of the Spitfire and Hurricane as well as for the heavy bombers.

As is often the case, it was only through the generosity of a public spirited person, in this case Lady Houston who donated a hundred thousand pounds to the Schneider Trophy Project, that it was possible to proceed, as the Government of the day was not prepared to provide the necessary finance. Had it not been for this generosity, who can say how long delayed the Spitfire would have been and if it could have been available in time for the Battle of Britain in which it played such a decisive part. A number of such opportunities have been either missed or delayed through Government parsimony or lack of courage. Frank Whittle's jet engine could have been put into Service use much sooner had the Government been prepared to provide the necessary support, with the probable effect of shortening the war. The resulting financial savings would have been far greater than the development costs, let alone the savings in lives and misery. Air Commodore Frank Whittle, now Sir Frank, was an ex Aircraft Apprentice trained at RAF Halton who went on to RAF Cranwell after being awarded a cadetship. He battled with authority to have his jet engine developed, but it was not until May 1941 that the Gloster Whittle aircraft first flew. Eventually, the Meteor was developed from this modest beginning, but who can predict the effect on, again, the Battle of Britain if Frank Whittle had been supported more vigorously and jet powered aircraft been available years earlier. Many such opportunities have been missed and one that is dear to my heart is that of the Halton Aircraft Apprentice Scheme which has been abandoned during the time I am writing. Surely the Royal Air Force needs the highly skilled tradesmen which the scheme has produced over the years, many of whom have reached Air Rank as Trenchard predicted. The war record of these ex 'Brats', both in the air and on the ground, has proved that a boy of sixteen years of age trained in this way is of immeasurable value. I just ask the simple question, 'How will the "Brat" be replaced?'

RAF Calshot was a flying boat base in Coastal Command at the time I was posted there. It was divided into two camps; the living accommodation was situated about a mile away from the hangars and workshops. Some was provided near the workshops site for the marine section and for two duty fitters who had to be available to start the engine which provided the auxiliary electricity supply when it was needed. This lower camp was known as the

'Spit' since it was positioned at Spithead opposite the Isle of Wight. A narrow gauge railway, used in the main to carry stores between them, connected the two sites. We paraded on the square at the top camp and marched down to the Spit behind the band each morning. They had the advantage of being entitled to make use of the train on the journey back from the Spit to main camp to convey their instruments; the midday meal was provided in the dining room at the lower campsite where there was a NAAFI for our requirements. Having arrived at Calshot I reported to the admin. section and having had a bed in the Engine Repair Shop billet allocated to me, all my particulars were then recorded in the usual way on arrival at a new Station, although of course all of this was new to me at the time. I was instructed to catch the train to lower camp and report to the O/C ERS (Engine Repair Shop). I caught what proved to be a rather 'Heath Robinson' train. As a matter of interest, the train driver had to be paid union rates since the train had to cross a public road. It must have been the cushiest train driver's job in all of Southern Railways.

The living accommodation on main or top camp was a great disappointment after the brick barrack blocks at Halton where we were provided with central heating and adequate ablution facilities with plentiful hot water. At top camp it was in dilapidated huts, twenty to a hut with three wash basins at the end. Hot water was only available in a separate block which also provided the lavatory facilities and was some distance from the huts. Only here was it possible to get a bath which, considering the nature of our work, could hardly be considered satisfactory. A small round stove in the centre of the hut provided heating. On cold winter nights the two forms and two chairs which were all we had to sit on, hugged this stove and those lucky enough to get a seat tended to keep it for the night. On one memorable occasion an armourer in the room who had managed to collect a few rounds of ammunition threw them into the stove and grabbed the seat that had been vacated by the previous occupant in panic, not realising that there was very little danger, only a few bangs. It worked once, but only once. Conditions were primitive in the extreme, but the airman of the thirties accepted them, albeit reluctantly and with the occasional moan, or 'bind' to use the accepted term of the time. Those of us who had not got the necessary qualifications for the next step up the ladder attended evening classes, thankfully held in heated classrooms, which were run by one of the SNCOs on the station. Sport on Wednesday and Saturday afternoons provided the exercise we needed, as well as the daily mile long march down to the Spit and back again. During the summer months we used to swim in the sea off the beach opposite the lower camp barracks. So all our spare time could be occupied away from the cold, depressing and soul destroying barrack rooms.

I duly arrived at the Spit and reported to the Warrant Officer in charge, and after a short interview was appointed to work with an LAC on the Napier Lion engine bench. I regret to say that his name escapes me, but because of his red hair he was obviously known as 'Ginger'. He had recently returned from the North West Frontier where he had been a fitter/air gunner in a Wapiti Squadron. At that time it was common for one of the tradesmen who serviced the aircraft to take a course in air gunnery and fly with the pilot of his particular aircraft as his gunner. This was rewarded by an increase in pay of one and sixpence (7½p) a day. A brass flying bullet to indicate he was a trained air gunner was worn above the cloth propeller (props) that indicated he was a Leading Aircraftsman. In those days a pilot generally had his own aeroplane, aircrew and ground crew, the whole working together as a team and taking great pride in the aircraft. He had a wealth of experience and I learnt a great deal from him, not only about engines, but life in the Air Force in general. His hometown was Plymouth and he inevitably supported Plymouth Argyle football team. We got on well together, working on Rolls Royce and Napier Lion engines. Ginger had been an LAC for many years; it was not unusual in those days for an LAC to serve as much as ten or twelve years in the rank, promotion was so slow. He told me of trips as an air gunner in Wapitis on the North West Frontier's mountainous regions; the tribesmen were hostile and, with rifles that they had probably stolen from our troops, were crack shots. Using the novel technique of lying on their back and holding the rifle between their feet they often managed a hit on the Wapitis. I think it was Ginger who told me that promissory notes, known as 'goolie chits' were carried by crews as an insurance policy in the event of being shot down or making a forced landing from other causes and being captured by the tribesmen whose women had nasty habits with one's private bits, generally starting with their removal without anaesthetic or sterilisation of the instruments. The 'goolie chit' promised to pay fifty rupees if the airman was returned complete. It is interesting to know that in the Gulf War in 1991 the SAS carried ten gold sovereigns for exactly the same purpose. The more things change the less they seem to change.

The three year Apprentice training at Halton provided the necessary grounding in engineering, but a further period was required for recognition as a fully trained FAE (Fitter Aero Engine), my trade designation. I had passed my trade test for LAC at the Central Trade Test Establishment, West Drayton and I was now the happy recipient of a weekly pay of thirty-eight and sixpence. Shortly after gaining my 'Props' I was put in charge of the radial engine bay in ERS. The radial air-cooled engines for which I became responsible were seven cylinder Lynx, nine cylinder Jupiter and fourteen cylinder Jaguar (two banks of seven cylinders), the same engines that we had been trained on at Halton; these unfortunately were not being dismantled on a daily basis and therefore presented us with rather more difficulty than the demonstration models in the training workshops. This was quite a responsibility for a young man not yet twenty-one years of age. Much of the work could be described as semiskilled and it was considered wasteful in manpower to employ highly trained engine fitters on such work. It was therefore decided to introduce a new trade of Fitter's Mate for such tasks. These chaps had had some basic training but their skills did not permit them to sign for work; they could do it, just not sign for it: only a qualified aero engine fitter could do that.

One of these lads was assigned to me; he was a keen young man anxious to gain as much experience as possible to enable him to take the exams necessary to remuster to the higher trade group. He worked hard and as a team we became the blue eyed boys of ERS, producing reconditioned engines in record time. Job sheets were required to be completed for each task on each engine and the work was inspected by the Sergeant Fitter in the workshops, so there were no short cuts or skimping. We just worked well together which made us extremely efficient. We both enjoyed our work and working together as a team. Like everyone we enjoyed receiving praise for the work being of a high standard. I do not know if my 'mate' was able to re-muster and I am sorry I was never able to check, but I am certain that in the period of expansion that was then upon us that he did and made a good aero engine fitter. I hope he learned as much from me as I did from Ginger. It was at about this time that the Apprentice training at Halton started to train what were known as 'Fitter IIs' which combined both engine and airframe training. Fitter II mates assisted these highly qualified tradesmen.

Another trade that existed at that time, but which I suspect is no longer is existence, was that of Wader. These chaps, garbed in a thick waterproof suit, were employed to take the cradle down the slipway and position it under the hull of a flying boat which was to be brought up for servicing. This entailed going into the water up to their armpits and the procedure generally took some time. In the winter the water was extremely cold and so were the Waders; as a result they were allowed a ration of Royal Navy rum to bring back their circulation. The pleasure had not yet been spoiled by the scientist who discovered that this treatment does more harm than good; one or two of the young boys would refuse this very strong rum and although normally they were required to drink it in the presence of the issuing officer, on one occasion it was passed on to a fellow Wader who had already downed his own ration; he crawled away and was oblivious to all around him for the next three hours. These chaps also went out to the floatplane aircraft, a few of which still operated at Calshot, and carried the pilots pick-a-back from plane to shore. Some servicing could be undertaken when a flying boat was moored afloat; on these occasions all the tools being used were attached by cords to the tradesman doing the work to prevent their loss if dropped, a common occurrence when working in a cold wind.

Work in the Engine Repair Shop at Calshot was not particularly exciting, but I enjoyed the responsibility of the radial engine bay, stripping an engine down to the last nut and bolt, ensuring that all the parts were sound and within the prescribed limits, reassembling them, ensuring that the valve and ignition timings were correct and then taking it to the Heenan and Froud test bed to ensure the correct power was being obtained. Finally, at the end of this procedure, I would return it to the workshop where it remained installed on its engine stand until required by one of the squadrons. Perhaps the thrill of flying off with the flying boats, particularly when they went away on their summer cruises, was more exciting, but the satisfaction in turning out a good engine from the one returned for major overhaul, was to me very rewarding. An even greater challenge and cause for satisfaction arose when one of the floatplanes dug in the tips of its floats and put the engine in the sea. It is a well known fact that seawater is very corrosive and the sooner one is able to deal with an engine which has been immersed, the better. Usually, by the time the engine had been recovered and delivered to ERS, it was late afternoon. However we had had time to make the necessary preparations. It was all hands to the pumps as the engine had to be dismantled quickly and each component inspected for corrosion. Some metals corrode very quickly indeed and cannot be salvaged, so no time is wasted on them; magnesium is a prime example. Each part that looked as if it could be saved was attached to a wire and immersed in a tank of boiling caustic soda solution; the length of time the part was left in this solution depended entirely on the metal it was made from. Steel required the longest time, aluminium like magnesium was unlikely to be salvaged. As a result of working at speed, the surrounds of the tank became wet and slippery and on one occasion a chap slipped when extracting a heavy item and was scalded when he put his arm out to save himself. The problem of course is twofold, as the caustic soda burn is as devastating itself as the fact that it is boiling. He was quickly washed in clean cold water and taken to casualty. Apart from a badly scarred arm he suffered no ill affects, but it did provide a lesson to us all to be more careful. When the parts were extracted from the caustic solution they were immersed in boiling water, dried and inspected. If passed as salvaged they were oiled and put away for a further inspection after about forty-eight hours and if they passed this they were fit to be used as spares.

These incidents usually happened late in the afternoon and the whole procedure took at least twelve and often as much as sixteen hours. On one particular Friday we started on an immersed engine at about four in the afternoon and it was after eight o'clock next morning before I had bathed and got to bed in my billet. An hour later I was told to stand by for CO's inspection, a normal Saturday morning routine. One did not argue in those days: I got up, folded my bedding in the prescribed manner, 'kit will be laid up as laid down' still held true, and stood by my bed. The CO, Group Captain Callaway, noticing my dishevelled state, asked why I was there as everyone else had laid their kit out for inspection and left for work. When I explained he told me to carry on, for which I was very grateful since I had been on the go for over twenty-four hours.

The fitters in ERS were responsible for the engine positioned in its own little hut at the Spit which provided power for the station in the event of normal power failure. To ensure that this engine could be started in an emergency it was run for a few minutes on a daily basis. This was easier said than done as the problem lay in starting the beast which was only ever achieved with difficulty. Firstly the priming had to be absolutely right; this was followed by turning the single cylinder engine using a large starting handle similar to that used on early motor cars. It was crucial to be prepared for the vicious kick-back that occurred when the engine did not fire. One chap had his arm broken in this way through being a bit too casual. It is interesting to think that in those days accidents like this and the poor chap with the caustic soda scald were taken as part and parcel of everyday life and a result of pure accident or carelessness; no one gave the slightest thought to suing the RAF, in fact there was a certain amount of trepidation as to whether or not we would be placed on a charge for our stupidity. It seems to me that these days the first port of call would be a solicitor to see how much compensation could be expected. I think the world's gone mad.

During Christmas breaks two ERS fitters had to stay behind to start this engine and also to turn the serviceable engines in the Engine Repair Shop to ensure that the oil was circulated. The fitters responsible for these engines did this job during normal working hours, but the ERS Workshop was closed during the Christmas break and the job fell to the two duty fitters who remained behind to start the auxiliary engine. To make life easier they moved down to the bottom camp for this period, which usually lasted a week depending on the day on which Christmas fell. I volunteered twice for this duty; the accommodation was far superior to the pre-war huts that we normally occupied and ablution facilities made one feel almost human. Provided the two duties assigned were carried out our life was free and easy; in fact, there was enough free time to make it possible to carry out work on our personal motor bikes using the workshop facilities which were not normally available to us. Since the period of time spent on duty over the Christmas period could be taken afterwards as leave, it seemed to me that I gained all round.

Christmas Day is a great occasion in the services; the dining hall is decorated, as is the NAAFI. The RAF cooks always excel themselves, producing the traditional dinner of turkey with all the trimmings in large quantities. Traditionally the SNCOs and officers who are in married quarters on the station serve the other ranks. Two NCOs joined us for the meal on my last Christmas as Calshot, having got to know some of us through sport. A fair quantity of beer was consumed, but bearing in mind the donkey engine's kick I decided that discretion was the better part of valour and did not overdo it. On future Christmases I helped serve the Christmas dinner both as an NCO and later as an officer. It is a great tradition which is enjoyed by everyone, except possibly the wives who have little idea of when their husbands will get home and what condition they will be in.

My time at Calshot was fully occupied in work, sport and my motor cycle. I had managed to buy a motor bike when I became an LAC, the increase in pay being put towards this purchase for the princely sum of fifty pounds. With petrol at 11½*d.* a gallon, less than five pence in today's money, and with tax and insurance in about the same proportion, I was just about able to manage. I was not able to afford more than one outing each week, so many evenings were spent in the company of a number of other motor cycle owners dismantling, cleaning and tuning, and discussing the merits of our steeds, all great names in the British motor cycle industry that have sadly disappeared: names like Norton, Aerial Square 4s, Rudge, BSA, Velocette with their fishtail exhaust pipes and a number of others. Great social evenings.

The two sports on which I concentrated, rugby and athletics, were well supported at Calshot and the young officers attending the flying boat school of navigation that was based there generated a great deal of competition for places in the rugby side. I managed to make it in the first season I was on the station, playing in the forwards, but next season, having shown a burst of speed at the station sports the following summer, moved to the three-quarters, either as wing or centre. The station rugby side played a number of local club sides as well as nearby RAF Stations. Coastal Command stations are widely spread so in the Command championships we often had to travel great distances. On one memorable occasion Calshot was drawn against Pembroke Dock in South Wales. We left on Tuesday and played on a very exposed ground on the top of a hill in a strong wind, with nothing having seemed to stop it all the way from Siberia; it was the one called a lazy wind, because it is too lazy to go round, it just goes straight through you. After the first half the officials decided to provide a tot of Navy rum in lieu of the normal slice of orange. It certainly got the circulation working again. But rugby is a religion in Wales and since most of their team was Welsh, we lost. They are also good drinkers and we joined them that evening for a few 'jars'. The coach was very quiet on the way back next day, but never the less a match to be remembered, if I only could.

I mentioned that I produced a burst of speed at the station athletics and did well in the 100 and 220 yard sprints. This should have come as no great surprise as I had done quite a lot of training as a schoolboy and achieved some success at that level, as well as competing during my time at Halton, but somehow it did. I also had a go at the long jump which was new to me and did well in that too. At that time the RAF Championships were held at RAF Uxbridge and each RAF Station sent a team. I was a member of the Calshot team and represented it in the long jump and 100 yards with little noticeable effect. The team did not disgrace itself. My chief memory is of Don Finlay, then a Sergeant Pilot, winning the 120 yards high hurdles, the event at which he was to achieve Olympic fame. Great Britain dominated this event for some years, first with Lord Burghley and then with Don Finlay. One of the sports halls at Halton today is called the Finlay Hall in his memory. I wonder how many of the recruits who use it these days have the remotest idea of who their predecessor was or how great his sporting achievements were?

The highlight of my athletic career was winning the Victor Ludorum Trophy at the Calshot sports in 1935, winning the 100 yards, the 220 yards and the long jump. My second place in the shot put, which I had taken up that year, gave me sufficient points to win the coveted trophy. The ERS team won the section cup and the evening was spent in celebration. The Team Captain, Flight Lieutenant Jordan, a very able high jumper, asked if we wanted beer or champagne. I opted for champers. This was my first taste and I have been hooked on it every since; unfortunately I cannot afford it as often as I would like. I did play the occasional game of soccer but only at Flight level.

At about this time there was a notice displayed asking for volunteers for pilot training. I was very happy with my life at Calshot; I had got into a lovely rut at work, and was a regular member of the station rugby side during the winter and represented the station at athletics in summer. In a half hearted sort of way I considered applying but it was not until the chap who had been my Leading Boy at Halton, the same chap who had me in his room to get me on his side in order to control the other members of the room, applied that I changed my mind. It was not until some time later that I realised how childish I had been but equally how fortunate to have made the decision. Having applied, I discovered that I would be required to pass an aptitude test and I was sent to Eastleigh across the estuary from Calshot. I was put in the rear seat of the dual control aircraft, I have even forgotten what it was, and the Flight Lieutenant testing me seemed to expect that I could fly this thing, even though he never bothered to ask if I had any experience. He gave me no instruction at all and sent a report saying, 'This airman will never make a pilot.' How it was possible for him to reach this conclusion escapes me. Fortunately for me my superiors, and luckily his, thought otherwise and I was selected for pilot training in due course. I have been eternally grateful to LAA Smart who unknowingly contributed to my childish decision. My days at Calshot were coming to a close; they had been an enjoyable three years during which I learnt a lot. What now awaited me was going to be very different.

# *CHAPTER 4*

## *Flying Training*

### *Brough – No.6 Flying Training School – Netheravon*

*Oh, I have slipped the surly bands of earth*
*And danced the skies on laughter silvered wings*
*Sunward I've climbed and joined the tumbling mirth*
*Of sunsplit clouds – and done a hundred things*
*You have not dreamed of: wheeled and soared and swung*
*High in the sunlit silence, hovering there*
*I've chased the shouting wind along, and flung*
*My eager craft through footless halls of air*
*Up, up the long delirious burning blue*
*I've topped the windswept heights with easy grace*
*Where never lark nor eagle flew;*
*And while, with silent lifting wind I've trod*
*The high untrespassed sanctity of space*
*Put out my hand, and touched the face of God.*

This poem was written by Flying Officer I. Gillespie Maggee, a 19 year old airman who was killed shortly after leaving Rugby. It has been in my flying log from the day I saw it and cut it out.

After a very thorough medical at the Air Ministry Central Medical Establishment in London I was sent for Ab Initio flying training at Brough, near Hull, overlooking the Humber. This was one of a number of civilian flying schools commissioned by the RAF to train pilots for the expanding Service. Training was also provided for selected civilians who would be offered Short Service Commissions when qualified. This was a new form of engagement to provide the increased numbers of pilots that were obviously going to be required. Probably the most famous to enter in this way was Wing Commander Guy Gibson of 617 Squadron fame. They were known as pupil pilots until they qualified for their 'Wings'. A number of regular airmen were also included on these courses, almost all LACs who would remain in that rank until they qualified at one of the RAF advanced training schools, following the award of their 'Wings'.

Because these were civilian schools we wore civilian clothes and were accommodated in 'digs', those of the pupil pilots being rather better than ours which were rather cramped. The bedrooms were satisfactory, one or two to a room with a common dining room which was adequate; but the shared bathroom caused some difficulty when early flying was the order of the day. Facilities in this area were sparse in the extreme and in the early morning the bath, shower, wash basin and lavatory were all in use at the same time by one or other of the six occupants, in the rush to get ready for breakfast before early flying. Our uniforms had been packed away and we were free of all the restrictions associated with life on a RAF unit; parades, cleaning and similar chores were non-existent and we were learning to fly. Life was magnificent.

We were introduced to the Blackburn B2, a side by side two-seat bi-plane powered by a Gypsy Major. I was to be instructed by Flying Officer Morris now a civilian but presumably permitted to use his rank for disciplinary purposes: a stocky jovial man of about thirty years of age. We got on well together. The course was fairly concentrated and lectures and flying fully occupied our time. I was very concerned about my future when, in trying to help a friend, I stupidly put myself out of action and into bed for a precious week, fortunately in my room rather than being sent to hospital. One of my pupil pilot friends owned a motor cycle and was having some mechanical trouble and, being aware of my trade, asked me to have a look. I traced the trouble to nothing more than a sticking throttle cable which I soon freed. Having eased the cable I tried it on two or three occasions and, satisfied that the problem was cured, I decided to ride the bike round a small cinder track in front of a pavilion. I went round the circuit fairly carefully a couple of times, but the third time, going a little faster, the throttle stuck and I could not hold the machine. Not wanting to cause damage to either the machine or the pavilion, I tried to hold on; but on passing the veranda just caught my knee on one of the supports and as a result the footrest went through my leg just above the ankle, thankfully not into the bone, although it was exposed which was a fairly unpleasant sight. I was taken to the surgery by a colleague where the doctor cleaned up the wound, stitched up the gash and told me to rest for a week. I was more concerned at this stage about not being able to fly for a week than about the messy gash that was being cleaned up, but the colleague who took me to the surgery, watching intently, passed out in the middle of the proceedings. I would probably have been similarly affected by watching someone else having a wound being dealt with; it is always far worse to watch someone else rather than put up with the problem oneself.

Feeling rather fed up after four days in bed and envious of the other chaps continuing their flying and relating their experiences to me, even though they did bring the odd bottle of beer to provide me with some comfort, I was persuaded to join them on a visit to a pub that we frequented at week-ends. The landlord had two rather attractive daughters which, I rather suspect, may have had some influence on the popularity of his establishment. We spent Sunday afternoon harmlessly flirting with the daughters and overstayed our welcome with the result that the CFI (Chief Flying Instructor) was informed. He read me the riot act on my return to flying, although I think it was fairly tongue in cheek as rumour had it, though it was never

*The Blackburn B2 at Brough: Ab Initio Training*

substantiated, that he had been young himself once. Anyway, he flew my arse off for the last few days of the course, leaving a very shattered, but very relieved airman. I still bear the scar to remind me of my stupidity.

Early morning take-off always seemed to be across the Humber and the Gypsy Major in G-ACLD, the identification of my aircraft, disliked the early morning. In spite of the usual warm-up procedures there was always a splutter, either real or imaginary, when we were over the broadest part of the river, which caused me to wonder what the Blackburn B2 was like to ditch. Flying Officer Morris had no fears and laughed at my apprehension. My initial attempts at the slow roll also caused him great hilarity, especially when my safety harness was not tight enough and I ended up virtually on his lap, but this was the only disadvantage of the side by side seating. In all other respects it had advantages over the tandem set up; the instructor could see exactly how his pupil was coping, right or wrong, but most important of all was the fact that conversation was possible with no chance of the misunderstandings which occurred when we used the Gosport tube to communicate in the alternative set-up. It may be useful to explain the communication methods (or lack of them) used at that time. In the aircraft the 'Gosport tube' was the sole means of contact between pilot and instructor. This comprised a piece of tubing forming a 'Y' which was attached to the flying helmet and could be plugged in to the length of similar tubing between the front and rear cockpits; using this the instructor and pupil were supposed to be able to communicate, provided the connections were good, through a mouthpiece passing the sound through the tubing to the earpieces in the helmet. It is akin to children playing telephones using two tins connecting by a piece of string and about as effective, particularly when you add the noise of the engine and the slipstream in an open cockpit. Obviously communication was between poor and impossible. A couple of instances, allegedly authentic but probably apocryphal, come to mind, both occurring in the Avro Tutor which had this tandem arrangement. On the first occasion the instructor gave the normal order, 'It's all yours,' not aware that the pupil's helmet was not plugged in. The lovely docile Tutor flew for quite a while before the instructor realised something was wrong and took control back. The other instance was when an instructor with a pupil who lacked confidence but who obviously had ability decided to demonstrate his confidence in order to boost that of the pupil, disconnected his joystick and told the pupil what he had done without realising that the tube was not connected properly. Once again the Tutor made various gyrations on its own and the instructor, who could not replace the joystick, was forced to land using the engine and tail trim. The alternative to this version which I am sure is apocryphal is that the instructor after disconnecting his joystick threw it over the side of the cockpit and the pupil, thinking it was an instruction, followed suit. There is a lot to be said for the Royal Navy's system of repeating commands or in using side by side training aircraft like the Blackburn B2. As I said, the Avro Tutor was a very docile aeroplane which was a very good thing for all concerned. The advantages of R/T (radio/telephone) in both air to air and air to ground communication, as well as in the aircraft between crew members, are immeasurable, especially as an aid to navigation and landing. The chaos of the mass formation for the Hendon Air Display operating from Harwell was caused totally by lack of communication from the ground coupled with the inability to communicate between formations of different aircraft.

Not all the instruction was formal. On one occasion Flying Officer Morris looked over and said, 'Don't attempt this on your own,' and demonstrated a 'bunt', an outside loop. We climbed to about five thousand feet, throttled right back and just as we were about to stall he pushed the stick right forward, very exhilarating but the lasting memory is of a tremendous pressure on my eyeballs. I see from my Flying Log Book that in the last two days at Brough I flew for five hours on each day in a combination of instrument flying, aerobatics, advanced forced landings, cross-country and, finally, testing by the CFI (Chief Flying Instructor).

With a magnificent fifty-one hours and thirty minutes in my log book and an 'Average' assessment after having completed all the ground and flying tasks successfully I was posted to No.6 FTS (Flying Training School) Netheravon for continuation training. Incidentally I had gone solo in nine hours and fifteen minutes, a little better than the average. One of my great friends never did go solo, poor chap; mad keen, he just could not judge height and never made a landing unassisted. We all tried to help, but it is something you either have or have not got: the technical term is spatial awareness, I believe, and no amount of help will make any difference. It's rather like colour blindness, if you have it you have it, or in this case I suppose if you lack it, that's it. Many would-be pilots and many good tradesmen have been failed through being colour blind as well.

I arrived at RAF Netheravon, the home of No.6 FTS, on Salisbury Plain where Hawker Harts (T) for Trainer and (S) for Service, were the main training aircraft. In addition the Hawker Audax and Avro Tutor were used, mainly for night flying. We were introduced to the Hawker Hart which seemed so large and powerful after the little B2 that I had some qualms about my ability to fly this huge beast. As normally happens, once the immediate apprehension was overcome I wondered why it had existed at all and I took the philosophical view that it is generally safer to be under confident rather than over confident.

Sergeant Neal was to be my flying instructor and he took me on my first flight in the Hart (T) on 24th September 1936. We flew for thirty minutes to acquaint me principally with the aircraft but, just as importantly, the local area. I was given my first dual instruction on the same day, which covered the elementary handling of the aircraft on the ground and then in the air. My apprehension quickly disappeared and I wanted to be in sole charge of this beast as soon as possible. It was soon achieved; having signed to the effect that I understood the petrol system, wheel brakes and tail adjustment gear and following a low flying test, I was given instruction on the action to be taken in the event of fire and the procedure for stopping and starting the airscrew in the air. I was then tested by Flight Lieutenant George, the Flight Commander, and sent solo. After three hours and thirty minutes I had been allowed to take the beast I had been so frightened of into the air alone. The freedom and power of being in charge was thrilling and exhilarating. Flying on my own has always made me sing; anyone who has heard me will understand that it is the only time I dare, as the noise of the engine drowns out my voice so no one has to suffer.

After the comparative freedom of the civilian flying school at Brough,

*The Hawker Hart (MoD)*

we were now back to the strict discipline of the RAF, back into uniform with tunics buttoned up to the neck. Collars and ties were the privilege of SNCOs at that time and it was not until we had earned our 'Wings' and promotion to sergeant that the tunics which thankfully are now no longer in use, were discarded. Back to barrack-room accommodation, albeit less crowded and with Corporal 'Jacko' Jackson having the unenviable task of having to take charge by virtue of his two stripes. He did this difficult job well; after all, we were all in the same boat as far as our training was concerned. Sadly, he was to lose his life in a flying accident while on the course. Nevertheless, life was certainly easier and the accommodation better than at Calshot.

The Hawker Hart and the Audax were biplanes and very similar to the Fury and Hind which were from the same stable. The taxi skid, nothing as advanced as a tail wheel yet, and high fixed undercarriage gave a pronounced nose up attitude on the ground which made it necessary when taxiing to swing the aircraft to the left and right in order to see where one was going because the beautiful Rolls Royce engine was pointing to the sky and obscuring the view ahead. The same problem occurred when landing. In those days flying in to land using engine power was frowned upon and the procedure was to judge the distance from the landing spot on the down-wind leg; that is when you are flying parallel to the runway in the opposite direction to the direction in which you will land, you throttle right back and make the approach and landing without engine. Of course if the judgement had been bad, engine power had to be used before touchdown, but the system was to turn in higher than was necessary and side slip any excess height off by use of rudder and control column. This also had the effect of getting the nose out of the forward view for landing. The show offs, which we all were in the early days, would slip to the right, then the left, until at the correct landing height, we would kick the rudder to get the aircraft straight for landing, essential on the small grass airfields of the time; this was known as the falling leaf approach. Since it was also *de rigueur* to make a three point landing, that is touching the wheels and the tail skid simultaneously, the later the aircraft was straightened up the longer the view ahead was available.

Night-flying in these nose up aircraft was made even more difficult by the flame from the exhaust stubs. For night-flying, goose neck flares, paraffin cans with rags stuffed into the necks and set alight, were placed at a distance of one hundred yards apart aligned into the wind, with two flares adjacent to the last flare to form a 'T'. Landings were made on the right-hand side of the flarepath, the pilot looking out to the left, judging his height with reference to the first flare and distance by the number of flares passed. It sounds complicated but one soon got used to it. The main problem was that the flame from the stubs ruined the pilot's night vision every time he looked out to judge the reference points. Early night-flying instruction was given in that lovely docile aircraft, the Avro Tutor, so kind it almost seemed to fly itself. Powered by a Lynx radial engine, with no exhaust flame or nose up attitude to contend with, it generally only required a short period of instruction on this beauty for sufficient confidence in night-flying to be built up to allow the pilot to progress to the Hart and Audax. The average time on the Tutor at night was a mere five hours before going solo and a further four hours before achieving it on the Hart. Night flying is a thrilling experience, particularly seeing the street lighting in towns; the whole landscape unfolds as a series of patches of light with intense darkness in between, very spectacular.

Instruction in instrument flying was achieved by covering the pupil's cockpit with a large green hood, making it impossible to see outside. The instrument panel was rudimentary and obviously had to be improved. However there was a turn and bank gauge, a rate of climb meter, an altimeter and a compass. Initially we flew on each instrument in turn followed by carrying out turns, plain spins, spins and recovering on a heading and finally take-off. All this was quite an achievement with those antiquated instruments. Throughout this time we had periodical tests by the Flight Commander and by the Chief Flying Instructor (CFI). I was naturally very pleased to be given an assessment of 'Above the Average' with no faults at the end of Flying Training and again at the end of the Advanced Flying Training. Group Captain ap Ellis was the Commanding Officer of RAF Netheravon, who pinned on my 'Wings' on 9th January 1937. I offer my heartfelt thanks to Sergeant Pilot Neal who must have had many frights at my expense as my instructor. I am proud of my above average rating, but it could not have been achieved without his patience and skill.

Sergeant Neal recommended me for my first solo in the Hawker Hart (T) after four hours and ten minutes dual instruction. I was tested by the Flight Commander, Flight Lieutenant George, and was passed to fly solo. I then passed on to the standard flying practices. On certain of these practices further instruction was given by Sergeant Neal and tests were made by Flight Lieutenant George and the Chief Flying Instructor, Squadron Leader Toogood. Aerobatics had to be demonstrated by the instructor: side slipping, cross wind landings, forced landings and so on. Everything was religiously recorded in my Flying Log Book; the flying hours were checked each month by Sergeant Jenner, a flying instructor in 'B' Flight; he seemed to have been delegated the unenviable task of checking the flying hours of all the pupils before they were signed as being correct by the respective flight commanders and the CFI, Squadron Leader Toogood.

Having successfully passed all the tests required for the award of the Flying Badge, the coveted 'Wings' in the training squadron and having been assessed as 'Above the Average' for that stage of my training, I moved on to the Advanced Training Squadron. The CFI was Squadron Leader Ivelaw Chapman and Flight Lieutenant Lousada, the Flight Commander in 'E' Flight. We continued flying the Hart (T) the Training version and the Hart (S) the Service version without dual control, the rear cockpit being fitted with a gun turret in place of the rear seat. The Hawker Audax was also included in the flying programme. These practices will appear simple and strange to today's pupil pilots but it must be borne in mind that the aids which are available today give considerable assistance both on the ground and in the air to the pupil, even though flying is more complicated and demanding. The instrument panel in 1937 only comprised a magnetic compass, an altimeter, a turn and bank indicator and a simple climb and descent indicator. None of them were gyro instruments and therefore tended to be rather sluggish in their responses.

Anticipating the extra money we would be getting on promotion to Sergeant Pilot, a number of us bought old bangers to provide us with some mobility, as the public transport on Salisbury Plain was not too plentiful. We were all technical tradesmen so the cars would provide the means of keeping our hands in and our skills honed. The vehicles varied from a Bugatti with all its copper pipes to keep polished to the Riley 9 owned by my great friend and rugby colleague Arthur 'Darkie' Clowes, the one on my right in the photograph of our rugby 'Sevens' side. We dismantled the Riley down to the last nut and bolt, replaced all the worn parts and generally refurbished it until it was in first class condition. The aim was to have it ready before we were due to go to Practice Camp at Penrhos, near Pwhelli in Wales, so that we could use it to get to the Camp and then have it for week-end trips while we were there. Permission was obtained for it to be used to convey four of us on the trip; it came up to all expectations and we were happily travelling along a main road into Wales, making good time as the road was wide and straight, when some hundred and fifty yards ahead of us a large Austin saloon started a 'U' turn. Darkie, who was driving, assumed that the driver could see us approaching and kept going, tooting his horn to make sure that he was aware of us. The Austin driver took no notice and continued his manoeuvre; we saw that the Austin was unable to get round in one lock, so steered to pass in front of it; but the driver, still apparently oblivious to our presence, started to move forward leaving insufficient room for us to pass, either in front or to the rear. Inevitably we crashed into him, damaging the Riley sufficiently to make it impossible to proceed. We telephoned the Duty Officer at Penrhos to inform him of what had happened and also that there were no buses or trains which could get us there on time. We received no sympathy and were ordered to get to Camp as soon as possible. As a result all privileges were withdrawn for seven days. At the local police station we learned that the Austin owner was a local doctor and the chances of compensation were negligible; the fact that he was deaf and seldom wore his hearing aid would carry no weight. Darkie's insurers were equally unsympathetic. Heyho, forty or more hours of work, considerable expense and no car. It was adding insult to injury that we had to take the blame. I suppose we should have stopped, but we had the right of way. It was the other driver who should have been charged with careless driving, but in those days young RAF pilots, particularly NCOs, had no chance against a local doctor; the scales were weighted totally in his favour as doctors were, after all, considered to be close to gods. Funny how things have changed; being a local doctor wouldn't cut much ice nowadays, yet the skill level

*Rugby at No. 6 FTS Netheravon 1936. Four of the winning Sevens Team; I am third from left.*

required is infinitely higher.

The Practice Camp was established to test the ability of pilots using live ammunition in the role in which they had been trained. As trainee pilots and not yet allocated to front line squadrons we were to be tested on the aircraft on which we were training. Therefore we were all tested in bombing, front gun and rear gun on either Harts or Audaxes.

There were a number of Practice Camps in the UK, all situated on the coast to permit safe gunnery and bombing over the sea in areas not frequented by shipping. Our camp was Penrhos, near Abersoch in mid Wales. Practice Camps had a permanent staff who were responsible on the one hand for all the various equipment, things like the targets, observation towers and drogues, and also for the pilots and aircraft to tow them. On the other hand they had to assess all the results. Drogues were trailed some one hundred and twenty feet behind the towing aircraft along a set path and the pupil fired at the drogue on a signal from the drogue pilot. Of course, because there was no R/T in those days, the signals were purely visual. The trainee fired the Lewis gun from the rear cockpit of the attacking aircraft from various positions and hits were counted on the drogue after it had been dropped near the permanent staff huts. Targets anchored out to sea were used for bombing from heights of six, eight, and ten thousand feet. Wind speed and direction had first to be calculated, normally using the three-course pattern which had its limitations, and this was used to calculate the bomb run. We were still using the old bombsight which also had serious limitations. Pupils were paired, one flying the aircraft while his partner practised bomb-aiming and similarly turns were taken firing the guns so that an assessment could be made of each pupil and each pair, because the pilot's ability could affect the gunner or bomb-aimer. Results were checked from the control hut and at the end of the camp were discussed with each pair. Bombing results, as can be expected, were far from good; if one managed a group within twenty yards it was good. Dive-bombing was much more satisfactory and a number of hits were recorded, but with no enemy fire against us our life was made easy.

As the bomb-aimer I found the trajectory of the bomb fascinating. On release a bomb appeared to drop vertically. When I released my first bomb I felt I had made a bad calculation and the result would be a miss well short of the target but as it descended the trajectory seemed to adopt more of an angle until just prior to impact it seemed to travel almost horizontally and to my great surprise, made impact beyond the target. My partner in these exercises was a fellow LAC who was a very steady pilot named Woods; obviously we christened him 'Timber'. For high level bombing it is essential to keep the height steady and certainly just before bomb release not to make rapid course correction or the bomb will be thrown out of line. On the run-up corrections are made by the bomb-aimer giving the commands: left, left or r-i-g-h-t, then STEADY, pause, bombs gone. The last to allow the pilot to relax from his concentrated flying. The whole process can be likened to the rally driver and his navigator with the pilot merely reacting to the commands and taking little or no independent action. Perhaps Timber and I ended up in the same newly formed Coastal Command GR Squadron 217, because we had obtained good results together at Practice Camp.

The flight back to Netheravon at the end of our time at Penrhos was an experience. We were to fly back in our aeroplanes, but because it was considered unwise to allow a formation of pupil pilots loose on their own, an instructor was detailed to lead the small formation of six Harts. We duly set off, but somehow the instructor managed to get lost when we ran into cloud and since we were merely flying in formation, that is effectively following our leader and not map reading ourselves, we could not help. We had no R/T so he could not let us know what the problem was. He tried to use signs to let us know that he was going down to have a look at the sign on a railway station, but with no success; so down he went to read the station name; down we all followed one after the other on a beautiful 'Beat-up' of the station. We were good dutiful airmen and said nothing on our return to Netheravon and no one at the station reported us. If it happened today all hell would be let loose, not least in the press. To the modern pilot this must seem like Fred Carno's Army, but our navigation was largely by road map and the use of the 'iron beam', perhaps better known as the railway line. We were little better equipped two years later when we went to war.

# *CHAPTER 5*

## *The first ground based Coastal Command Squadron*

### *Tangmere – St Eval*

On 21st May 1937 with an overall assessment of 'Above the Average', I was selected to join one of the newly formed Coastal Command land based squadrons. Hitherto, flying boats had been the only aircraft used by Coastal Command. 217 (GR) Squadron was formed at Boscombe Down operating the Avro Anson Mark One, an aircraft of mainly wooden construction

*RAF Tangmere 1937*

powered by two Cheetah engines, but at least with an enclosed cockpit as everything I had flown to that point had been open to the elements. Boscombe Down was a Bomber Command base deemed to be too far inland for a Coastal Command Squadron with aircraft of limited range. At that time there were no Coastal Command aerodromes for the simple reason that there had been no land based aircraft and we were forced to be a lodger unit somewhere. On 27th May therefore we moved to Tangmere, a Fighter Command Station accommodating Numbers 1 and 43 Squadrons, both with famous histories. At least it was by the sea. Soon after we arrived, the 'A' Flight Flight Commander, 'Nobby' Clarke, took me up for my first trip in the Anson. I just sat in the right hand seat and watched as there was no dual control in the aeroplane. This was hardly ideal in daylight, but was positively dangerous when learning to fly it at night.

We settled in at Tangmere quite happily considering the rawness of the flying personnel most of whom were young, newly commissioned officers, and some Direct Entry Sergeant Pilots who were awarded their rank on qualifying as pilots but with no experience of the Service. We were fortunate in 'A' Flight in having the regular 'Nobby' Clarke as Flight Commander. The other two Flights had newly promoted junior officers in charge. As I said, Coastal Command hitherto had not had land based squadrons and thus had no experienced officers to call upon for these newly formed units. At the same time, Bomber and Fighter Commands were loath to lose any of their experienced officers and the Anson Squadrons being formed were forced to rely, in the main, upon young newly commissioned Short Service Officers. On the whole the newly promoted Flight Commanders justified their appointments but those of us who had seen service had reservations as to their abilities in man management which in the Service requires a special understanding of airmen, who are generally a breed apart. The man who is best able to provide this in depth knowledge of the individuals is the Flight Sergeant, as he is the person who works most closely and directly with them. Each flight has one; they know their men, know the service and its funny ways and their advice is invaluable to the inexperienced officer in charge of a flight. Those prepared to listen to and learn from the 'Chiefy' made good flight commanders; those who thought they knew it all made a big mistake and in one case I recall, completely lost the support he needed. In 'A' flight we were again lucky when 'Nobby' Clarke was posted after being promoted in having a Canadian, 'Arnie' Arnold, getting his own promotion and being appointed as our Flight Commander. I served with him for the next four years: a good flight commander. Later, at St Eval, after he was married, he lived in a bungalow just below ours and the families became good friends.

The members of the Sergeants' Mess were not so happy: invaded by young Sergeant Pilots who had come from the ranks to become members of a Mess occupied by SNCOs who had served for many years with little promotion and had been members of the Mess for longer than those newcomers had served. They resented the fact that the newcomers were on equal terms with the 'Old Sweats', a term which I think they richly deserved. Worse was in store; it had been decided that the number of pilots required to meet the expanding Air Force could not be obtained through the SSC (Short Service Commission) Scheme, so a Direct Entry Sergeant Pilot scheme was instituted. This was really hard to bear for the 'Old Sweats'; young men straight from Civvy Street were given three stripes and automatically made members of the Sergeants' Mess: sacrilege. In time they moulded into Mess ways and became accepted, albeit reluctantly. The Officers' Mess on the other hand did not have this problem since it was normal for a steady flow of young officers to become Mess members and their equivalent of the 'Old Sweats' was a very small number by comparison; the Station CO, the OC Squadrons and Flight Commanders being the only likely long term members.

Squadrons in peacetime used flying personnel in a variety of duties which had to be abandoned when they were kept fully employed in their main role. It was the duty of sergeants in the Squadron to maintain the engine and airframe log books; these provided an historical record of the life of an aeroplane. Records were kept of every servicing or repair carried out, the engine numbers and any engine changes, any compass swings that were carried out and so on. Major repairs to the airframe or engine were recorded as well as all regular servicing and inspections. In those halcyon days each crew had its own aeroplane and was responsible for its cleanliness and general serviceability. This included general maintenance of the wireless and instruments; there were few of these anyway, the magnetic compass being the main item that needed any work, and a compass swing at regular intervals generally kept this in order. The engines were maintained by the fitter who also flew as a gunner and the wireless equipment by the wireless operator. These records were usually the responsibility of one of the sergeants on the crew of that aeroplane. When war arrived the tradesmen obviously could not be responsible for this work and be expected to fly as aircrew as well. Soon after hostilities began they were made full time aircrew, promoted to SNCOs to give them some standing as PoWs if they were captured and their tradesmen roles were taken over by others.

An historical record, Form 540, was maintained in every squadron which was kept up to date by a squadron member, usually in those days, a Sergeant Pilot. Similarly, the station maintained a record of events at station level; for instance, the numbers of the squadrons operating from the station. It would, for example, have been recorded that a Coastal Command (GR) Squadron was a lodger unit on the station at Tangmere; special flights such as the occasion when Squadron Leader F.R.D. 'Ferdy' Swain landed at RAF Tangmere following his setting of the world height record in an aircraft specially designed for that purpose. War changed this recording procedure. Forms 540 were made the responsibility of the newly established operations room staff. In fact the old system would have been impossible at Squadron level, as owing to war casualties there would have been a lack of continuity: on 217 Squadron, we lost eight crews in a matter of weeks, thus the Squadron 540 would have been passed from one to another losing all threads and with the inevitable omission of important items. Both Station and Squadron 540s referring to the operation from which I failed to return are included as an Appendix and give an indication of the differing detail that was included in each.

Sergeant Pilots were kept fairly busy in those days. With no control tower and therefore no air traffic controller, some other form of control was necessary and this was carried out by the Duty Pilot. At squadron level a small analysis section was established to plot our air searches, to locate faults and so on. When a number of aircraft are engaged to carry out a search covering a large area of sea with no reference points, things can go wrong; the analysis usually indicated how, why and where this happened. It must be emphasised that aids to navigation were virtually non existent; R/T was yet to come as were the aids like radar and sonar, which became indispensable. They always had been, of course; it was just that no one had realised it. Indeed they were introduced rapidly because of their vital necessity in war. In those pre-war days we had to rely on Wireless Telegraphy, bearings and amateurish wind finding. It is a sad but true fact that the advance in all technical fields is remarkable during a war, as it is only under those conditions that advances can be tested properly and the real necessities discovered. Although we practised instrument flying using the very limited instrument panel then fitted in the Anson it was extremely difficult and I suspect we were not far removed from the days of flying by the seat of the pants. Although this term is used as a colloquialism, it has a basis in fact; it is comfortable if you are flying correctly, especially when making turns when a steady pressure on the seat is felt which lets you know that all is well. A clumsy turn which was fairly easy to make rapidly turned into the well-known 'split arse' turn, the flying equivalent of a skid, which you could feel coming through the seat of your pants well before the instruments indicated any problem, hence the term. Basically, if it felt all right it probably was.

The Avro Anson had started life in civil aviation as the Avalon; the RAF, desperate for a suitable land based aeroplane for Coastal Command duties, deemed it to be suitable for the job. The crew of four comprised two pilots, both of whom were qualified navigators as well, who alternated the flying and navigating, and two other members who were a wireless operator who was also responsible for the servicing of the wireless equipment in the aircraft and either a rigger or a mechanic who was responsible for servicing the aircraft and acting as the gunner when in the air. All this was rather primitive and had to be changed when war made it impossible for other rank crew members to service their aeroplane as well as carrying out their flying duties. In fact, it was not long after the start of the war that they were promoted to Sergeant and employed solely on flying duties. The Anson remained in service with the RAF, with modifications like variable speed propellers, hydraulically operated landing gear and interior changes to suit the many different roles the good old 'Annie' was called on to fulfil, throughout my remaining years in the Service and beyond: a truly remarkable aeroplane. To me it became like donning a favourite old jacket to get into the Anson and I made a point of flying in one of the later Marks on the last day before my retirement in 1959. I had flown over twelve hundred hours in a number of different Marks. Probably the greatest relief of flying this aircraft came with the introduction of the hydraulic undercarriage as we no longer had to make the one hundred and fifty-seven turns of the handle to retract the undercarriage and the same number to lower it when landing; exhausting for the co-pilot who had to perform the task and potentially dangerous as will be seen. The variable speed propellers provided a better performance and in particular permitted feathering and thus a better single engine performance in the event of engine failure.

Tangmere was a very pleasant and happy station and we soon established a relationship with the fighter boys from whom we learnt a lot about throwing the Anson around and particularly in copying their formation flying at which we became very proficient. This ability to fly in very close formation, largely due to watching and hopefully emulating 1 and 43 Squadrons, was probably the reason for 217 Squadron being selected for escort duties for Royalty and celebrities whenever a sea crossing had to be made which, Britain being an island, was of course nearly always the case. 217 provided escorts for King George VI on his return from both Canada and from France; for the King of Belgium and for the King of Rumania. Other squadron strength formations were for the King's Birthday, for the Hendon Air Display and other similar important occasions.

Mainly through playing rugby in the station team I got to know a fellow 'Brat', who had been a fitter on a Hawker Fury Squadron, had qualified as a pilot and returned to Tangmere to the same Squadron, 43, and was by now a very experienced fighter pilot. Sergeant Frank Carey, known universally as 'Chota' because he was so small and with the Indian influence from colonial days still remaining strong in the services, played rugby as a scrum half and since gum shields were not then worn had a couple of front teeth missing, but that's by the way. I had come to love performing aerobatics and when I suggested and 'Chota' agreed, that he let me have a go in his Fury in exchange for him borrowing my Anson, I was delighted. I had twenty-five glorious minutes throwing the Fury about in loops, slow rolls and rolls off the top. Chota Carey was commissioned early in 1941 and ended the war as a highly decorated Group Captain. The days of being able to borrow an aircraft are long since gone. The aircraft of today are complicated and expensive and it is necessary to attend a flying course on type before taking one up. Modern pilots no longer have their own designated aircraft, so approaching an individual is no longer an option. This came into force just after the war and I was stopped from flying a Mosquito which a friend, who was at that time commanding a squadron of these beautiful aircraft, had agreed to let me try. The order was issued just before the date of the arrangement: a real shame; I would have loved it.

I'm afraid I spent little time on my old 'banger', a two seater Morris 8. It got me about although there were difficulties in getting it to stop, other than rather slowly. The braking system was by wire cables, which tended to stretch, operating brake shoes in brake drums. If the cables were adjusted fairly frequently and the brake shoes roughened, again frequently, all was well; but I'm afraid I spent more time on the far classier cars of my friends than on poor little 'Angela', the name I gave her for no apparent reason. In those days most of us seemed to name our cars, a habit that has virtually died out. I suppose that they had much more character than the mass produced and very similarly designed models of today. Mind you, the modern ones do tend to be more reliable and the brakes tend to work.

I have to feel slightly guilty at the way I may have neglected her, as Angela was responsible for the best decision I ever made. I had heard that my girl friend of Halton days and in fact even earlier than that, since we were at school in Ramsgate at the same time, had completed her course at Kerr Sanders Secretarial College in London and was now working as a journalist on the *Western Morning News* in Exeter. She was living with her sister and one weekend I pointed Angela in that direction. Gutless individual that I have always been in these matters, though I hope not in others, I persuaded myself that I was going to see the sister and her new baby. What nonsense, I wanted to see Marjorie after a break of three years. The candle had not gone out and thereafter Angela made frequent visits to Exeter and the *Western Morning News* reporter had a 'makey learn' Sergeant Pilot as her taxi driver on most weekends. The taxi driver drove Angela over much of Devon and some of Cornwall, taking Marjorie on her journalistic assignments. It was during these trips in the narrow country lanes that I found that the brakes needed some assistance and often the car had to be nudged into the hedge to slow it down.

On one return trip to Netheravon, I left Exeter rather late and was pressing on a bit in order to get back in time for a few hours sleep before the morning flying. I was tired and it was dark and I was not concentrating fully. I skidded, hit the verge and turned Angela over. Thankfully neither of us was damaged and I was able to lift her back onto four wheels and continued my journey. When I watch the 'strongest man' contests on television, I am able to recall that they are not the only ones who can roll a car back on its wheels, even if Angela was much lighter than the models they lift. Those were the days when a gallon of National Benzole petrol, a brand that has disappeared in one of the many changes in the oil industry, cost less than a shilling, five pence now. It looks remarkably cheap until you consider that as a proportion of income it represents about ten pounds a gallon. I once proffered a five-pound note, one of the beautifully etched, large white notes that seemed the size of a handkerchief, that were in circulation in those days and which I had to desecrate with my signature before it was accepted. They were treated rather like cheques are today.

Soon after qualifying I was posted to 217 Squadron and in November 1937 married Marjorie in Exeter with Timber Woods – it wasn't just our cars that had nicknames in the RAF in those days – as my best man. I also borrowed his Morgan 4/4 to drive back to our cottage after the wedding and from that day on never had less than total support from a truly remarkable woman, who even treated the frequent moves that are part and parcel of service life as an adventure instead of the enormous upheaval that they in fact were. I could never have achieved what success I had without her unstinting help and unswerving belief in my ability. I cannot thank her enough. One of the few tragedies in my life is that she died just as I retired from my second career.

Almost immediately after my wedding I was attached to RAF Manston where the central navigation school was training GR pilots as navigators.

We were flying in Ansons and I take my hat off to the pilots who were flying us around in all sorts of weather, since we were learning the art of navigation and were still not very accurate, particularly in the early exercises. It was often up to them to get us home. We often made landfall some distance from the spot we should have, yet these pilots were able to pinpoint exactly where they were, even with weather conditions closed in below the height of the cliffs, and get us back to Manston airfield. This must sound rather ridiculous with all the modern aids to navigation that are in aircraft today, but at that time it was pure dead reckoning, with no means of finding exactly where we were apart from getting the wireless operator to give us a cross bearing on two wireless stations. I managed to complete the course successfully and the examination at the end of the course gave me an above average rating as a General Reconnaissance navigator. This was essential since we were flying two pilots to an Anson with one acting as the navigator. At least the Ansons of 48 Squadron at the GR school had a full instrument panel, while ours at Tangmere had a very limited one indeed.

Slowly things were being improved; one by one we took our Ansons to Woodford for more modern gyro-driven instruments to be fitted, which was all completed within a few hours. Instrument flying, under the hood, still caused a sweat, but was much less hazardous than with the old panel which only had an altimeter, air speed indicator and a turn and bank indicator, very primitive, and we felt a lot safer in poor weather conditions. Finding the airfield in poor visibility or low cloud was not easy; W/T bearings from the airfield and when closer, a station flashing beacon helped, but landing aids were non existent. With the weather deteriorating as rapidly as it does on the coast, it was often not possible to recall aircraft quickly enough to avoid very difficult landing conditions. The need to get aircraft which had been away from base for long periods down safely, which was typical of the nature of the work of Coastal Command, made it imperative to provide landing aids to achieve this. Now, with modern instrument panels and aids to enable a return to base in any weather coupled with the landing aids which enable blind landings and take-off, an Air Force is never grounded. A system of instrument ratings permits airfield controllers to decide on the pilot's ability to take-off or land in conditions for which he is qualified. I am proud that I qualified for a 'Master Green' card which qualified me to take-off in nil visibility and land with the cloud base down to one hundred feet, and these conditions applied up to the time I retired.

There have been occasions when I have been more than lucky: in the front of my Flying Logbook I have a newspaper cutting which states, 'Eternal vigilance is the price of safety'. I am ashamed to admit I have not always

This i[illegible] that

Name and Rank

[illegible]OYAL AIR FOR[illegible]

[illegible] MET T[illegible]TS FOR

[illegible]RUME[illegible] [illegible]IL[illegible] RA[illegible]

[illegible]GREEN[illegible]

[illegible]CORDANCE WITH AIR M[illegible]
ORDERS.

FOR A[illegible]
TECHNICAL TRAINING COMMAND

Date 22 DEC 55 VARSITY

R.A.F. Form 5214A (M)

SERIAL No. 34571

COASTAL COMMAND
ANSON

Signature of Holder

Wg Cdr.

RENEWALS

| Date | Signature of Commanding Officer | Station |
|---|---|---|
| | 6 month renewal | |
| 3 JUL | | ST EVAL |
| 21/1/56 | | ST EVAL |
| | 6 MONTHLY RENEWAL | |
| 31/7/57 | | ST EVAL |
| 20/1/58 | | RAF St Eval |
| 10/7/58 | | RAF St Eval |
| | | |

(S.15686)

*My green card*

adhered to this tenet for I was not only endangering my own life, but more importantly, that of those flying with me and as captain of the aeroplane my responsibility was for them and to them. I had been guilty of over confidence on a few occasions and got away with it. In retrospect it appears that these lapses occurred about every five hundred hours. The first was in an Anson when flying out of sight of land over a very calm sea at nought feet. At the best of times flying at this level in bright sunlight requires concentration to be of paramount importance, but on this particular occasion, becoming overconfident, I leaned forward to adjust the gyro and pushed the control column forward with me. Although the whole process took only a fraction of a second, the tips of the propellers just touched the sea; another fraction of a second and we would have crashed: lesson learnt, I never did it again.

The second lapse, again in an Anson, occurred when we were on detachment at Bircham Newton and the CO asked me to fly him back to Tangmere for the weekend as his wife was expecting a baby and he wanted to be with her. This done, I was returning to Bircham with my crew when some distance out my co-pilot started to wind down the undercarriage, the whole one hundred and fifty-seven turns you will remember. I suggested we leave it until nearer the airfield and did not insist that the process was reversed; we then both forgot the remaining turns. The undercarriage was not locked in the down position and I made the smoothest landing possible but not on the wheels: the two propellers bent at their tips and both of us had very red faces. Later Ansons had lights to indicate that the undercarriage was down and locked but the Mark 1 relied on a couple of green balls popping up and these were a rather haphazard reference. Fortunately for me a number of similar occurrences of undercarriages not properly locking down had happened and I only received a mild reprimand. Those to the Flight Commander and to the CO were more severe and stricter control of aircraft about to land was put into effect. The duty pilot using the Aldis Lamp was to give a green light if the wheels were seen to be down in the correct position and a succession of reds if they were not: the origin I suppose, of the term 'to get the green light' when you have permission to do something.

Landing wheels were again my problem in a Bristol Beaufort, although in this case I did not and still do not, consider myself to blame. Two incidents occurred when I was instructing 217 Squadron pilots at St Eval; in each case one wheel failed to lock down and in spite of operating the laid down procedure it proved impossible to achieve this. The choices open to me were either to raise both wheels and make belly landings or to attempt a landing on the one locked down wheel whilst holding the wing of the other wheel up as long as possible and letting it gently come to rest as speed and thus lift was lost. I managed this on the first occasion with the result that the only damage was to the wing tip and the tips of the propeller on the side of the unlocked wheel. The damage was minimal and far less than would have been the case had I made a belly landing which would have caused damage to both the propellers and the belly of the aircraft and with the distinct possibility of the aircraft catching fire and being a write-off. I therefore used the same technique on the second occasion which caused very similar damage. Although the station were happy with my decision, Coastal Command Headquarters thought otherwise and instructed that a Red Endorsement be inserted in my flying logbook. I reported to the Station Commander who inserted the endorsement but said, 'I will write it very small so that it can be erased at a later date.' I think it is important to consider two things: firstly, the airfield was far from smooth, and secondly, the radius rods supporting the separate wheels suffered from some structural weakness. It is possible that the combination of these factors caused the radius rod to bend and therefore make it impossible to lock the wheel down. It is interesting to note that the radius rods were later strengthened.

The last of my foolish acts was when attacking the port of Brest. Having made our attack and dropped our bombs, I was being kept in the beam of a searchlight. Annoyed and frustrated at not being able to shake it off, I dived the Beaufort on to the beam firing the solitary front gun but with no result, I suppose there was never really any likelihood of any. The effect however was much more interesting. I was now at fairly low level and leaving Brest between two islands with flak coming from each of them. I felt that if I flew low enough as I passed between them, the two flak batteries would be firing on each other and hopefully causing some damage, or at least consternation when the gunners realised what they were doing. Wishful thinking no doubt, but it gave me a feeling of elation and justification for my foolishness. My crew were good enough not to comment on my actions either at the time or later.

I previously mentioned the Duty Pilot briefly and it is probably worth elaborating on this role which would be found laughable by most modern service pilots. Before the Second World War aircraft movements were infrequent and aircraft speeds were fairly low. As a result the need for air traffic control was limited and would not have been possible anyway because of the lack of communication facilities, as there was still no radio-telephone between ground and air available. Airfields were of grass and about eight hundred to a thousand yards square. The entire area could be seen from a small hut, usually positioned in front of one of the aircraft hangars. In front of this hut was a square outlined in white containing the station identification letters and a large arrow which could be swivelled to indicate the wind direction. All of this was in white and large enough to be seen at a thousand feet. Windsocks were at the extremities of the airfield and also gave wind direction and an indication of its speed.

A pilot from one of the squadrons on the station occupied the hut for the day's flying and was known as the Duty Pilot. He logged the take-off and landing times of all aircraft movements and these times were available to pilots for their flying logbooks. Aircraft movements to another station were passed by telephone to the receiving station stating the estimated time of arrival (ETA). Similarly an air movement with its ETA from another station was received by telephone. If the aircraft had not arrived within thirty minutes of this ETA a search was instituted. The Duty Pilot also had responsibilities to the local Meteorological Office. At hourly intervals he would pass a report to them giving the weather conditions observed at the station. This would include the cloud cover and type of cloud in tenths of sky covered (this figure is now given in eighths), and the estimated wind speed and direction. The following factors were passed by reference to a code held in the Duty Pilot's hut: drizzle, rain, hail, snow and with each of these whether it was heavy, light or intermittent; the visibility with the following classifications: if it was estimated to be at less than one hundred yards, fog; over one hundred but less than a thousand, mist; and above a thousand, good. All very haphazard, mostly guestimates but adequate for those days. After all, at the time very little flying was attempted in poor weather since no landing aids existed and navigation was, in the main, visual either by iron beam (railway lines), or main roads. Railway station boards were sometimes used to check position and I have often wondered if that is why the old-fashioned station signs were so large; I cannot think of any other justification. The habit of carrying out the role of Duty Pilot came in very handy in PoW camp when we posted a look-out by the main gate to keep a record of the movement of German personnel where he was still referred to as the Duty Pilot.

It was customary for a small number of Sergeant Pilots to be recommended for a Permanent Commission and I was fortunate in being one of them on the recommendation of my Squadron Commander. I was to be interviewed by the C in C, Coastal Command at his Headquarters. Fully booted and spurred, I presented myself at the appointed time. There I met the other candidates, all Flying Boat pilots. All had more experience than I had, having served in their squadrons for some years and were also a little older than I was. From the outset I felt the odd man out, especially as the Air Marshal carrying out the interviews was more in tune with sea going craft than the new land based aircraft. Air Marshal 'Ginger' Bowhill was said to be an old sea dog and a bit of a martinet. I was apprehensive but I would have been of any officer of that seniority at that time; indeed even today, possibly irrationally but I think correctly, I am aware of the disparity when I am with officers of Air rank. I discovered that two of the Flying Boat Sergeant Pilots were successful, but I was not. I was obviously disappointed, but under the circumstances felt that I had done myself justice and fervently hoped that there would be another opportunity. The chance of obtaining a Permanent Commission had been missed, but since war was imminent, I was commissioned 'for the duration of the hostilities'. However, my Permanent Commission was granted at the end of the war and very thankfully I was able to continue in the service I loved and enjoyed for many more years.

Navigation out of the sight of land with few aids was haphazard to say the least. An example of how inefficient we then were is demonstrated by the experience in one of our exercises. Part of our job required us to locate enemy vessels, or in the case of convoy escort, our own. A series of search patterns had been devised to cover the circumstances existing at the time. The parallel track search was one which was used to locate a vessel reported to be in a particular position. The report would be out of date by a few hours by the time it reached us from the time of the sighting; the vessel could therefore have travelled some distance in any direction. As a result a large area had to be searched. The number of aircraft to be used was dependent on the visibility in the area and its estimated size. Each aircraft would start from a datum point; the distance between aircraft would be twice the visibility which in theory meant that any vessel between any two aircraft should be sighted. This was obviously true provided that each aircraft kept to its track and groundspeed. Unfortunately this was seldom achieved owing to inaccurate wind finding by individual aircraft and the tracks calculated by the search controller not being maintained. Our wind finding on such a search was confined to judging strength and direction from observing wind lanes on the sea, at twelve hundred feet, our operational height. We became quite accurate as far as individual aircraft were concerned, but it was too haphazard for such a precise operation when the compounding effect of small individual errors meant that large errors occurred. The squadron had a navigation office in which an analysis of all searches was made. The Squadron Commander knew of the interest that a great friend and fellow sergeant, Arthur Southall, and I had in this subject, so we were given the job of analysing, in particular, the parallel track searches and found, not unsurprisingly, that large errors were normal due entirely to inaccurate wind speeds and directions being used although the flying itself was accurate. This just proved that there is not much point in flying accurately to an inaccurate course.

Estimating wind speed and direction by referring to wind lanes could not be relied on and the other methods of finding winds could not be used if parallel tracks were to be maintained. The squadron navigation officer decided to send six aircraft on a parallel track search using a standard WS&D (wind speed and direction) supplied by the Met Office to be used throughout. The result was a disaster; landfalls were made over a very wide area, one aircraft actually running out of fuel and having to ditch in the sea; fortunately, the Anson Mark One was mostly constructed of wood and would float for lengthy periods. Analysis showed that the wind had veered through almost one hundred and eighty degrees during the search. We had adhered to the given wind with the resultant disaster. Such was the state of navigation just before and even during the early stages of the Second World War.

*A typical Coastal Command pilot – why me?*

We normally flew as settled crews and with some six hundred hours flying together in the Squadron were able to produce reasonable results. Although not crewed with Arthur Southall, we arranged to fly together occasionally in order to attempt Astro navigation. The Anson is not a steady enough platform, a six shot sextant and a poor dome gave poor results, but we learnt a lot from the tables and the stars. Arthur became a highly decorated wing commander gained mainly when flying 'Leigh light' Wellingtons; these were Wellingtons fitted with a floodlight to aid bombing accuracy.

Originally 217 had been formed as an RNAS squadron in France in 1918, but it had been disbanded after the war and a request was made to return to the original aerodrome to celebrate the reforming of the Squadron. The Air Ministry refused, but when we pressed our case they agreed that we could go to Jersey. It was arranged with the authorities in the Channel Islands that we would go one flight at a time, A Flight on one day, B Flight the next and C Flight on the third day. It so happened that even though we were in A Flight the weather was bad on the first day that we could not go and ended up as the last flight to make the visit instead of the first as had originally been planned. The other two flights had told us how successful it all was and told us the best places to visit. We set off, landed in Jersey and had an extremely interesting and 'thirst quenching' day out; in fact the corporal wireless operator who had joined my crew instead of my usual W/O had indulged rather too freely and I had some qualms about him being able to operate the wireless and establish contact on the way back. There was no R/T, it all had to be done on the key by morse code and we had to pour this poor chap – why poor chap I don't know, he had had a lovely time – into the aircraft, but as soon as he got into his seat you would not have believed that he had had a single drink and he operated perfectly all the way home.

When we were leaving Tangmere the CO had asked me to collect his macintosh which he had left in the control tower on his visit the previous day. This I did, along with half a dozen bottles of champagne which we had bought on our stay. I wrapped the CO's mac around the champagne and stowed them in the bomb bay which in those days was operated by allowing the spring loaded doors to be forced open by the weight of the bomb; as we had enjoyed ourselves so much in Jersey we decide to give them a traditional 'beat up' by way of a thank you. As I pulled out of the last dive which I suppose I had overdone a bit and which forced me to pull up sharply, out went the CO's mac and our champagne, right in the middle of Jersey airport. Fortunately the CO did not press the point of my failing to bring his mac back, but I was pretty apprehensive for quite a long time afterwards. I was fairly annoyed about the loss of the champagne, but of the two the CO's mac was far more valuable from the point of view of my career.

The decision to send Bristol Blenheims to RAF Habbaniya in what was then Mesopotamia involved sea crossings and it was decided that crews accustomed to operating over the sea should undertake this ferrying operation. Three Blenheims were to be ferried on each flight and the first three crews were selected from 217 Squadron at Tangmere. We were attached to RAF Thorney Island which was very close to Tangmere for conversion to the Blenheim and it was there on 6th April 1939 that I started my conversion. Although a much larger aeroplane than the Anson, the Blenheim proved not to be too difficult and I flew solo in a matter of two hours. This was followed by cross country exercises, fuel consumption tests and full load tests. Our three aircraft took off on 9th April on the first leg from Thorney Island to Marignan, a flight of some four hours and fifteen minutes. Flight Lieutenant Gordon was on an exchange posting from the RCAF and was 'A' Flight Commander. He was the senior officer of our three Blenheims and we flew together with Sergeant 'Gracie' Field who was i/c technical matters during the delivery flights and a w/t operator. Sergeant Field had an uncomfortable time sitting on the mass of spares necessary to cope with all possible emergencies. Reaching Marignan in time for lunch we were entertained by the French Air Force in their mess. We were to stay the night and an RAF liaison officer had been attached to Marignan to ensure the crews passing through were adequately catered for. Marignan is the military part of Marseille airport on a joint user basis. The sight of some of the French aircraft on the airfield, most of them even more old-fashioned than ours, was not very encouraging when war was declared a few months later. The casual attitude of the mechanics servicing their aircraft, Gauloises dangling from their lips, made me pleased to have our own servicing airmen under Sergeant Field to ensure all was correct with our Blenheims.

The next leg to Halfar in Malta was another four hour and fifteen minute flight over the Mediterranean and was without incident. We stayed at Halfar for two days and on the 24th, the next leg to Mersah Matruh took three hours and fifty minutes. There was only time for lunch which we enjoyed in an hotel near the sea in a gorgeous setting. That afternoon we took off for Ismalia, an RAF station where we stayed the night before leaving the next day for our ultimate destination, Habbaniya, where we landed on the 25th and handed over our Blenheims which looked very modern beside the old Valencias which were operated from this large depot in the middle of the desert.

The RAF station at Habbaniya was just north of the lake from which it got its name but is no longer shown on maps and of course Mesopotamia is now known as Iraq. It may be useful to include a few details about Mesopotamia. It was part of the Ottoman Empire until 1918 when having been occupied by the British during the First World War it became a British Mandated Territory in 1920, with Faisal as King from 1921 to 1933. The country became independent in 1932 but was again occupied by the British from 1941 to 1945 after a pro-Nazi coup in 1941. Habbaniya was situated to the north of Basra, which was an RAF station at that time and was between the Tigris and the Euphrates and some thirty miles to the south of Baghdad. Habbaniya was a desolate spot where the tour of duty had been reduced to two years as opposed to the five years at most overseas postings because it was classified as a non-accompanied posting. The number of relationships broken off by girls left behind caused by this posting brought about the term 'Messpot Letter' as the equivalent to the American 'Dear John'. The Blenheims were delivered in 1939; I spent two very boring days at Habbaniya and was thankful that I was not posted there. Flying time to the depot was eighteen hours and forty minutes which could be achieved nowadays in less than half that time and without the necessity of the stopovers. Indeed, during the Gulf War American B52 bombers were doing the round trip nonstop in little more than half the time.

We were to be returned to Heliopolis in Egypt in one of the Valencia transports. Reputedly they took off at eighty knots, cruised at eighty knots and landed at eighty knots. A slight exaggeration perhaps, but not much, an incredibly boring aircraft. On 27th April, Pilot Officer Honor and his co-pilot, Sergeant Maunder, with myself and six other passengers took off from Habbaniya, and after two hours flying using the oil pipeline for navigation we landed at Rutbah Wells, I'm not sure why, possibly to deliver something. We got airborne again but made a forced landing after fifteen minutes owing to a violent duststorm. After the storm had subsided we took off again but landed, yet again, after another fifteen minutes of flying. On this occasion, although not a soul could be seen when we landed, a number of Arabs suddenly appeared on the horizon. Honor ordered us to keep out of sight while he negotiated. We were very apprehensive. We had all been armed before entering the aircraft as the Arabs were hostile, or so we were told. However, Honor distributed a few cigarettes from his Players flat fifty and we were free to take off again. We had been airborne for only forty minutes since leaving Rutbah, had forced landed twice and been scared three times, enough excitement for any journey. Another scare was on the way, however, for after another fifteen minutes a very heavy rainstorm caused another forced landing. Today, of course, none of this would have occurred; firstly it is doubtful that a modern aircraft could land in the desert and if it did would almost certainly not be able to take off again; and secondly the weather conditions would not make it necessary as, if not already doing so, a modern aeroplane would simply climb above the weather with no fear of getting lost with modern navigational aids.

I was by now beginning to wonder if we were ever going to reach our destination, or if perhaps it might have been quicker and even more comfortable by camel; this was not the end, however, for we were to force land on two more occasions owing to heavy rain storms. Eventually we reached LG4H, the point on the oil pipeline at which a number of the oil company personnel resided. They were overjoyed to have the company of a few new faces and when they learned that we were to stay the night, really pushed the boat out. A few years later, when I was an unwelcome guest of the Luftwaffe in a PoW camp, I realised the importance of fresh faces and fresh conversation. Living cheek by jowl with people, however well one gets on in normal circumstances, certainly frays the nerves with day after day of contact in confined conditions. Every move can be predicted and conversation becomes stereotyped and stilted with nothing new left to say. We got the same kick as the pipeline personnel did when a new batch of PoWs arrived in the camp. Oh, yes, I understood their elation.

We took off the following morning bound for Amman which, wonder of wonders, we reached without mishap in one hour and thirty minutes. After refuelling we took off on the last leg of our journey, but engine trouble caused the pilot to return to Amman after only twenty minutes. At last we were airborne again from Amman and this time we arrived at Heliopolis without further trouble, in three hours and forty-five minutes. The next time you experience a delay in an airport, just remember that however dreadful, it's a great deal better than it was. I was hoping to be flown back to England, but no such luck, I was booked to return to Southampton on a P&O liner which was just sailing. At least it was more comfortable and faster than it would have been on a troopship which was the normal method of transporting service personnel in those days: a great waste of service time. Eighteen hours to Singapore by air against six weeks by troopship; the saving in pay alone more than justifies the cost of air transport apart from personnel being idle on board ship for long periods. At last, back to the Squadron, now fully engaged in working up for their role in support of the Royal Navy: navigation exercises, exercises with submarines and destroyers, exercises in support of seaborne trade, searches for submarines and so on.

In September 1938 Mr Hitler was getting a bit stroppy and signs that war was imminent were growing. To operate a Coastal Command Squadron from a Fighter Command station would have been impossible and 217 Squadron was moved to the only airfield able to accept us so to Warmwell in Dorset near Dorchester we went. Warmwell was a field much the same size as Tangmere but lacking in repair facilities for our aircraft, and having poor accommodation. In general we were more than happy when Neville Chamberlain returned with his 'piece of paper', and we returned to the comforts of Tangmere. Our return to Tangmere was short-lived. We were soon to be sent to our war station, St Eval in Cornwall.

... Fighter ... station would have ... and 213 ... was moved to ... to ... [illegible] ... in ... [illegible] ... [illegible] ... more than happy when Neville ... returned with ... piece of paper ... we ... [illegible] ... was ... We ... station ... in Cornwall.

[illegible]

... [illegible] ... quite ... the ... was ... [illegible] ... in ... [illegible] ... but any ... essential.

St ... [illegible] ... Accommodation for the ... was poor in the extreme and the ... grass ... developed muddy areas especially at dispersal and servicing ... it became necessary to put down strong wire mesh to prevent ... bogged down. Conditions for the ground crews were appalling in spite of which their esprit de corps and cheerfulness was

# CHAPTER 6

## *War time operations in Coastal Command*

It soon became evident that war was inevitable and 217 was again on the move, this time to a war station being prepared for us in Cornwall. St Eval was the usual grass airfield of the time, situated on the clifftop near a small bay on one side of which were a number of holiday bungalows, now empty since it was out of season. Mawgan Porth is about ten miles north of Newquay and only a couple of miles from St Eval. Those married were permitted to live out and the bungalows at Mawgan Porth were soon fully occupied. The young estate agent, an attractive lady, had never achieved so much business in such a short time as the Squadron and station personnel took over the whole site, at a time when normally most would have been empty for the winter. I arranged for our Anson to be flown down to St Eval by my co-pilot, Sergeant Hayes, while I drove down with our two wives and my small daughter. I rented two small bungalows overlooking the bay and 'Sunnyside' became our very happy home for just over a year. Cornwall was quite a pleasant neck of the woods, rationing was less severe than in the highly populated towns and food was certainly not in short supply. When hostilities started in earnest we could see and hear Plymouth being attacked but only on rare occasions were we subjected to the same and then only by 'hit and run' short assaults.

St Eval was no more ready than Warmwell had been. Accommodation for those living on camp was poor in the extreme and the far from level grass airfield soon developed muddy areas especially at dispersal and servicing points. It soon became necessary to put down strong wire mesh to prevent aircraft becoming bogged down. Conditions for the ground crews were appalling in spite of which their *esprit de corps* and cheerfulness was fantastic; living in poor accommodation, working in wind and rain for very long hours and still showing the greatest interest and pride in the achievements of the flying crews was an amazing experience for me. I had once been one of them, had experienced some of the hardships, but nowhere near as severe, that they were enduring; I knew what it was like to work in the open for long hours when spanners were difficult to hold with cold hands and with the frustration of getting to awkward pieces of equipment, but the Squadron were never late in taking off or forced to abort any missions. My admiration was boundless.

One of these airmen who had worked on my Anson during those difficult times was later trained as a pilot in Canada, I suspect under the Empire Training Scheme, towards the end of the war. He retired to Canada and continued flying with one of the Canadian airlines. He discovered my address after my retirement and wrote to me asking for a photograph of the old Mark One Anson as he was building a model for his grandson. Naturally, I was only too pleased to help and sent a photograph as requested and was also able to give him the war-time Squadron identification letters MW which he could paint on to the model. He too is now retired and we exchange Christmas cards and family news each year. Unfortunately, the bond which then existed between the groundcrew working on a particular aircraft and the aircrew who flew it is no longer possible; the introduction of Planned Flying/Planned Servicing which ensured that the majority of aircraft were available at any one time, removed this link and has in all probability been superseded by another more efficient system for getting the most out of an aeroplane since my retirement. It may be more efficient technically but I wonder what the loss is in terms of morale when the link with the people who actually fly the aeroplane is no longer there?

As I have said, the living accommodation on the camp was poor, but it was soon decided to billet aircrews and key personnel in hotels some distance from the camp when the bombing of the station started, since it was thought that direct hits on the various messes could put a high proportion of the experienced crews out of action. The journey to the camp was a two-mile trip by car and although petrol was severely rationed, additional coupons were issued to allow private cars to be used for these journeys. Strict black-out rules were in force and car headlights were dimmed by fitting a black metal screen over each headlamp with a small slit in the centre which was hooded at the top so that only a tiny shaft of light penetrated downwards, rather like the aperture in a small post box. Whether or not it was effective in preventing the Luftwaffe from seeing our roads being used I know not, but it certainly made driving difficult on pitch-black nights. I discovered this in no uncertain terms when I received a call from the Police Sergeant at Bodmin saying he had a young lady there claiming to be my sister and could I collect her. My sister, as far as I knew, was in Ramsgate, but it transpired that she had been told to leave as the evacuation from Dunkirk was in progress; after dispensing soup, sandwiches and tea to the unfortunates arriving in Ramsgate, she put her cat and a modicum of clothing into her Austin Seven and set off for Cornwall where she knew I lived. That she had got as far as Bodmin, the latter part of the journey being in darkness, was remarkable. It was only when I set off to collect her, a journey of less than twenty miles against hers of some two hundred and fifty miles, all on single carriageway roads, none of the luxury of motorways, that I realised just how remarkable. It should also be remembered that all the signposts had been removed, making it extremely difficult to find the way. During my journey, which took place completely in the dark, I encountered numerous very keen members of the Home Guard who took quite a lot of convincing that I was on legitimate business and therefore entitled to use the petrol. Once at Bodmin police station and having established that the lady was my sister, I was allowed to leave with her and the cat for St Eval which we reached some five hours after I had left it. My wife meanwhile was getting concerned about my safety; after all, I had only gone twenty miles, and she was used to my flying over to France, dropping my bombs and getting back in less time.

Another rather silly incident occurred at Mawgan Porth: just after dawn one morning I heard a strange engine noise and getting up saw a Dornier flying up the bay at low level. Always having my revolver loaded, I fired at the Dornier. It was so close that I could see the pilot but obviously, apart from giving me the satisfaction of having a go, little was achieved, or could have been, with a pistol shot at an aircraft flying past at some two hundred miles an hour. It was not the only occasion that St Eval was subjected to dawn raids, one or two causing damage and casualties, one rather bad one hitting the entrance to an air raid shelter causing several WAAF casualties. It seemed natural, and was accepted that airmen might be injured or even killed, but it was difficult to accept casualties among airwomen. I wonder at the present decision to allow women in the front line, or has the male protective nature disappeared completely? After I had been shot down a Junkers 88 landed at St Eval, obviously having got lost and thinking he was over France, I suppose, and for him that well known phrase, 'For you the war is over', was trotted out; or did we use a different cry of welcome? Whatever it was, the answer is the same; the war is never over for a PoW, the fight goes on, it's only the circumstances that are different. It does appear, though, that we made more escape attempts than German personnel in spite of their treatment being rather more lax than ours.

It was a great pity that Hitler could not have delayed the war for a few more months to allow St Eval to have been better prepared and conditions made more endurable for the groundcrews in particular. For that matter it would have allowed all three Services to prepare because, as usual, they were woefully ill equipped as a result of the politicians' desire for expedience over practicality. In spite of everything, the Squadron never failed to carry out its role of escorting convoys and searching for enemy 'U' boats, not that we saw many, and the monotony of searching was broken only by meeting incoming convoys and giving them the latest news by dropping the day's newspapers on to the naval escorting vessels. Not all of these hit the target of course, since dropping a bundle of newspapers on to the deck of a moving destroyer is not easy and many ended up in the sea; but hopefully enough got through to serve their purpose. We witnessed the results of 'U' Boat attacks on our merchant shipping, and the bravery of the merchant seamen whose ships were such an easy target for these marauders. I can only hope that the presence of Coastal Command escorting aircraft kept the 'U' Boats from attacking and provided some feeling of security to those brave chaps; it certainly made us give the utmost concentration to our task.

The Anson was capable of only six hours flying time and when meeting an incoming convoy, the escorting period was often very small and a large number of aircraft were inevitably employed if the convoy was to be escorted from as far out as was possible. The Flying Boat Squadrons with their greater range were able to provide escorting duties of a much greater range. The best height for spotting 'U' Boat periscopes had been calculated as twelve hundred feet and it was at this height that we always flew when on patrol: at that stage of the war there were no aids other than the Mark One eyeball for detecting submarines.

This operational height of twelve hundred feet reminds me of a story told by a Coastal Command pilot who had flown a Sunderland flying boat to the USA and was being debriefed by the Americans. Asked at what height he had made the crossing he said, 'Twelve hundred feet.'

'You mean twelve thousand?' enquired the American.

'No, twelve hundred,' replied the pilot.

'Please be serious,' said the debriefing officer.

'I flew at twelve hundred feet which is the normal height at which we fly in Coastal Command. You understand about the curvature of the earth, well, we climbed to twelve hundred feet and set course, which means that taking the curvature into account, about midway across the pond we were just skimming the waves.' The debrief ceased at this point.

As I have already said, there were no aids to navigation or landing such as we have today which enable aircraft to home on to the airfield and then obtain a ground control approach to bring it in to land without a sight of the runway until down to two hundred feet or less. However, we became quite used to returning in poor weather, and coming in from the sea as was usual, we became adept at finding Mawgan Porth Bay and flying to the airfield and making landings with cloudbase over the airfield as low as a hundred and fifty feet. On one occasion, however, after four hours on patrol out of sight of land we received a message that St Eval was obscured by cloud down to ground level but that we were to continue in the hope that clearance would occur. We had insufficient fuel for a diversion to another airfield so continued as ordered but with little hope of getting into St Eval. We were at two thousand feet, just above a cloud layer, when suddenly a gap in the cloud exposed a nice long stretch of beach. I requested permission by W/T to land on this beach but the reply was not positive: I was told to use pilot's discretion which means that if it went wrong it was my fault; but at least this allowed me to have a go without disobeying orders, so down I went. The beach was at least a thousand yards long, an unusual occurrence in North Cornwall where the majority of the bays tend to be very narrow. Thankfully the tide had just ebbed to create this width and also leaving a nice solid looking area to land on. The cloud base was about three hundred feet and I made a quick dummy run to ensure no rocks or debris lay in my way and came round to make my landing. Wheels down, half flap, approaching from the sea as there was a cliff projecting just out of the cloud at each end requiring a late turn, deliberately a bit 'split-arse', to line up with the tide line and we made a perfect landing. The surface was better than that at St Eval. When the tide is in only a small area of sand is left and I realised that my guardian angel had looked after me by ensuring the tide was out for my landing.

I taxied up on to this strip of soft sand and was starting to secure the aircraft when a small schoolboy appeared and began asking a lot of questions. He obviously knew quite a lot about the Anson, some technical details which surprised me. I asked where he had obtained all this information and he said, quite innocently, 'From the back of cigarette cards.' So much for 'Dangerous talk costs lives'; twenty cigarettes will tell you all you need to know. In the meantime St Eval had been contacted and told there was no damage to the aircraft or crew and that we would be able to take off next morning at ebb tide, and asked if in the meantime could they arrange for the bomb load to be collected and the aircraft refuelled. With this done and the aircraft secure, we found we were invited to various hostelries in the town, which turned out to be Perranporth, where we were treated as some sort of heroes. We lapped it all up and the only casualty was our wireless operator who fell into the small stream leading down to the beach, when we made our last inspection of the aircraft at about midnight to ensure that all was secure. We took off next morning, gave the town a bit of a beat up as a thank you and got back to St Eval in time for lunch.

Back to convoy escorts and anti-submarine patrols, often flying every day. It was on one of these sorties just south of the Scillies when flying over a destroyer, that there was a big bang and the cabin filled with smoke.

The bastards have fired at us,' I said, and was about to send a rude message to the destroyer, which would have had to have been by Aldis lamp and had little impact anyway, when we realised that we had been struck by lightning; we were in cumulus cloud conditions. The wireless operator had his trailing aerial out which had collected the charge and conveyed it through his seat and out through the wing tip. Aircraft are bonded against this occurrence and it was the paint on his seat being burnt which had caused the smoke in

*I landed on Perranporth beach. The young man quizzed me. He knew as much about the Anson as I did – from cigarette cards!*

the cabin. We continued our patrol since, on this occasion, we were not going out of sight of land. However, compasses are affected by lightning strikes and the next day it was necessary to check the compass on a compass swing, a technique no longer used so worth explaining. To check the magnetic compass by compass swing the aircraft is positioned on a base which has the magnetic points marked on the ground with great accuracy. The aircraft is positioned facing north and the compass checked and calibrated if necessary. It is then moved in a clockwise direction through the compass positions from north west to north east with any necessary corrections being made at each position.

A certain amount of excitement occurred when the Squadron was detailed to attack the French port of Brest in daylight at Squadron strength. Our CO requested the attack be given further consideration since an attack on this highly defended port in an aircraft which was capable of carrying only two 250 pound bombs and whose defensive armament amounted to only one mid upper turret with one gun and a fixed front gun, had little chance of success. Faced with the fact that at least one and possibly two squadrons of Bf 109s protected this important port, it was inevitable that very high losses would be sustained on the highly trained crews in the Squadron. No alteration was considered and the CO offered to make the attack himself with a volunteer crew but not to commit his Squadron. He was immediately relieved of his command, court martialled and as a result reduced in rank to Squadron Leader.

My wife was friendly with his and visited her during the time he was at Uxbridge, which was used as a centre for court-martial at that time. On his return, we were at his house in Mawgan Porth when his wife was replacing his Wing Commander's rings and sewing on those of a Squadron Leader. We conveyed our sympathy and that of all the aircrew, who realised what a great sacrifice had been made on their behalf and the numerous lives that had been saved. That he was justified in his action was vindicated when I was later detailed to lead an attack on the German battleship *Hipper* in Brest in daylight and the three Beauforts making the attack were all shot down by 109s and only three of the twelve aircrew survived. The daylight Anson attack was cancelled and the Squadron was detailed to make the attack at night. This was more realistic as fighter protection of Brest did not include night fighters, in fact I do not think there were night fighters at this stage of the war. I think nine Ansons attacked and all returned safely with no casualties at all. It was interesting that the crews I spoke to had the same experience as I did: that the 'flak', although quite heavy, all came up ahead of the aircraft and we presumed the batteries could not believe how slow the Anson was.

It was appreciated that the Anson had to be replaced and it was decided to re-equip us with the Bristol Beaufort. It was also decided to convert the Squadron at St Eval and to this end some Squadron pilots would be trained to convert the remainder. As one of the most experienced pilots, with over a thousand hours in my logbook, I was selected to take the course at Silloth in Cumbria just off the Solway Firth, to qualify as an instructor for the conversion of the Squadron pilots. An officer from another flight and myself were given rail warrants for Silloth. We stayed overnight at a friend's flat in London and continued to Silloth the next morning. Silloth was a bleak airfield and we were accommodated in tents. It was May and the weather was cold and it rained quite a lot. The Beaufort could be quite vicious and occasionally would develop a swing on take-off. The undercarriage was operated hydraulically, a nice change after the early Anson, but sometimes would not lock down, which then required a manual operation, so we did not escape completely from the chore. The aircraft was not good on one engine until later in the war when Pratt and Whitney engines replaced the Bristol Taurus.

The Beaufort Instructors Course at Silloth started on 27th May and was completed on 23rd June. I went solo after three hours and twenty-five minutes and after a few hours of circuits and bumps was able to carry out single engine flying tests flying from the right hand seat, a little different, but the trainees would be in the normal captain's left hand seat and we had to be

*The Bristol Beaufort*

able to deal with emergencies from the wrong place so to speak. During the course I managed to get a trip in a Hudson, another aircraft for Coastal Command to replace Ansons. I was interested in flying this aeroplane because of the new technique required in landing as it had a nose-wheel instead of the tail-wheel which most aircraft had at that time. All modern aircraft now have nose-wheels. In fact the technique is only different in so far as it is necessary to push the stick forward after touch-down instead of pulling it back to keep the tail down: it was quite fun to make the approach in the normal way, round off as one reached the landing point and as flying speed reduced and the main wheels touched and rolled, push the stick forward to keep the nose-wheel on the ground.

With a Beaufort Instructor qualification in my logbook, I set about converting the Squadron pilots. Starting with the Flight Commanders followed by the more experienced pilots. I achieved a good rate of instruction and conversion. The tendency to swing on take-off that I had seen during my conversion had not been cured and there were occasions when it became vicious and I had to consult the resident Bristol Aircraft Company Representative at St Eval to give advice on the aircraft and its performance. His advice was to open the throttles more slowly to keep the engine revs equal. This was fairly easy on a long concrete runway, but much more difficult on a short uneven grass field like St Eval. Another problem with the aircraft which required a trip to the factory in Bristol was the rear facing gun positioned in the nose, which had been designed to deter fighter attacks from below and was operated by the navigator. Unfortunately this single gun was prone to stoppages, mainly I think as a result of the ammunition flow jamming for one reason or another. In any event I put it to the Squadron that it was a useful deterrent against fighter attack and that we should try to find out if it could be put right. I was given permission to take an aeroplane up to Bristol, where the armament section manned by civilians could look at this gun and perhaps provide the answer. I landed at the Bristol Aircraft Company airfield at Filton on a beautiful long runway which was so very different from the grass field at St Eval. This was the runway that was eventually used for the first flights of both the Brabazon and Concorde, amazingly both flown by Brian Trubshawe. I went to the section dealing with the armament of the Beaufort and explained the problem to the man in charge. He asked me to go to the range where a gun had been set up in what he claimed to be exactly the same way as in a Beaufort and fired it nonstop without any problems at all. I suggested that he come with me in the aircraft over the Bristol Channel where we could get permission to fire the gun at some object out of sight of land. He refused to come, saying that if the gun fired on the range it would fire in the air. At this I got a little heated and said that it was all very well for something to fire on the ground in ideal conditions, but we were concerned with defending ourselves when being attacked and if the wretched thing jammed then it wasn't much help to know that it worked perfectly well in test conditions. This cut no ice with him and he was adamant that it would work. In practice we didn't bother to take ammunition for the gun as we felt it was a liability, but I expect he slept well in his bed knowing that he had done a good job and that if I or my colleagues died that was not his problem.

We ran into further mechanical difficulties of various kinds with the Beaufort and conversion was suspended until 22nd September, when we started again in earnest. For the next three months I was giving dual instruction both night and day and most of the Squadron was by this time converted. We were engaged at the time in attacks on the 'U' Boat pens at Brest, Lorient and Bordeaux, the latter being at the limit of our range, and for this had changed our operational height from the twelve hundred feet of convoy escort and patrol to fourteen thousand feet for bombing. I continued to give dual instruction to new pilots, and check dual to pilots who had got a bit rusty as a result of the pause in conversion owing to the technical difficulties with the aircraft, while at the same time I was flying on the raids with the Squadron. The CO suggested that I concentrate on instructing and relinquish the raids: I said I could not agree to this since I felt it was my duty to take my share of the bombing raids. It was only after I was shot down that I realised how much had been taken out of me by flying in the conversion role virtually every day, sometimes as often as three times a day, as well as taking my share of raids. I slept for most of the day after I got to hospital. I have no regrets, I would have felt as though I was shirking my responsibility had I not taken the decision I did.

Our new Squadron CO, Wing Commander Guy Bolland, was converted by me and later flew with me on two attacks on the submarine bases. Coastal Command was opening a new Group Headquarters at Mountbatten in Plymouth and the AOC designate, Group Captain Hopps, flew with me on a raid on Brest. The target was covered in cloud so we continued to Lorient which was also obscured by cloud; I decided to try Brest again, but although cloud still covered the area we encountered pretty heavy flak giving Group Captain Hopps some idea of what raids on these ports were like.

It had been decided to replace the second pilots with navigators. Although we had all been trained in navigation it was decided that a crew member trained specifically to concentrate on this would prove more efficient; in addition, pilots took longer to train and to lose two on each sortie that

THE TIMES FRIDAY JANUARY 31 1941

# "FLAK"

# A NIGHT RAID ON BREST

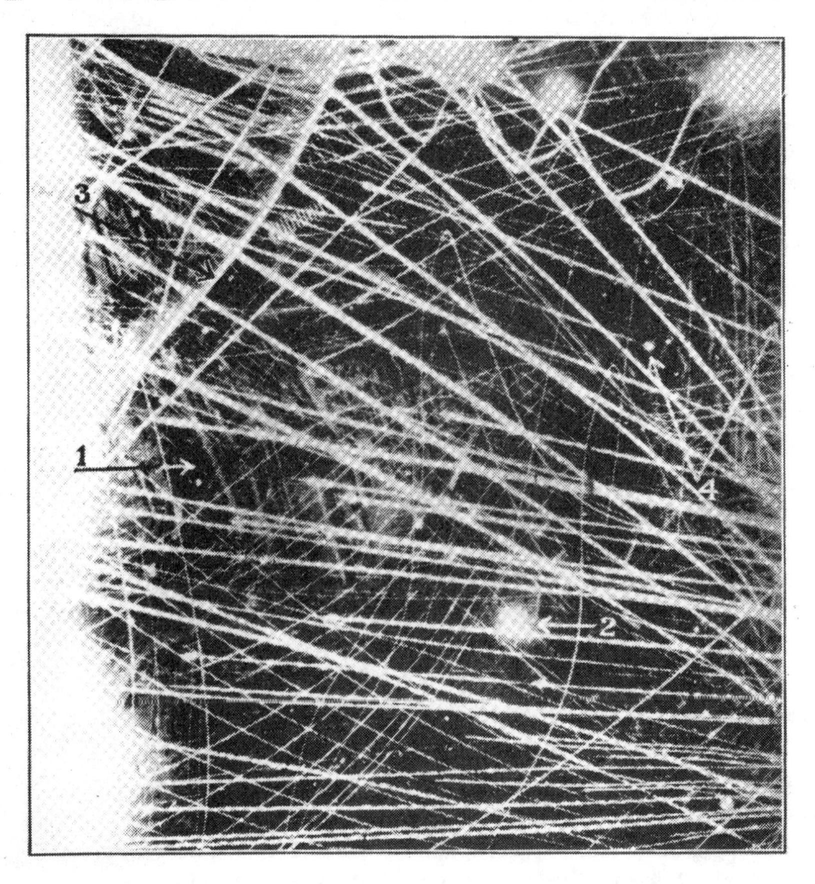


*A remarkable picture taken during an air raid by the RAF on Brest, giving a graphic impression of what 'flak' (anti-aircraft fire) looks like from the air. The fine lines of light show the paths of tracer shells and the broader lines those of heavier guns. Factories and buildings can be seen. 1. The Port Militaire. 2. Flashes of anti-aircraft gunfire. 3. Searchlight. 4. Point of origin of two tracer 'flak' positions.*

involved a lost aircraft ceased to be acceptable. Some crews had already had the second pilot replaced with a navigator but Flying Officer Stratford had not been replaced and was part of my crew when I was shot down, as was my Wireless Operator Sergeant Cannon who had been with me since the early days; both were taken prisoner after bailing out of the shot up and burning Beaufort over Brest.

My long time gunner, a jovial and efficient cockney called Brown, had been taken off flying temporarily because he had a bad cold and a young nineteen year old boy took his place. It was the first time he had flown with me and he was killed in his turret. The 109 pilot, who came to see me in the Kriegsmarine hospital in Brest, told me he had put his first burst into the turret, then a second into the port engine which he set on fire and then into the cabin; what he did not know was that he severed the elevator controls leaving me without any control over the pitching movement of the aircraft. We went into a steep dive, the port engine was on fire and I gave the order to 'Abandon aircraft.' Stratford and Cannon went out of the top of the cockpit: I had to give each a push to get them out, then attempted to get out myself, but the aircraft was diving at great speed by this time and I found myself trapped by the slipstream against the back of the upper hatch and push as I might I could not budge it. Suddenly I was thrown clear, why I do not know; I was told the aircraft had exploded but I believe more likely that the slipstream eventually aided my getaway. And so, after some twenty operational sorties and one hundred and ninety-five hours day and night on Beauforts, that was it. The other two aircraft were not so fortunate and were shot down with a total loss of their crews. So much for daylight raids without fighter cover on a heavily defended port. Copies of the Station and Squadron records, Forms 540, tell the story as others saw it. More particularly a letter I received from a member of the French Resistance who witnessed the attack gives an eye witness account of what happened:

> On Saturday 15th February 1941 at about 17:00 two British prop aeroplanes flew over the Elborn at low altitude towards Brest with DCA shooting. One of the British aeroplanes had to turn round as it was being followed very closely by a German fighter plane shooting non stop at it. The two aeroplanes were at a height of two thousand metres. Suddenly the leading plane's tail was on fire but it carried on its flight without changing its path. The shooting carried on, the British plane exploded, splattering bits everywhere around Gerrus. That was the end of the fight. Three white misty lines appeared in the sky; nearly all the crew managed to jump out. The south-west wind

changed the parachutes' path and the German plane did a few somersaults in the sky to show its triumph. The first one was captured rapidly in a Jew's house while he was washing the scratches on his face with water, another one was arrested in a field near Fessiou as he was making some enquiries waiting for nightfall, pretending to go to Brest. The third one was picked up by the Germans quite quickly.

A second eye witness also reports seeing the aircraft explode, so perhaps my impression of being sucked out by the slipstream was wrong. Squadron losses had been mounting fairly alarmingly up to this point and I am told that this last loss of three aircraft with their highly trained crews had a great effect on morale in the Squadron. It was a great relief to me to read in the letters from the Resistance that the body of my gunner Sergeant Sheridan was discovered some six weeks later, as I had never been able to discover what had become of him and had been concerned that he had not been able to get out of the aeroplane when I could have been of some assistance to him. This confirmed what I was told by the German pilot.

For my part, having been blown out of the aircraft I tried to gather my thoughts. I had always considered that my chances as an operational pilot were not high but I had never taken into consideration the possibility that I might become a PoW. I was reluctant to accept the fact and was not disposed to pulling the rip-cord to open my parachute. I then thought that I could evade capture; after all I had got maps sewn in my jacket and a button compass, besides which, the ground is very hard. So I decided to pull the ripcord. On a pilot's seat type parachute the 'D' ring, pulled to release the parachute, is on the left breast; when I tried to reach it I found I could not raise my right arm. I then panicked; from not wanting to live I now desperately did not want to die. Eventually I flicked it with my left thumb. The action, rather like Alfred Doolittle in *My Fair Lady* with his thumbs hooked into his braces, worked and the parachute opened and after the noise of battle all became quiet and serene. I looked up at the canopy above me and noticed one of the panels had split; this did not worry me too much as I still had some distance to fall as I had started at about fourteen thousand feet. What did cause concern was the 109 which was circling my descent as I had heard that the Luftwaffe had been known to put a burst into pilots descending by parachute. This proved false in my case and I suspect in all others, as there is a fellow feeling in pilots both friend and foe. All the chap was doing was indicating to a party of troops on the ground where my likely landing spot would be. In fact I landed alongside a road and within a couple of minutes I was looking at half a dozen rifles being aimed at me

*Grave of Sgt. Sheridan, my gunner killed in the first burst.*
*The French found him in the Beaufort.*

and hearing the inevitable, 'For you the war is over.' Yes, they really did say it.

*Note*: Group Captain Guy Bollard CBE, my CO at the time, discovered my address when attending a Beaufort Association Reunion and wrote to me. He had strong views on the use of the Beaufort on daylight raids, particularly against such heavily defended targets as Brest. He was of the opinion that our attack was not a justifiable risk (Forms 504 refer). On the day following our disastrous sortie he went to 19 Group at Plymouth to remonstrate with those responsible. This resulted in Guy Bolland's removal from the command of the Squadron and it is likely that his career would have progressed beyond the rank of Group Captain in which he retired, had he not taken this action. At least, he said, daylight raids in these poorly armed aircraft were not ordered again and he felt his action achieved something and saved some lives. Having heard from G. Hayworth – extracts from his letter are attached as an Appendix – the reasons for this attack on the *Hipper* were obvious, even though the desired result was unlikely and the exercise prove to be futile.

We exchange Christmas cards regularly and I hope Guy now accepts that it just had to be and neither he nor anyone else could have stopped it.

# *CHAPTER 7*

## *Prisoner of War*

I was put into their lorry and transported to the Kriegsmarine hospital in Brest. There I was taken to a casualty room where all my clothes were removed before I was placed on a bed to have the large number of pellets removed which had lodged in my legs from the explosive bullets used by the fighter aircraft. Afterwards I was injected with anti tetanus in each spot, or so it seemed. The main injury however was to my right wrist and hand. This was obviously the reason I had not been able to raise it to reach the parachute 'D' ring after I had baled out. It was carefully inspected and put in plaster, leaving a gap where the skin was broken due either to a bullet or to a piece of the aircraft hitting it. Up to this point none of my wounds had given me any pain, but I now felt all of them, especially the wrist. A nightshirt was provided and I was taken to a ward occupied by German sailors. A guard was placed at the foot of my bed and later, I suppose at about nine o'clock, a pilot came to see me accompanied by, as I later discovered, his engineer officer. They obviously came to quiz me about the Beaufort, although I soon discovered that the pilot, who had been the one who had shot me down, already knew a great deal about its capabilities, weak spots and so on. He was quite keen to tell me how he had first attacked the gunner, then the port engine and so on. It became a monologue as soon as he discovered I would not answer any questions. He told me of a number of Beauforts with our Squadron letters had been destroyed by his Squadron.

In the next bed to me was a young man who had recently received a Christmas parcel from home containing a cake. Using nothing but sign language, his English being just as non-existent as my German, he gave me a piece of his Christmas cake. Such is war: one of my bombs could easily have been misdirected and killed him a few hours earlier and here he was sharing his precious cake with me. I don't know if I was given anything to make me sleep but I certainly did until the next morning when my clothes were returned, unfortunately without the maps and button compass, and I was told to get dressed. I was taken to a staff car which called at a barn where my two colleagues had spent a very uncomfortable night lying on straw under guard. We were taken past the *Hipper* which seemed completely undamaged!

The staff car took us to the railway station. We were met by two very burly guards and at once embarked in a separate carriage on a train; the guards made it clear that conversation was *verboten*. We realised when we were some way on the journey that they could not speak English and were therefore suspicious of any conversation we might have. We were naturally all very thirsty after our ordeal and as a result of our wounds; my two colleagues, although not suffering gunshot wounds, had suffered bruising and Cannon had problems with his back which made him very uncomfortable. Asking for water was a waste of time and it was not until we reached a main line station where we had to change trains that we had an opportunity to stretch our legs, which we had not been permitted to do in the carriage. We were given soup in an army canteen which was very welcome. The guards kept a close watch on us, but were happy to let us have the soup, which was very sustaining, especially for my two colleagues who had not eaten for twenty-four hours.

We had been travelling for about two and a half hours and it was by now late afternoon. Stratford and Cannon had had no food and I had only had a piece of cake since leaving St Eval over twenty-four hours earlier. We boarded another train which took us to Frankfurt-am-Main, the nearest railway station to Dulag Luft, which was the interrogation camp for RAF personnel. We were met and taken over by Luftwaffe personnel who took us to a large Mercedes staff car which was driven at break-neck speed; it was now dark and the journey of about half an hour was frightening. I was separated from the other two and put into a room about eight feet square. Feeling very tired, I lay on the bed and went to sleep.

Next morning a mug of ersatz coffee made from roasted acorns, and two slices of black bread were delivered to my cell and I was left to dwell on my fate; looking round the room, which was bare except for a chair and a bed, I noticed the boards forming the walls were nailed and that a previous occupant had counted the nails and written the number down. With nothing else to do, I started to do the same thing but soon gave up this rather useless time waster as my wounded arm was beginning to cause me considerable pain.

I suppose it must have been late in the afternoon that I had a visitor, a Luftwaffe Major who I later learnt was the Commandant of Dulag Luft, Major Rumpel. He offered the inevitable cigarette and noticing the plaster on my right hand asked how I felt. Strangely, he made no effort to question me; instead he told me what aircraft I had been flying, where I was stationed and so on. He seemed to know all about the Squadron and what our role was. Whether he was going through this merely to watch my reactions I do not know, but he certainly had all the facts and confirmed that German intelligence was very efficient at that stage of the war. He noticed that I was in some pain and said that he would arrange for me to go to the local hospital where a section was reserved for wounded POWs.

And then I slept and I slept and apart from meals and visits from the doctor I slept. My right arm was strapped in position above my head and I watched the multi-coloured bruising start to spread from the damaged wrist and creep down to my shoulder. I began to doubt if in fact the damage to my wrist had been caused by an explosive bullet which had been my first thought. There was a small open wound which had prevented the plaster cast from covering the whole of my wrist and I now thought this might have been caused by a part of the aircraft hitting me as I baled out. Whatever the cause the end result was spectacular. The bones at the base of my thumb are fused into one solid mass which has left me with little movement in that area. It is somewhat unsightly but does not restrict the use of my right hand to any great extent.

I suppose the bruising lasted for about three weeks and I stayed in the hospital where life was reasonably comfortable. I was not able to use my right hand for normal everyday things such as writing, shaving, combing my hair or cleaning my teeth, but I did manage to write a letter to my bank with instructions to allow my wife to draw on my account, as foolishly I had not had the common sense to make it a joint account at the outbreak of war. I need not have been concerned because the RAF Benevolent Fund had provided the necessary funds to enable my wife to survive during the four weeks before my letter to the bank made it possible for her to draw on my account; incidentally, the bank were very accommodating in accepting a letter written with my left hand. I suppose the fact that it was written on a PoW letter form had some bearing on their trust and of course the Red Cross had confirmed that I was a PoW. In fact the first news of my capture had been given on the German radio by Lord Haw Haw who used the technique of listing captured British servicemen as a way of getting an audience, improving his ratings I suppose it would be called these days. Shaving was no problem, I didn't. The resulting beard was passable to look at but a coil grew which acted like a spring, where I had a small piece of shrapnel in my jaw, and this made sleep uncomfortable when my right side was on the pillow.

PoWs always received pay in the form of what we called *Lagergelt,* paper money which had no value outside a PoW Camp. It was intended for purchases in the Camp canteen, but fairly quickly there was nothing to buy and the paper was worthless. The equivalent of this paper money was deducted from our pay at home and although representations have been made to our various governments no repayments have been made. Parsimonious in the extreme, a truly generous thank you from the Government for our efforts. However, in the hospital one of the orderlies would buy items when he went into the local town. I expect the exchange rate was in his favour but at least we got some return for our money. I decided to do away with my beard and asked him to buy a razor for me on his next visit. This he did and I became the proud owner of a pair of electric clippers similar to those used by barbers, still, close enough for what I required. I put it to use without first trimming the by now fairly luxuriant growth. The result was painful and non-effective; the razor dug deep into the beard and stuck. It took a long and painful twenty minutes to dislodge and made me more careful at the next attempt. This was the one and only occasion on which I was able to spend my *Lagergelt.* For the remaining four years of captivity it was useless to me and I threw it away. Considering the result of my effort to shave, none of it did me any good.

The period in the PoW ward of the hospital gave a false idea of life as a PoW. A snapshot of my fellow inmates in the hospital taken at the time indicates that we were not too harshly treated. The purpose of the photograph was to show our relatives how well we were. When it was shown to my niece, then aged about five, she wanted to know if I was the one in the uniform who was in fact the German doctor. This chap was a bit scared of being sent to the Front and some of the other doctors in the hospital decided to pretend to have him posted to the Russian Front. We got to hear of it through the orderlies and made the most of the prank, suggesting he had volunteered in order to get an Iron Cross and surely he was looking forward to going? His state of nerves increased daily until at last he was made aware of the leg-pull when he became extremely brave, saying how disappointed he was having to remain in the mundane job of caring for a few PoWs. He got his own back by pretending to arrange the posting of two of our number to one of the most notorious camps. He allowed the hoax to continue until the morning they were due to depart. It was only when the goodbyes and good lucks had been completed that he announced it was a leg-pull. So much for the Germans lacking a sense of humour; he was a basically decent chap without any of the arrogance that tends to be associated with his countrymen; equally, so much for generalisations. Although it was a difficult place from which to escape, a plan was in progress at about the time I left, indeed wherever I was a prisoner there was always some escape plan afoot. The two officers who had been longest in the ward were to make the attempt, but as we were on the third floor the only possibility seemed to be out of a window as all other routes required having to go through wards occupied by staff and patients. I suspect it failed, although I never knew.

During my time in the hospital an incident occurred that was particularly frightening and potentially dangerous. An ultra violet lamp was sent to the hospital for the use of 'U' Boat crews, but as there were only a few in the hospital at that time the equipment was sent up for our use. It was installed in our ablution area which was covered throughout with white glazed tiles. One person was in the treatment room and two of us were in the next room waiting our turn; there was no screen and the ultra violet rays could be seen clearly on the glazed tiles. Rather stupidly we did not protect our eyes as we did when under treatment where we were supplied with protective goggles. That night my friend and I, who were in the same room, turned and writhed all night in agony until eventually we exchanged views on our symptoms. It felt as though sand was being rubbed into our eyes and we

*Dulag Luft; in hospital 1941. German doctor standing. Here I sport a beard: fourth along from him. Three other Squadron members also here. My W/Op is sitting next to chap with cushion over his foot stump which he was hiding.*

both felt that we were going blind and blamed the Germans, thinking that we had been used as guinea pigs in some experiment or other without our knowledge. It took twenty-four hours before, to our great relief, it cleared.

I was sent to Dulag Luft, the 'Passing Through' Camp, near the hospital and where nearly all aircrews arrived, although in the early days of the war, during the battle for France, some were sent to Army PoW Camps. It was not until later that they came under the control of the Luftwaffe in camps run specifically for captured aircrew. These ultimately included members of the Fleet Air Arm, Royal Marines and all those flying with the Royal Air Force who had been enlisted by their own countries and included Canadians, Australians, New Zealanders and in particular not forgetting the Polish crews, many of whom joined us in Stalag Luft 3 at Sagan. Later United States aircrew also arrived and were originally put in with the other Allied aircrew. This was a mistake on the part of the Luftwaffe because while they were with us they learnt so much of what can only be learned from people who themselves have learnt the ropes the hard way, from experience. As their numbers increased they were transferred to camps specially prepared for US personnel.

At Dulag Luft, I was seen by 'Wings' Day, a senior Wing Commander who had been shot down in a Blenheim in the very early days of the war. He was one of the permanent staff retained at Dulag Luft by the Luftwaffe Camp Commandant, Major Rumpel, the one who had interrogated me when I arrived. Other members of the permanent staff included Flight Lieutenants Harvey, Bourne, and Mike Casey who eventually was one of the fifty prisoners who were shot by the Gestapo after the 'Great Escape'. These officers organised the arrival arrangements of aircrews who had recently been shot down. We were accommodated in rooms of four; Red Cross parcels and rations were pooled under the control of Flight Lieutenant 'Bacchus' Bourne who was detailed as the catering officer. Meals were provided in a central dining room, prepared by other rank aircrew volunteers who were also part of the permanent staff. They also cleaned our rooms and made our beds, in fact acted as our batmen. This was before the wops. and gunners were promoted to NCO rank. Meals were sparse, but were far better than we were to have in any of the main camps where each room was responsible for drawing rations, receiving Red Cross parcels, which contrary to popular belief appeared very seldom, and eking them out among their roommates. Cooking was carried out, when possible, on the one communal hut stove and generally caused difficulties as there were some twenty rooms in each hut which allowed only twenty minutes each on the stove. The allocation of Red Cross parcels was intended to be one per man per week. In fact this was seldom, if ever, achieved in the camps in which I was accommodated, with the possible exception of Dulag Luft which was I suppose, closer to the source of supply.

Life at Dulag Luft was, in comparison with the main camps, very pleasant which led some people to the erroneous opinion that 'Wings' Day and his staff were collaborating with Major Rumpel. In fact, security under Day was so efficient that none of us passing through was aware of any underhand activity; tunnelling was in progress all the time and the resulting tunnel was eventually used by the four staff, but like most escapes, getting out is just the start of a multitude of difficulties. For 'Wings' Day this was the first of six attempts and the report made by an officer passing through Dulag Luft to higher authority that Day was taking advantage of his position there resulted in the officer and not Day being reprimanded. 'Wings' Day was respected in every camp throughout the period of his incarceration; he was recognised as the Senior British Officer (SBO) at Stalag Luft 3 even though he later no longer held senior rank in the camp. There was one occasion when there were two group captains in the camp, who did not assume responsibility for the running of the camp because they realised the respect which Day commanded.

After a few weeks at Dulag Luft the time came for a number for us to be transferred to Stalag Luft 1, at Barth on the Baltic. We were transported by train. We were well guarded and our boots were removed as a deterrent to those bent on train jumping. The journey was far from comfortable and we were somewhat apprehensive as to what this journey had in store for us since no news had filtered back about conditions in this particular camp. Eventually, we reached our destination and were marched from the railway station to the camp, past the guardroom, and then through the main gates and into the compound. There were two sets of gates and on entering the first gate we, the new arrivals, were faced by a number of dishevelled individuals wearing an assortment of garments, many in a very poor state of repair, and the individuals themselves presented a haggard and sad looking bunch.

On entering the second gate this motley crowd greeted us, all anxious for the latest news from home; some had been captured in the first few weeks of the war and at that early stage their only news had been from German news bulletins which those in charge were only too keen to broadcast since they were all of the enormous success of the German advance. Depression was deep, but as always not in front of the Germans. As new arrivals we were each allocated a bed in rooms already occupied. We were questioned on a number of subjects, not least the state of the war, and when an individual was from the same station, for information about friends and so on. I should emphasise that the rooms had been checked thoroughly for any bugging so that we were quite free to speak at this stage of the war. These initial meetings were also used to inform the new boys of camp procedure in general and of how the camp was secured by guards, 'ferrets', security officers and so on. This method of putting each new arrival into a room occupied by older 'Kriegies' (we shortened the German word *Kriegsgefangener* meaning prisoner of war to make this diminutive to refer to ourselves), made it possible to establish if the new arrival was a plant or genuine aircrew. At this stage of the war it was probably not necessary for the Germans to use such a method, but later at Stalag Luft 3 a plant was exposed and kept in confinement in a room in the camp, a PoW of PoWs so to speak. He disappeared during one of the 'goon' searches; we were told he had reported sick.

The permanent PoW camps in which I was a forced resident were all of similar pattern: huts of wooden construction some forty to fifty yards in length and ten yards wide, raised on stilts about three feet above the ground to allow the security people, known as 'ferrets', and their dogs to search for unusual activity underneath them. Incidentally we found that the dogs could be fooled more easily than the ferrets. There were some areas which could

*My room mates at Stalag Luft 1; I am third from the left, back row.*

not be searched under the huts; for example the water from the ablutions in each hut had to drain away and the drains were surrounded by a brick wall. The heating in each room was provided by a stove which had a brick plinth to support it which obviously went down to the ground, both of which provided exceptional means for the camouflage of tunnel trapdoors. Each hut had a similar lay-out, a central passage with rooms on either side which were about twelve feet by twelve feet, intended originally for four occupants, but this soon became six and then eight and sometimes more. Also in the room were a small table and four chairs. The stove which I have already mentioned was in the corner of the room nearest the corridor. Originally, two double tier bunk beds complete with bed-boards, mattress, pillow and sheets were provided. Later these were increased to satisfy the increase in population of the room. Later still we rebuilt the beds to form three tiers, a very rickety arrangement but it served two purposes; it provided much needed surplus wood for tunnel construction and gave the room additional free floor space. Eight guys occupying twelve feet by twelve with a table, chairs, three three tier bunks, the unused top of one being used for storage, was a bit of a crush and living in such close proximity soon made one aware of the slightest idiosyncrasy in speech, gesture and behaviour which would probably never be noticed in normal conditions. One knew what a fellow member would do or say on any occasion and anticipated what would happen to such an extent that if for some unaccountable reason it did not it became even more annoying. To alleviate the irritation we used various diversions, the principal one being circuit bashing, which served the dual purpose of giving us exercise while talking without fear of being overheard and more importantly an excuse to disperse the sand that was being dug from the tunnels by letting it out through a contraption hanging down our trouser legs. This was very slow and tedious and had to be discontinued when the circuit became discoloured. Escape activity and goon baiting were our other methods of preserving our sanity. For some the strain became too much, but fortunately only a very few became unhinged. Incidentally, all discussion of a classified nature was conducted while bashing the circuit. This was especially true when the 'X' organisation and its activities were under discussion.

On one side of the central passage there were between ten and twelve rooms for accommodation; on the other side were six for accommodation, an ablution containing three wash basins and a central drain over which we made our own shower by perforating tins and connecting up to the water supply by means of a rubber hose. The final room contained a cooking stove. Each room had a window and an external shutter which the goons secured each night. Use of the cooking stove was limited to twenty minutes for each room. There was little to cook but potatoes were usually available. A system was developed to utilise the twenty minutes to the best advantage. The first room on the stove boiled a large pot of potatoes, extracted those for their room, leaving the water for the next room and so on. By the end of the evening the constant potato boiling left a potato soup which the last room to cook were able to enjoy and it was for this reason that cooking times were rotated. I had a special interest in the stove which I will come to later. At Stalag Luft 1 there were only four huts but at Stalag Luft 3, both the north and east camps had sixteen in lines of four with a latrine in the centre which we called the forty holer which can at best be described as an open cesspit and when the spring brought the flies it was just hard luck.

It is well known that when captured the duty of Commissioned Service personnel is to escape; he is required to give the enemy only his Service number, his name and rank. 'For you the war is over,' so often repeated by our captors, was just not accepted. The captor has guns, bullets, spies, dogs, barbed wire and countless refinements of mental oppression which make life as a PoW a special sort of hell. The captive has only his wit, inventiveness, his brains, endurance and mental attitude as well as pure cussedness, a particular asset of the British, never admitting defeat or letting the enemy think he is defeated and more important than anything, unlimited time to plot and scheme.

On our PoW Camps there existed a vast quantity and variety of knowledge: individuals from all walks of life including lawyers, accountants, civil and mechanical engineers, student doctors and teachers. Many could speak three or four languages and classes were arranged for the study of any of these subjects. In fact life as a PoW was not conducive to study and although some persevered and obtained good results, few continued. I knew of one whose nervous system gave way under the strain of study, not of being a PoW. The PoW had twenty-four hours a day in which to make use of his skills and greater knowledge against his captors who apart from anything else were outnumbered and of lesser intelligence. This is not a slur on the German people, merely on the guards, as they tended to be the least able members of the German forces, garrison troops who were unfit for active service. Even so guards with loaded guns ordered to shoot if a Kriegie stepped out of line, for example if he got within twelve feet of the wire, did have certain advantages.

I had never considered being taken prisoner. I did accept that, as a pre-war regular airman, my chances of survival were not great and it was a great shock, as it was to most of us, that suddenly we were going to spend one knew not how long pushing back the barbed wire and tormenting the goons detailed to keep us inside, and in trying to escape. From tea and cakes, eggs and bacon and dates with girl friends one minute to being shot down, caught, and put behind barbed wire a few hours later. The sheer speed of this was traumatic in itself and the fact that the transition was never contemplated automatically meant that one was a reluctant and awkward captive. Bloody minded in fact!

At both Stalag Luft 1 and Stalag Luft 3 north, the NCO aircrew were in separate compounds, but close to us. In fact, in Stalag Luft 3 north the compounds adjoined one another and it was quite common to see an individual on our side of a ten-foot high wooden fence apparently talking to himself as he walked up and down the fence. On the NCOs' side of the fence the same thing was happening and a great deal of useful information was exchanged in this way. We were not close enough at Barth but information was exchanged by arranging sports matches against each other.

Life as a PoW is dull and frustrating. Christmas Eve was the only time of the year at which we really escaped. A bugler was allowed to open his hut door and play 'Silent Night'; for once the camp was absolutely still. He was a very good bugler, but it would not have mattered if he had been appalling as we were all at home in England, Australia, New Zealand or his case

*Stalag Luft 1 – in the NCOs' compound. A good way to exchange information between camps. Author on extreme right.*

South Africa, thinking of our loved ones and hoping that next year we would be there in person. You could have heard a pin drop. The days pass very slowly indeed and the indeterminate nature of the incarceration is an added anxiety; for my part, and I think for many of us, the cry as each Christmas arrived was, 'Home for Christmas', because to accept a period of longer than twelve months was too much to bear, although in our heart of hearts we knew, in the early days of our captivity, that the only possibility of the period being less was for us to lose the war. This was too horrible to contemplate and certainly not an option entertained by any of us, though for the first two years of my captivity it was certainly a distinct possibility; the daily news, broadcast by the German radio, was far from encouraging, our forces on all fronts were having little success and it was not until the Russians held out at Stalingrad that the Germans suffered any setback. Eventually the toing and froing in North Africa seemed to have been resolved at last by the Eighth Army under Montgomery and later by the invasion of Africa in Algiers by British and American Forces to squeeze the German North Afrika Korps to its surrender. And so for the first time in almost three years of war a glimmer of hope was with the PoWs who had never given up in spite of the jubilant German reports of the successes given out daily by the Obercommando der Vermarkt over the radio. By this time we had our own radio giving us the BBC news which was relayed to us covertly through our internal intelligence organisation which I enlarge on later. It must be said that the BBC news bulletins also exaggerated Allied achievements and negated our failures so that the Kriegie, who received both, probably had a more accurate view of the war than the civilian populations of either of the combatant nations who were being given only what those responsible for propaganda permitted to be published.

# *CHAPTER 8*

## *Coping with captivity*

This then was the PoWs' lot, short of food and hope; living in cramped conditions but continuing to remain certain of eventual success and never failing to let the Germans know our feelings. Once 1943 arrived and with our successes growing on all fronts – I exclude the Japanese theatre – we were able to obtain more contraband from certain weak Luftwaffe personnel who were anxious to be in our good books when the war ended. Pieces of equipment for our radio, and cameras to take photos for the passes needed for escape and many other items difficult to obtain by fair means, were now made available. Quite simply, it was possible to blackmail a Goon who fell for the offer of a cigarette which were in short supply for non combat troops, or a cup of coffee in a Kriegie's room: once they had accepted they were doomed. Obviously we had experts in this field and the unfortunate victim could be made to supply what we wanted or be reported for acceding to bribery. They were usually young men who had no wish to be in the Forces and were thus easy prey. A fascinating conundrum, 'If you don't give in to blackmail we will tell your superiors that you have and you will be punished for doing what you have refused to do, but if you do give in we won't say anything.'

The majority of those ensuring we were kept in were good loyal soldiers; they knew our little antics and accepted them. One security man in particular, a Feltwabel, the Luftwaffe equivalent of a Flight Sergeant, called Glymnitz, spoke very good English, having been summoned to return to the Reich from South America on the outbreak of war, and was in the habit of making use of our 'Duty Pilot', as he was known, to discover if any of the ferrets were in camp and was usually given the information since no harm could come from him knowing. Incidentally, the Duty Pilot could not, and even if he could, would not, provide any information on the whereabouts of any goon, only if he was in or out or whether or not he was in the compound. The Duty Pilot was named after the peacetime flying days when a pilot sat in a hut to record all the coming and going on an airfield. A further check on the exact whereabouts of any foreign body was available to us through the security system provided to each part of the compound. A Kriegie passed this information rapidly to the secure area which was obviously essential when tunnelling, photographing, counterfeiting, deciphering, forging or any of the other subversive activities which went on whenever it was safe to do so. The tailoring department was another section which had to be secure and the system of warnings proved foolproof over the years. When one considers that it takes several minutes to recall tunnellers who may be up to fifty yards in a tunnel, give them time to wash off the sand, close down the tunnel and conceal the entrance, the system has to be efficient. There were occasions when a tunneller had to be left in the tunnel owing to the lack of time available to get everything done before the ferrets arrived, but this entailed an added risk since a snap roll-call might be called and it would then be necessary to arrange a manipulation of the count. At these roll calls we would line up in three ranks by huts and the German Sergeant would go along counting the front row. We sometimes moved about just to disrupt the count; we had nowhere else to go and it would cause some irritation. More importantly, we used to have, from time to time, what we called 'ghosts'. These were prisoners who hid after an escape in order to convince the Germans that more escapers were on the loose than was actually the case. They then of course had to keep hiding whenever there was an Appell (roll call) which could be quite difficult if it was of the snap variety. However it did mean that when there was an escape we could disguise the fact for a while as we brought the ghosts out of hiding which meant that the count was again correct.

Mention has been made of Red Cross parcels which were intended to have been sufficient for an issue of one parcel per man each week, a rate which was seldom achieved. This applied to the British Red Cross. Parcels from Canada, America and the Argentine were usually provided in bulk rather than on an individual basis and had to be broken down and shared. To achieve this a PoW parcels officer was appointed and approved by our captors to ensure the proper distribution of all food parcels. The benefit of having our own representative was considerable, particularly after it became possible to send messages from our camp to the authorities in England and to receive them in return. Personal parcels from families and friends could also be received; I believe that there was a limit to these but I was not aware of it. In any case most items were on ration at home which in itself placed a limit on them. Distribution of parcels was made by the security people and entailed reporting to a centre where on the shout of 'Parcels up', one member from each room would collect the allocation for his room's occupants. After the discovery of a tunnel in which the air supply was provided by using tins from the parcels which had been soldered together to provide an air duct, we were no longer given the tins; the contents were emptied onto plates and since there were insufficient plates it meant that the room's 'duty stooge' conveyed a plate or plates containing jam, margarine, stew, raisins, sugar and so on, all mixed up. Disgusting, but it was food. The duty stooge was the chap appointed on a weekly basis to provide the meals for the occupants of that room. Rations from the Germans were supplied to us on the same basis as garrison troops, the lowest of all, and even this meagre ration was reduced as the war progressed. These varied according to the time of the year. The basic ration of bread, meat and potatoes did not vary to any great extent, but a glut of cabbage in the market gave us a bonus of greens. The standard ration of black bread was one sixth of a loaf a day. It was more filling than our bread, not as palatable but one got used to it. To give some idea of our rations I have taken a section from *My Secret Journal*, written by a squadron leader who had coincidentally occupied the camp at Barth which we had left three years before. He was an artist and produced a book of drawings and caricatures which includes various menus.

A TYPICAL RED CROSS PARCEL

1lb Tin Corned Beef or Stew
12 Biscuits
½lb Tin Salmon
4oz Powdered Egg
2oz Porridge Oats
1lb Tin Condensed Milk
4oz Sugar
2oz Cocoa
1 Bar Soap
1lb Sausages
½lb Meat Roll
½lb Bacon
1lb Tin Vegetables
6oz Cheese
1oz Tea
½lb Prunes or Apricots
4oz Powdered Egg

GERMAN WEEKLY RATIONS (in grammes)

Margarine 150
Fat 42
Potatoes 3290
Sugar 155
Sausage 100
Black Bread 1960
Cheese 27
Vegetables 70
Jam 155
Barley 57

The meat ration supplied by our captors was so small that an arrangement with a number of other rooms in the block made it possible for a small joint to be made available on a roster basis, the meat ration for all members of these rooms being pooled to provide, about once a month, sufficient for each of the rooms in the scheme to have a piece of meat large enough to be seen; I presume that the same ration provided for the guards was made into a stew mixed with their vegetables, not really possible for a room of eight or nine Kriegies. The bread ration was spread over the day by having two slices for breakfast with a cup of tea or coffee if our Red Cross parcel had not run out and ersatz coffee if it had, another two slices at lunchtime and that was the day's ration gone: however, we later purchased a bread slicing machine and placed it in one of the central huts for the use of us all. It was soon noticed that quite a few crumbs accumulated under the machine which was similar to a bacon slicer and it was not long before another roster allowed these crumbs to be collected and rather peculiar bread puddings started to appear on room menus.

The lengths we went to in order to ensure equal shares of food were apportioned in the room whether it was an eighth of a meat loaf, an equal portion of jam or indeed anything edible were quite remarkable. Shares were measured to the nearest millimetre and even then lots were drawn for first choice; it was also remarkable how suddenly one changed one's mind about one's likes and dislikes. As an illustration, a recently shot down group captain was allocated to a room of seasoned Kriegies for messing purposes. Swede was available on the menu for his first evening meal and the duty stooge served the groupie with his share, at which point the said groupie declined, saying that he disliked swede, to the joy of the others who absorbed his share into theirs. A fortnight later swede was again available. Groupie was not given any and complained vehemently, 'But you don't like swede, sir,' said the duty stooge, a squadron leader. 'Maybe not,' says Groupie, 'But I likes me wack.'

In one room I was responsible for the trap door to a tunnel and during my duty the occupants, and thankfully there were only two, usually had their evening meal and the share-out went something like this:

'Give me a word, Jack.'

'Susceptible,' said Jack.

At this point George the second member would start spelling out the word between the two of them in the same way we all did as children when playing a game of tag, until the last letter had been allocated which gave the holder first choice of plate over an item that had been divided to the last millimetre anyway. Day after day I watched this absurd charade with complete understanding.

An incident involving what we euphemistically referred to as the forty holer was amusing but could have resulted in something very serious. It was the practice to make use of this communal latrine just before dark when we were locked in, since it is reasonable to engage in this operation as privately as possible. It was nothing more than an open pit and the resulting none too healthy stench which filled the building made it a normal practice for most participants to light a cigarette when taking their place. I should add that this place was merely a position on a wooden pole extending the length of the pit, with another pole to lean against. To set the scene, the pit was due to be cleared and was therefore particularly full. As was usual it was a full house in all respects until someone dropped a lighted match into the pit which set light to the paper that had accumulated. This was not too far below twenty bare arses which were removed extremely rapidly as the conflagration took hold. Unfortunately it burnt itself out, against the hopes and wishes of the whole camp. No one lost his balance and fell in, which would have been a disaster, but on another occasion the back rest had been removed to provide wood for tunnel props without ensuring that a general warning was circulated and one man only just managed to save himself from toppling in, almost literally in the fertiliser business! Another sight which one did not expect to see was a senior officer with a loo roll under his arm on the way to the forty holer; there is of course, nothing wrong in this but somehow it is totally unexpected. It was however quite understandable as this commodity became very precious and it was necessary to ration oneself.

On associated subjects, a very proper lieutenant commander, RN was seen following the horse drawn carts in the camp collecting the droppings which he used on his gardens. With the help of the horse manure the tomato plants which refused to grow in the sandy soil which had recently been supporting a pine forest, produced tomatoes. Such was life; but we learned many things which would not have been possible in normal circumstances and useless though they might be, they were useful at the time. We had no fridge to keep food fresh in summer, so instead a box was covered with cloth which was kept wet by having water dripped onto it and placed in the sun where it would keep items cooler than in the sweltering rooms, by using the cooling effect of evaporation. The technique was originally used by the Romans, and possibly even before that, but we found it very effective fifteen hundred years later. Washing machines were replaced by 'dunkers': a small tin was fixed inside a large tin and secured to a pole to agitate one's washing, rather like the old 'dolly', which was in use before the present day washing machines.

Then, of course, there were all the skills which were developed by Kriegies in support of the escape organisation, digging tunnels, shoring them, providing an adequate air supply and making use of everyday items for the purpose; making clothes from blankets, dyeing them in the correct colours after experimenting with extracting the dye from other materials: strangely enough book covers were the best source of these dyes; forging passports and producing rifles from wood, the metal parts taking hours of rubbing with pencil lead to make the end result indistinguishable from the real thing.

It became evident that control of escape activity was necessary if one escape was not to jeopardise others: to this end an organisation was set up under 'Wings' Day, the same one who had been so wrongly maligned as a collaborator in Dulag Luft. Following his escape attempt from that camp he came to Stalag Luft 3 north and from there to Luft 3 east. He was the senior ranking officer up to that time and although outranked later, continued to be recognised as the Senior British Officer by the two group captains who came to the camp about midway through his time at east camp. He was certainly the most knowledgeable and experienced Kriegie and was respected by all. He was shot down in the early months of the war as a wing commander and without doubt would have had promotion to ranks well above group captain had he not been a PoW and I think this was generally recognised. 'Wings' Day set up the 'X' Organisation with its head designated as 'Big X'. This was designed not only to approve any escape project, but to assist in every way possible in the success of that escape and in particular to ensure that it did not conflict with any other escape projects. In every hut one officer was designated as 'x' (Little 'x'), and it was their responsibility to keep Big 'X' informed of all escape bids. Big 'X' responsibility was vested in Squadron Leader Roger Bushell, a very able officer who was a member of the Royal Auxiliary Air Force, part time fliers, mostly in fighter squadrons flying at weekends and only becoming full time members of the service at the outbreak of hostilities. His civilian profession was that of a barrister; he was older than almost all of the other fighter pilots who tended to be very young, and indeed most Kriegies. He spoke fluent German and was an imposing and forthright character which made him an obvious choice for this responsibility. Roger Bushell was certainly the man for the job, not least because like 'Wings' Day he had escaped a number of times. He was shot by the Gestapo following his capture after the 'Great Escape', one of fifty who suffered the same gangster treatment at the hands of Hitler's henchmen.

It was essential to know what was going on so in addition to the escape committee we had an intelligence organisation organised on similar lines and each hut had a Little 'i' reporting to a Big 'I' who was a member of the escape committee; this committee discussed matters while pounding the circuit so as to avoid the risk of being bugged in a room. One would see 'Wings' and 'X' or 'Wings' and 'I' or 'X' and 'I' walking round deep in conversation. They also walked round with others to avoid the Goons noticing the same important people going round together and surmising that something was afoot particularly since Bushel was known as a troublemaker. Under the direction of this committee, several specialist departments were set up. There was a clothing department which could produce clothes to suit a labourer, a city gent, a Luftwaffe uniform, in fact whatever was required. Blankets were useful for this and dyes were obtained from soaking colours from the covers of books. Most important was the counterfeit department who could produce passes that were as good as the originals, which had been left on a table, generally unwillingly, while the owner had a cup of coffee; maps, routes, rail time tables, border crossings were all produced by these ingenious and skilful men. High energy food, which was a mixture of chocolate, oats and glucose was produced, which when the general lack of food that was available is taken into account was remarkable; yet everyone gave up their share in the interest of aiding an escape even though we knew that most were destined to be unsuccessful. It was claimed that one large square of this chocolate provided sufficient energy for three days march and since we had student doctors and a dietician among our number it was doubtless true. The ingenuity of the Kriegie had no bounds even to the extent of building radio sets, three of which were hidden away in various hidey holes in different huts, operated only by the person who knew of their location. Every item was made in the camp with the exception of the valves.

Since we were in a position to provide intelligence back to England, information both from and about shot down aircrew, as well as defences round the various cities that were being attacked, an organisation had to be set up to coordinate this. Inevitably this was done by 'Wings'. I do not know precisely how it was set up or how the codes were agreed, but I can explain how the messages were sent as I was directly involved in it. All those of us sending messages were married as it would not be suspicious if we were writing on a regular basis to our wives. My wife received notification from the Air Ministry that sometimes my letters would be delayed and that they would have been read. I used a Spanish/English dictionary and I was given a list of Spanish words which I then translated into English. I had a frequency of six, which meant that the translated word had to occur as the sixth or multiples of six in the letter. I had no idea what the message was and I suppose that it went through a further translation when it was decoded. Two others in my room were also sending messages in this way, but how large the organisation was, I have no idea.

The BBC News was received and was read to each hut under strict security throughout. Lookouts were doubled for the entire operation because this contact with 'Home' and our version of the news as opposed to the German news was a very prized link. Strict rules also existed for the destruction of the written news should discovery seem likely at any juncture. As I have already said, the BBC News contained elements of propaganda and it was possible to get a pretty accurate picture of events by listening to both bulletins. Once the tide had turned in our favour a large map, referred to as the Ops Map, was kept up to date on a daily basis from the information obtained from the German wireless and papers. We could not use the combined information for the obvious reason that it would have alerted the Germans to the fact that we were getting additional information and that that could only have been from an illicit radio; we could however mentally

RED CROSS AND ST. JOHN
PRISONERS OF WAR DEPARTMENT
ST. JAMES'S PALACE, LONDON, S.W.1

PW/RAF/O/318.

P/O. F.A.B. TAMS.

**KEEP THIS CARD CAREFULLY**

The above particulars must be written at the top of every letter you send to us about this prisoner.

**IT IS TO YOUR AND HIS BENEFIT TO DO THIS.**

PW/4019

*Passing coded messages to my wife*

apply the data. Most of us visited this map room daily. Tactics were discussed and theories as to possible strategies to end the war occupied many hours.

The theatre which we built kept a large number of enthusiasts busy: those who were concerned with the construction and those who produced the plays, some twenty-two all told, ranging from *Blythe Spirit* and *Pygmalian* to *Saint Joan*. We also produced some rather coarse, but to us extremely funny, productions. To give an idea of the quality and tenor of these shows, they were written by Talbot Rothwell who made his name after the war writing shows like *Up Pompeii* for Frankie Howard and several of the *Carry On* films. It took 'Tolly' two years to get his typewriter, but once he had it, it was never idle. The theatre staff worked practically full time; there were carpenters, electricians, metal workers and wardrobe wizards all producing all manner of clothing including shirts, pyjamas, handkerchiefs and many other things. The theatre director was Kenneth Macintosh, a professional actor from before the war, who both produced and acted, as a patient organiser who produced a play every fortnight. It may be wondered how the female parts were filled. In fact, although our memories might have dulled somewhat over the years, it was difficult not to believe that these hairy legged men were the attractive girls in the plays; it is remarkable what expertly applied make-up, a wig and female clothes can do. The theatre provided entertainment of high quality and took us out of the wire for an hour or two once a fortnight. From the early days at Stalag Luft 1 we had musicians; in fact, one of my room-mates got hold of a saxophone and with a few other instrumentalists used to practise two rooms away from ours and now I cannot hear the opening bars of 'In the Mood' without remembering how it used to drive me mad, being repeated time after time. But all this changed under the direction of Arthur Creighton who had been a professional musician before the war. He formed and conducted a forty piece classical orchestra which gave us many hours of pleasure.

It was when I was detailed as the hut adjutant at the time we moved to Stalag Luft 3, the camp from which the tunnels Tom, Dick and Harry were dug and from which the 'Great Escape' was made, that I decided to put the stove to a use other than cooking potatoes. We had been receiving Red Cross parcels fairly regularly for a change and I thought we might use some of the contents to lighten our dull lives a little. The Polish contingent, who occupied one of the huts in the centre of the camp, incidentally the hut from which one of the tunnels started, used raisins and sugar from parcels to produce wine. Having tasted this I decided it was too sickly and decided to distil this product after all the rooms had completed their cooking; the stove would be red-hot and very little coal would be required and 'What the hell did it matter anyway provided we got the right result?' The Germans issued jam in large metal containers of about two gallons. I obtained one of these from the German cookhouse, made the lid a tight fit and soldered an outlet tube to the top of this container. This metal tube was fed into a trombone which was positioned in a wooden trough filled with water. An extension soldered to the trombone outlet allowed the 'hooch' to drip into our bottles. I collected a quantity of raisins and sugar from each room in the hut and made the wine; each room had a spherical globe covering the light bulb and these globes, capable of holding about five pints, were put to better use than their original purpose. The raisins and sugar were placed in the globes which were three quarters full of water and were placed behind the heating stove in each room where they started to ferment; after three weeks the fermentation process had been completed and the great experiment started. Yeast was not required as the natural bloom from the raisins served the same purpose.

The wine was drained into the still, connections were made to the trombone and the trough filled with cold water. I had no idea what the correct temperatures were, and little means of control apart from lowering or raising the heat from the stove. I did know that alcohol vaporised at a lower temperature than boiling water. I progressed through the night making periodic tasting checks; unfortunately the metallic taste of the trombone came through very strongly and it was not until after two or three bottles that I got rid of this flavour. I decided to distil this batch again and was so pleased with the result that in all future distillations used this double distillation process. It was of course sacrilege to use food in this way but three good snorts of this reduced the duration of the war one day at least. I persuaded the hut to have one more go for Christmas when we would all have a party. One of our parcels contained dried apricots; I chopped these into small pieces, diced is I believe the technical term, and I put the equivalent of two halves into a bottle and left it for a couple of months. I opened the bottle for Christmas and we were able to kid ourselves that we had an after dinner apricot liqueur. Another day lost, or gained I suppose, depending on your viewpoint.

Once inside a PoW camp there are only three ways of escape: over, under or through the wire. There are a number of ways of achieving any of these. We were enclosed by two rows of barbed wire, ten feet in height and the two rows about six feet apart and containing large coils of barbed wire some five feet in diameter. Each row of barbed wire was supported on poles similar to telegraph poles placed about twelve feet apart. The wire stretched between the poles was latticed to form squares of about a foot. Guards in raised sentry boxes placed at fifty to sixty yard intervals overlooked the compound and the wire. At a distance of about five yards from the wire, a wooden guardrail was positioned to prevent prisoners approaching the wire without permission being obtained from the guard. To recover a football for instance, a request was made to the guard, and when it was given it was safe for the ball to be recovered; without permission the guard had authority to shoot the offender.

There is always a way to beat the system. When we were due to move from East Camp to North Camp at Stalag Luft 3, Commander Jimmy Buckley asked to see the new camp which was supposed to provide accommodation far superior to what we had had up until then. Jimmy was our security officer. He praised the new camp and then asked if he could look at a sentry box. Strangely, the Germans agreed and Jimmy was able to confirm what he had suspected which was that the sentry box was placed in such a position, midway between the two rows of wire, that the line of poles created a blind spot halfway between two sentry boxes. Thus, if the sentries in two boxes could be distracted for a short time, a prisoner could jump over the warning rail and be hidden from the guards in both boxes. Provided the camp was clear of ferrets and our strict security system could ensure this, the blind spot could be utilised. Soon after this Jimmy Buckley escaped, I don't know how, and nothing was heard of him again, either from German sources or

*Just out of hospital, viewing the wire at Dulag Luft.*

our own. We did hear his intention was to steal a boat and suspect he did this but sadly did not make the sea crossing. Unfortunately he was also unable to witness the use to which his discovery of the blind spot was put.

Two prisoners decided to test the system and armed with wire cutters, which were made on the camp by a Kriegie with an engineering background, an ex 'Brat' no less, whom modestly precludes me from naming, and pegs to lift and keep the centre coil of wire in place, planned to cut through the wire and walk away. The operation was approved by the 'X' Committee. Timing was critical. The sentries had to have been on duty long enough to be bored and not due to change for some time and the compound had to be free of ferrets. The day arrived when the conditions were right. A German speaking prisoner engaged one of the sentries in conversation and the other sentry saw two prisoners start to argue and then resort to fisticuffs, quickly joined by a crowd cheering them on. Standing in a sentry box is a boring pastime and these guards, mainly old men, became interested in the slightest diversion. When the guards were properly occupied the two escapers leapt over the guard rail, ran to the fence at the blind spot and started to cut the wire; it had been calculated that only three cuts were necessary and that the wire could then be bent up to give an opening large enough for a man to crawl through; the inner coil could then be propped up with the pegs, again allowing room for a man to crawl underneath before again cutting the outer

*'Just try cutting your way through!' It will be seen that the sentry box is positioned in the centre of the wire, the sentry looking down the row of supports at an angle producing a blind spot about midway.*

lattice. The noise of the fighting and general hullabaloo rehearsed for these occasions drowned any noise caused by the wire being cut or the propping up of the inner coil and the escapers wriggling through.

Mission accomplished, both escapers stood up and adjusted their caps and clothing, all of which had been produced by the camp tailors. At this point one of the sentries was seen to look in their direction. He obviously did not believe what he saw, or if he did could not decide what to do; he was in a no-win situation. If they were prisoners how did they get there without him challenging them and if he now took a pot shot at them why did he let them get that far? In fact, he did nothing and the two escapers walked away. The urge to run must have been overwhelming. They were back in camp within a few days and occupying the cooler for the mandatory fourteen days; but they had had a few days of fresh air at least.

Probably the most hazardous and courageous attempt I knew about and witnessed also involved the warning rail. The German security had decided to make use of a seismograph to try to detect our tunnelling activities and to this end dug a trench to a depth of about six feet, just inside the warning rail into which they planned to lay a line later. Always looking for ways to escape and seeing a way to make a quicker exit than by weeks of tunnelling, two individuals put forward a plan to the 'X' Committee. If they could get into the trench at dusk without detection they could tunnel underneath the wire, pushing the spoil behind them like moles, and be out by dawn. It was agreed and the usual complete assistance was given.

A similar method of getting the attention of the sentry box guards was provided as had been used in the 'blind spot' escape and the two moles jumped into the trench just before we were locked into our huts for the night. The intention was to dig out the entrance, putting the initial extraction of sand in the trench. The camp had been built on what had been a pine forest, which had taken most of the body from the soil leaving a light sand down to quite a depth and it was this lightness of soil that made the idea viable in the first place. Having made an entrance, they then moved forward, pushing the newly dug sand behind them like moles. Since they had calculated that the whole operation would be completed by first light they had no misgivings about making air holes with a rod, believing that neither the rod nor the condensation from their breath would be seen in the dark since the guards in their boxes normally swept the compound with their searchlights but not the wire area.

The following morning those of us aware of the attempt took an early walk round the circuit as soon as the huts were unlocked and 'Appel', morning roll call, was over and were appalled to see vapour coming from an air hole along the line of the tunnel. Obviously progress had been slower than had been anticipated; it was equally obvious that the moles were still working. We calculated the time of their expected breakthrough outside the wire and organised a distraction of the sentry box guards to coincide with it. Our calculations were not far out and the two moles duly clambered out of their hole, stood up, adjusted their caps and walked off. As one who could not even take on normal tunnelling duties because of claustrophobia, this moling operation was the ultimate in courage to me. Throughout the whole escape, for those of us who knew it was under way, the hardest part was not to keep glancing at the line of the tunnel to assess the progress of the moles. As I said earlier, getting out, however difficult, was the easiest part of escaping and like most others these two were soon back inside the wire. Lack of success was never a deterrent to the hardened escapers.

The 'Wooden Horse' was another escape designed to reduce the amount of digging required to get beyond the wire. This escape received almost as much publicity as 'The Great Escape'. It took place in Stalag Luft 3 East Camp and the horse was placed in front of the spot where my photograph was taken of us enjoying the sun. Not being able to tunnel, I devoted my time to carrying the horse to and fro and taking part in the vaulting exercises over it to justify its existence. It was remarkable that the ferrets were not

*In front of the 'Wooden Horse', author third from left.*
*Looks like a holiday camp!*

sufficiently suspicious to investigate our actions. The system that we used was to carry the horse out each day with a tunneller inside who opened up the trap door entrance and dug the tunnel, putting the sand in bags which were carried back at the end of the session in the horse. A long and tedious procedure, but we had time to spare and were doing our duty, helping someone to escape.

The 'Great Escape' took place after we had left East Camp and moved to North Camp. In this case, three tunnels were being built at the same time code-named, 'Tom', 'Dick' and 'Harry', each starting from a different hut and with different hiding places for the trap doors. Too often we had had a tunnel discovered and had all our hopes dashed; with three on the go even if one were to be discovered the 'goons' would not think we had others being built at the same time. My contribution was simply doing what some five hundred others did, anything but tunnelling itself. One of the duties was guarding the entrance to one tunnel which was under the stove in the room where my colleagues used spelling games to decide on the allocation of food.

Disposing of the sand was always a problem. The quantities involved made it impossible to use the old bag down the trouser leg method especially as the colour of the sand lower down the tunnel was of a different colour to the sand on the surface and the ferrets would soon cotton on. We resorted to storing it in hut ceilings until it was obvious that the weight was so great that serious damage had become a distinct possibility. It sounds odd but we were saved from disaster by the discovery of one of the tunnels which put the ferrets off the scent. The building of the theatre provided us with much needed space for the disposal of large quantities of sand. We constructed a sloping auditorium so that everyone had a good view of the stage which gave us a large space for sand dispersal. This together with the decision to concentrate on one tunnel and to use the remaining tunnel for storing sand made rapid progress possible on the third and ultimately successful one.

The 'Great Escape' has received so much publicity that it is unnecessary to record the details here. It was an enormous operation involving over five hundred of us on a virtually full time basis. Hundreds of tons of sand were removed and disposed of without discovery and but for a small error in calculation, not an easy task anyway, it would have been possible for twice the number to have got out. The opening which should have been in a wooded area fell some distance short of the calculated break-out which made it impossible for the steady exit that had been planned and the signalling system that had to be set up at short notice drastically slowed the speed of those getting out. The fifty who were shot, well over half the number who got out, leads one to wonder on what the resultant rage in the German High Command would have been and just how many would have lost their lives had the planned number of over two hundred escaped.

The escape of so many PoWs obviously caused quite a stir in high places in the German hierarchy and early in the morning following the escape several members of the Gestapo arrived accompanied by a posse of goons with loaded rifles and machine guns and we were herded out of our huts. We had little time for concealment but we were used to spontaneous searches and were fairly confident that the more important items would not be found. In the event the Gestapo thugs unearthed one or two items which they placed outside the doors of the rooms, much to the almost open glee of our own ferrets who were well aware of our antics and did nothing to assist the thugs. Very soon the items disappeared from outside the room doors, back into the safe custody of the Kriegies. The Kriegies took further advantage of the ineptitude of these Hitler henchmen when at about midmorning they enquired where the canteen was. Of course there was no canteen, but always on the ball, a canteen suddenly came into being and a quantity of cigarettes, coffee and chocolate from Red Cross parcels was being sold for real Reichsmarks, gold dust to the escape organisation. The thugs left us with far more than they discovered or collected. Some days later the Commandant, Von Lindeiner, requested that the Senior British Officer, Group Captain Massey, come to see him. Obviously ill at ease, he told the SBO that he had been informed that fifty of the escapers had been shot while attempting to escape after recapture and all had been killed. The SBO asked how many had been wounded, with the obvious inference that if some had been shot re-escaping more must have been wounded as it would not be possible to kill everyone. He was told that there were no wounded.

The whole of the camp was shocked and angered by this mass murder. We attached black squares or diamond shapes to the sleeves of our uniforms and flying jackets and it is fair to report that those Luftwaffe personnel who had been with us for some years were equally resentful of this murderous affair which could only have been the work of the Gestapo. They knew our duty was to escape and it was their duty to prevent this; in certain circumstances we could be shot at and killed or wounded, and both sides accepted this, but mass murder they did not accept.

Permission was obtained from the Commandant for a working party to build a memorial to the fifty and to this end a number of us gave parole each day to go to the chosen site for this purpose. The memorial was completed and the names of those who had been killed inscribed later. I have learned from the RAF Association that it is cared for by Polish colleagues as it is now in part of their country. They are anxious for anyone who was in Stalag Luft 3 to make the pilgrimage to the memorial, especially members of the RAF Escape Society. Many of those who were shot were from this brave country.

There were spur of the moment escapes which were unlikely to jeopardise any of the planned escapes being controlled by the escape committee. One such was when we were moved from North Camp to East Camp which had been a pine forest and although the hutted area had been cleared completely

This is a photograph of the Unfinished Vault, designed by F/Lt. Todd, himself a prisoner of war, for the Ashes of the Fifty Officers who were shot by the Gestapo, after their escape on the 24th of March, 1944. The Vault as it now stands has three granite scrolls rising from the granite slabs seen in the picture on which are engraved the names of these Officers.

**In Memory of**

THOSE OFFICERS WHO PAID THE EXTREME SACRIFICE AFTER ESCAPE ON THE NIGHT OF MARCH 24th 1944

*"Per Ardua Ad Astra"*

of trees, a large area still had the stumps in the ground. Permission was requested and given for this area to be used as a sports field and we agreed to dig up the stumps in return. Picks and shovels were loaned on a daily basis and used in the main for this purpose, but one becomes very cunning as a PoW and the tools were put to other uses as well, even though we were under the surveillance of guards and ferrets. In due course all the stumps had been dug up and the goons sent in horse drawn carts to remove them, together with the brushwood which we had also cleared from the area. Naturally, this provided a chance to get outside the camp and Kriegies jumped in the carts and covered themselves with the foliage, hoping to be taken through the main gates safely. Unfortunately the ferrets who had been with us for some years were not fooled and knowing our little ways had guards just inside the first gate prodding the contents with their bayonets. No one was hurt and it was all taken in good part by both sides and no one got through. A chap who obviously had a stomach of iron and no sense of smell made another attempt: the large latrine in the centre of the camp was cleared about every four or five months in the normal way of these things. The 'honey wagon' as it was called was also horse drawn and one of our number clung to something underneath the wagon hoping that the ferrets would think that no one would use this method and that the search would only be cursory, if at all. Wrong again and the poor chap only reached the first gate. These attempts did not incur punishment and were treated light heartedly by both sides, which was normally the case when the goons felt that they were in charge.

Two other spontaneous attempts received a very different response from our captors. About once a month a party of about twenty prisoners were taken to the Commandantur compound for a hot shower, a very welcome privilege since only cold water was available in the camp. On one particular occasion we heard that the bathing party had been cancelled. The devious mind of the Kriegie considered the possibility that the guardroom might not have been told since it had been a last minute cancellation; particularly since the bathing party had already assembled. Luftwaffe uniforms were always available at short notice and were provided for two German speaking Kriegies who were also provided with rifles, which were of course dummies fashioned by experts but from a distance of only a few yards indistinguishable from the real thing. The barrel had been treated with the carbon taken from pencils which was rubbed into the wood until the effect of a metal barrel was achieved and the butt and wooden parts were dyed and polished. With our towels under our arms and our 'guards' shouting at us in the normal goon manner, we marched through both sets of gates bound for the showers, but on the way a wood presented an ideal spot to break away and begin our escape proper, so off we went. We weren't away long, but it had caused some irritation. This was my first and last escape attempt; I restricted myself to the support role from then on.

On the same day senior officers in the camp were due to have a meeting with the commandant which was also cancelled. The senior officers decided to emulate the shower party and obtained a couple of German speaking Kriegies as guards who were armed with revolvers, manufactured of course in our own 'armoury', and proceeded through the first of the main gates. But on passing the guardroom their luck ran out in the shape of Herr Pieber, the officer who took our Appells, who emerged from the guardroom just as the party was passing; he knew most of the prisoners by sight since he saw all of them at least once a day and recognising one of the phoney guards, he exclaimed, 'Are you going for a walk, Mister Sadler?' at which the whole of the German contingent burst into jeering and laughter, the officers slapping our officers on the back and generally enjoying our discomfort.

This joviality lasted about ten minutes when it turned to rage and shouting, particularly at the guardroom personnel; one of the guards had been returning through the woods when he saw some of the clothing left by the shower party. He ran to the guardroom and made his report where it was recognised that they had allowed some twenty or so PoWs to walk straight through the gates past the guardroom without a word of challenge. One has to hear a German who has been made to look foolish shout and scream in a rage to realise that they lose all control in such circumstances. These were but two instances of the German loss of control in truly Teutonic character. From our point of view the whole episode was extremely funny; there had been little chance of the escapes succeeding, but it did allow us to annoy the Germans and it certainly did that.

Just after the Canadian commando raid on Dunkirk which went so badly wrong and where most were killed or captured some of the prisoners had their hands tied up. This was a reprisal for the alleged fact that the Canadians had captured some Germans and tied them up. As usual, with time on their hands, the Kriegies found a way to remove their hands from the ropes and put them back again undetected. One day a shower party went down to the showers with their hands tied, undressed and went under the showers with their hands tied, leaving the guards scratching their heads in consternation. These were the normal guards, not the ferrets who knew us well enough to have known what was happening.

As I have said, the security against bugging was established in every hut, but escape plans were nevertheless made outside on the circuit. An amusing incident as regards this aspect of our lives occurred in Stalag Luft 1 at Barth; one of the security officers asked if we would like to listen to programmes broadcast by the German radio station. This was accepted and in due course a receiver was put on the wall of one of the rooms. Unfortunately for the German officer we were not as naive as he had hoped and an inspection soon established that a two way system had been installed and back in the Commandantur building conversations from the Kriegies' room could be overheard; they obviously hoped to learn of escape plans or any other loose talk. They certainly heard our conversations, but they were not quite the sort they expected. A stream of invective and abuse was hurled at the receiver and guffaws greeted the programmes. Of course nothing could be said or done by the Germans without admitting that they had bugged the radio. The set was removed the next day amidst joyful mickey taking from the Kriegies.

Our captors failed miserably in all their attempts against us: the first American aircrews taken prisoner were accommodated with us in Stalag Luft 3, but as their numbers increased, which they did very rapidly as a result of the daylight raids with crews of twelve in a Flying Fortress, a separate camp was built alongside ours which they occupied. This was separated by only a single barbed wire fence instead of the normal two with coils in between. As I mentioned earlier, the Americans learned about being a Kriegie and how to thwart the Germans in their little tricks very quickly from us, who were after all the experts as we had had plenty of practice. Firm friendships were made, so much so that a number of the Americans who had been with us climbed the wire into our camp to celebrate Christmas with old friends. I mention this in order to show how fruitless it was of the Germans to try to play the USAAF against the RAF and they soon found this out.

There were times when depression became hard to bear, when it seemed that the war would never end and this tedious existence would go on forever and it was here that friends came to the rescue. I suppose they would call it counselling today, but in reality it was just understanding and a friendly ear. Another outlet was predictions made by an optimist in the camp as to when the war would end. He would bet hundreds of pounds on quite ridiculous dates. I imagine it gave him some comfort and I'm sure none of the bets were expected to be paid. A rather remarkable incident which occurred just after Christmas in 1943 is worth recording. A roommate woke up one morning with the news that he had dreamt that the Invasion had started on 6th June. He explained the Invasion and predicted the end of the war by the following Christmas and said that we had all been drinking in a bar in London. It was therefore quite remarkable that the Invasion did start on the 6th June, even more so since it was originally planned for the 5th but postponed for bad weather. Unfortunately the rest did not materialise but we were certainly full of hope for the rest of that year, particularly after the Invasion.

So the days, weeks and months went by with the same old routine. But now the Russians were advancing on the eastern front and the Invasion, after some dicey days, was also showing some signs of success and there was hope abroad. We could even hear the Russian guns in the distance. Then came the bombshell, 'You march in one hour,' and off we went on our first march.

# CHAPTER 9

## *Marching to freedom*

The order to evacuate all prisoners from the area arrived from the German High Command. Russian guns could be heard getting nearer day by day and the order to march was therefore a disappointment. I was in the theatre when the order came. The curtains were suddenly lowered and Herr Pieber appeared to make the announcement, 'Gentlemen, you march in an hour.'

A foot or more of snow lay on the ground and the temperature was twenty degrees below zero. We hurried back to our rooms and started to build

*Stalag Luft 3, Sagan. The last visit to our theatre before the march. Author on left.*

sledges. The eight occupants of our room decided to march in two fours with a sledge to each four. The parcel store was opened and we were allowed to draw two Red Cross parcels each which when added to the food we already had and with the addition of blankets and the heaviest of our clothes more than filled our sledges. These were made from the backs of the chairs in the room which were conveniently made in one piece, the back legs extending to form the back of the chair and being made with a convenient curve. We strengthened this frame, attached a couple of ropes, which we made from plaited Red Cross string, and *Voilà*! we had the means to convey our goods and chattels with only a small backpack each to carry. We were ready within the hour. It is amazing how quickly things can be done when there is a deadline. 'Needs must when the devil drives,' was certainly true here, but it was well past midnight before we eventually left Stalag Luft 3, six hours later than the scheduled time. Not that time mattered to us; indeed, the longer we took to leave the nearer the Russians were and the greater the likelihood of an early release.

Our light-weight sleds moved easily and it was when passing some mammoth contraptions which had disintegrated within half a mile of the camp that we realised how sensible we had been with our choice. The American owners of the ones which had not got very far lost most of their contents. Stereotypes are misleading, but Americans do seem to have a fixation with size which is not always the most appropriate. In fact our sleds served us well until the snow melted and they had to be discarded. One chap who had spent considerable time and effort on his, could not bear to leave it behind and continued to pull it until the runners were paper thin. Within a couple of hours ten thousand Allied prisoners were trudging through the snow. I was deputed to lead the members of our camp and to move in accordance with normal 'Route March' procedure: that is, fifty minutes marching and ten minutes rest in each hour. This works if everyone starts together and stops together, but in these conditions it became impossible and in a very short time the concertina effect on the two thousand from our camp applied to such an extent that when we stopped at the front, the back markers were still catching up and when we started again they had just started their rest. We got a lot of stick! The route march procedure was quickly abandoned as it only works in a correct drill formation and when the orders 'march' and 'halt' are obeyed instantly, and neither of these conditions could apply in our circumstances. We trudged for thirty-six hours with infrequent halts; the ten minutes rest per hour had gone by the board early on with the abandonment of the forced march routine. Hot water was obtained from *Hausfraus* in the small villages that we went through and the coffee we made through this kindness put some warmth into our cold, tired and aching bodies. Considering that we were all aircrew and the devastation that the bombing had caused throughout Germany, their generosity was amazing.

The authorities realised a halt had to be made and when we reached Mauskau, a small town with a pottery, a riding school with heated stables, and a cinema, it was decided to give us a rest. Our little party ended up in the cinema. All the seats had been removed and the whole floor area was littered with dog-tired prisoners who just lay down wherever a space could be found. I ended up on the lintel above the entrance door, a space eight feet long by two feet wide, ideal. I spent two days on my ledge getting warm and having cups of coffee and food passed up to me by my colleagues. After two days it was time to resume our trudging. In a very short time we passed through a party of Americans who were in a sad state, lying in the ditch beside the road. There was nothing we could do as we were being urged on by the rifle butts of our guards.

That night we were housed in a barn. A frozen earth floor and open brickwork provided us with little shelter from the cold wind which was now blowing. Desmond Neely RN, who had been one of those who had got out in the Great Escape and had also been one of the fortunate twenty-six not murdered by Hitler's thugs, agreed to combine his blankets with mine. We then sewed them together to form a sleeping bag into which we both managed to crawl. This proved to be another wise foresight, but the ground soon froze our hips and about every half an hour came the call from one or other of us, 'Two, three, over,' as we both turned simultaneously to present the unfrozen hip to the ground. This was not a very restful night and we were glad to get under way after receiving a frozen loaf of black bread to share among our roommates.

The march continued, but later that day a thaw made it necessary to discard our sleds and carry the load on our backs. It was only for a short spell however, for we soon reached a Panzer barracks where we were given a bowl of good hot soup which revived us considerably. This was just as well for a further ordeal was awaiting us. We were marched to the railway station where we were shut into goods wagons. We were packed into these wagons to such an extent that we were not even able to sit down. By this time some of our number had developed a mild form of dysentery which under the circumstances caused them the utmost embarrassment and shame. Inevitably the stench was overpowering. We were let out once during the two day journey. The only hot water available to us was from the engine which at least enabled a hot brew to be made; unfortunately this only made the poor chaps who had the squitters worse.

The wagons showed obvious evidence of air attacks and every time we heard an aircraft we were apprehensive that we would be strafed, but fortunately this never happened. After two days and nights of near hell we reached Bremen and were marched to another 'Wire Bound World', which had recently been evacuated by Merchant Marine internees and condemned. This was not surprising for the huts were polluted, bed bugs abounded and only six beds existed in the entire place. We slept outside until beds and mattresses had been provided for us and they had been cleared of bed bugs. After all we had endured our spirits were at a nadir. Food was short and our dietician informed us that we should spend the days conserving energy by lying in bed, but this was disregarded. I think we survived mainly because it was obvious that the war would soon be over and we refused to give in so close to freedom. A little black marketeering was started through Kriegsmarine sailors who would exchange eggs and sometimes a chicken for coffee or cigarettes, the items being pushed under the wire at a pre-arranged spot. One day an RAF Mosquito circled the camp at about a thousand feet with no opposition at all; we obviously had control of the air. We waved, hoping that we would be recognised as PoWs and perhaps this was established as he departed without firing a shot, to our great relief.

We had been in the camp for several weeks when once again our hopes were raised as we learned of the British advances, but just as quickly dashed as once more the order was given to march. This time we were having none of the forced march procedure; the SBO promulgated a movement order, which was to take effect in the event of another march. This order dictated the terms under which we would move: a limited number of miles per day, stops in the evening to allow sufficient time to prepare food and a camp for the night. From memory I think ten miles was the most we travelled in a day. Our little party of eight bartered cigarettes and coffee for two perambulators which carried all our belongings, rather more effectively than the sledges now that the snow was gone and much more comfortably than on our backs.

The march was towards Lübeck. Parcel collecting points had been arranged along the route and soap, cigarettes and coffee were in good supply. They were particularly valuable as we were able to barter with them, at first with the civilian population, but later with our guards, who at first were opposed to the trading, but when they saw what they were missing, made it their business to gather eggs and vegetables in order to exchange them for our products. Reggie Spear, our Aussie colleague who had been a school master and spoke fluent German, would visit schools and with a little bribery, obtain permission to talk to the class and inevitably concluded by asking for eggs which were invariably produced. We fed well as a result. Eggs, and I mean eggs in the plural, which when you consider what the ration was at home was pure luxury, poached and served with nettles which are young and tender in spring and taste like spinach which has been peppered, makes a wonderful meal. Life was certainly getting better, even if we did smell a bit. We slept under the stars and all was well, marching, which was I suppose more like ambling, towards Lübeck. We could hear gunfire once again and knew that this time it must be our own troops who would catch up with us. There was considerable excitement one day when some of our Belgian colleagues became very noisy in a ditch alongside the road; it transpired that they had found the right sort of edible snail which they gathered and cooked that evening. We were by now eating well enough to be able to resist the temptation to join them. Approaching Lübeck a message was received that the town was overflowing with prisoners, that there was an epidemic of typhoid and we were advised not to continue.

Through the Red Cross permission was obtained to find suitable accommodation nearby. A tobacco plantation at Trenthorst provided the answer: a lake, plenty of barns and in my case a pigsty which was tiled, clean and had a bed of straw, on a farm; it accommodated our eight well in complete comfort. We lived on our farm, sleeping in the pigsty and eating better than had been possible for all the previous years as prisoners, though this comparative luxury still lacked the one thing everyone prizes above all else, freedom. The desire to do what one wants when one wishes is a paramount requirement in human nature; this at last now seemed possible as once again artillery could be heard. The BBC news was received and read out saying that the end was very close, but remembering our disappointments in the past, the excitement was subdued and the hope that all this horror was about to end could not really be accepted.

On 2nd May, stragglers from the German Army arrived. Those with guns threw them down, others had already discarded theirs. '*Tommy Kommt,*' the Tommies are coming, they said, as they came through our makeshift camp. It was not long before the buzz went round that the 7th Armoured Division, the Desert Rats, had surrounded the area, but it was not until a Scout car arrived, 'Hello H2, X35 to H2, have just released second PoW camp,' that we realised that this was it, we were now no longer PoWs; a bespectacled Lieutenant in a Scout car had released us. I do not know what I expected, but it was not this supreme anticlimax. Our little group who had been in captivity for years could not accept this strange feeling immediately, and went back to a brew.

Later an Army major arrived and addressed a mob of cheering prisoners. 'I can promise that you will be in England in ten days. I have arranged for portable shower units to be made available in the meantime.' The reception to this announcement was not what he expected. Ten days was a lifetime to those of us who had spent up to six years longing for this day; quite unreasonably we thought we could be whisked away and taken home at once. There was still a war on since Germany had not yet capitulated, but that did not enter our thoughts, we just wanted to go home.

Appreciating our feelings, arrangements were made to take us out of the camp and on the way home. Convoys took us to a reception camp in which conditions were appalling and to cap it all we were told that a further delay of at least two weeks was likely owing to a backlog of many thousand prisoners ahead of us. Depression and despondency reached such a level that senior officers visited a local airfield where the RAF were told of our predicament. I do not know if it is true but it was reported that a message was sent to the effect that, 'You flew us in, now you fly us out.' And this they did. A call for volunteers produced sufficient aircrews to man Lancasters to take all of us to an airfield in England. Ground personnel serviced the planes and aircrew gave up leave to bring us home. Once again the Service rallied round for its own. For the first time for four years this Trenchard Brat donned his Mae West over his tatty Irvin flying jacket, still with the black diamond on the sleeve, climbed into a Lanc and was homeward bound. I do not remember the airfield at which we landed, who cared, all that mattered was that I was home. As we got off the plane ladies from the volunteer services were there to welcome us, but not before each of us had been subjected to DDT treatment, puffed up the arms, legs and front. We then went for debriefing, received a fresh battle dress, sent a telegram to our next of kin, in my case my wife, received railway warrants and set off to see and be with those we had dreamed of for many years. It had happened at last: I was on my way to see my wife and daughter.

The journey down to the London terminus was uneventful but, to me, it was strange to see men sitting and ladies standing. I understood better when one man offered his seat and received the rebuke, 'I am quite capable of standing, thank you.' Arriving at Waterloo station, I discovered that I had missed the last train to Barnham, my destination, and that the next was the milk train which would leave at five in the morning. I decided to stay on the station and wait for it. The station was soon invaded by crowds of revellers from all the Services; it was 8th May, VE Day. A large section had obviously, 'done the town'; members from all three Services were in a dishevelled state, tunics undone or missing, caps off and both men and women behaving in a manner quite alien to my ideas of decorum. The last straw was seeing a number of sailors of both sexes sitting on the platform, backs to a pillar, boots and socks off, wiggling their toes and giggling. They were, of course, letting off steam and certainly relief valves had been blown but to be pitched into this from four years in a prison camp and with memories of the England I had left, it all seemed so unreal that I genuinely began to doubt my sanity for the second time.

The mind can behave in strange ways in certain circumstances; in my third year as a PoW I had attended the sickbay daily for treatment to my back as I was suffering from sciatica. I was asked to accompany a young man whose mind had been badly deranged and was in need of medical care. He apparently trusted me. I collected him from his room and when we reached the parade area he stopped and said that we were to wait for a fly-past and that he was the reviewing officer. He was so convinced of this that I had some difficulty in persuading him that it was to take place later that day when we returned from sick quarters. The procedure was for those attending sickbay to congregate at the gate to wait for the guards to accompany us. While waiting on this particular day, one of those in the queue told me a weird story, about worms, that he had been reading. It was a strange yarn and I had already been affected by the chap I was detailed to accompany and now begun to wonder which of us was round the bend. On arrival at the sickbay I handed over my charge and went for my treatment. This required lying face down under a small tunnel of electric lights to provide heat for my back. Lying under these lights I kept very still and watched everything that was taking place until I decided that my mind was not affected. I relate these two instances to show how easily one can be affected when under conditions of stress. Some time later an RAF doctor told me that I was one of the sanest ex-PoWs he had seen. Some were very badly disturbed when they came home.

I gladly caught the five a.m. train for Barnham and again quietly reflected on the previous night's scenes and decided that I was going to have to get used to many of the changes that had taken place during the last four years. I reached Barnham, got a taxi and asked to be taken home. The taxi driver remembered me; he was aware, as were the whole village, of my homecoming. I arrived at the cottage where my wife and daughter lived at about seven o'clock. As I reached the cottage my wife had rented, a small girl was coming down the path; the taxi driver, seeing I did not immediately recognise her, said, 'Don't you recognise your own?' I had left behind a child, not much more than a baby, of two and here was a schoolgirl of almost seven. I was bewildered but recalling the photographs I had received

I caught up and said 'Hello.' She said, 'I'm just going to milk the goats,' and that was that. My wife explained that my telegram had reached them early the day before and I had been expected on that day. They had sat up to give me a small reception party and when I had not arrived by ten p.m. had given up and my daughter had formed the opinion I was never coming. She apparently had started to milk the goats at a friend's house and was very proud that her hands were now large enough to be able to do this – much more important than an illusive father.

After an absence as long as we had had, it was not unusual for both my wife and myself to feel strangely shy. We talked as though we had only just met. She had prepared a small homecoming, a cake and a few small bottles of sherry, and spirits which friends had collected and given to her. It was very difficult to get wine and spirits with rationing still in force. Jacqueline returned from her milking and our feelings fell into place gradually. As the days passed we became a family again and we returned to the relationship that had always existed.

We had no electricity and oil lamps provided the light in the evenings; washing clothes had to be done by hand and all the other amenities now accepted as standard caused my wife some hardship. I asked why the cottage was not connected to the electricity supply. The reply was astonishing and infuriating; the cottage had been occupied by the gardener of the owner of a large country house, and my wife rented the cottage from him as the gardener had joined one of the Services and it was unoccupied and likely to be so until the end of hostilities. A request to the owner by my wife for the electricity supply to be connected, at her expense, was refused on the grounds that he 'did not approve of servants having modern comforts.' I had just returned from more than four years of captivity, many of my colleagues and hundreds of others had given their lives, but this individual refused to allow the wife of one of those who had fought to retain his freedom the chance of modern amenities. At the end of hostilities, in spite of the shortage of accommodation, I am sure he would have had difficulty in employing anyone with the offer of that sort of housing and with this attitude.

# CHAPTER 10

## *Return to duty*

Generous leave had been granted to all ex PoWs but, to my shame, all I wanted to do was to return to flying. I talked it over with Marjorie and, as ever, she understood, although it must have been hurtful to her that I did not want to take full advantage of my leave and spend it with them. She understood my restlessness and agreed that it was what was best for me. I contacted the authorities to request the curtailment of my leave and a return to duty. The request was granted and I was instructed to report to a rehabilitation centre set up specifically for ex PoWs. This rehabilitation comprised morning PT, lectures and films on subjects we had missed during captivity and above all, visits to local centres to meet people, mainly ladies, which certainly attracted some members of staff. But I was once again separated from my family and after a very short time asked to see the CO of the unit. He was an air gunner wing commander which surprised me and was in fact the only thing I learnt on this so called rehabilitation course. The most senior air gunner I had known up until then had reached the dizzy height of flight lieutenant and an air gunner CO who was younger than me was strange. He was a nice chap doing a difficult job with a somewhat overbearing staff. I explained that in my case the course was not achieving what it aimed to do and my only wish was to return to the job I had been trained for from an early age and to try and retrieve some of the four years I had lost. He agreed that I could leave.

I went for an interview and was informed that it was unlikely that I would get a flying appointment. I was obviously greatly disappointed. I was posted to Rivenhall, a station operating Stirlings, as station adjutant. My predecessor handed over and departed the RAF to return to his job in civilian life. I lived in the Mess at first, as did the CO, and I suppose, because I was older than most of the other officers in the Mess, we spent quite a lot of time together. As his adjutant he got to know me fairly well in a very short time and he knew of my urgent desire to return to flying. Station Flight at Rivenhall had an Oxford and the CO agreed to allow me to be checked out on this aircraft. I had to learn the R/T procedures which were foreign to me, never having been under air traffic control up to this point, but after a few circuits and bumps and a Standard Beam Approach I was allowed to fly solo. The flying was not difficult, but the R/T procedures were, as neither they nor air traffic control had existed in this form before the war. It was only when I started to fly the Flying Fortress (B17) at Langham in Norfolk that I realised how useful the flights in the Oxford at Rivenhall had been.

The station flight Oxford enabled me to fly to Langham where my friend of early 217 Squadron days, Arthur Southall, now a well decorated Squadron Leader, commanded 521 Squadron, flying Long Range met. sorties and operating Flying Fortress (B17) aircraft. On one of these trips I broached the subject of joining his Squadron as I was desperately keen to get back to a flying posting, a sentiment which he completely understood. We had flown together a lot, had similar ideas on flying, particularly in bad weather and also in using astro navigation. He managed to arrange the posting and I reported to him for flying duties on 24th September 1945. He personally gave me dual instruction on the Fortress and after an hour declared me

*Flying Fortress (B17) 1945. Joy back to flying; 521 Sqn.*

suitable to fly as 2nd Pilot and in this role I continued to fly met. sorties code-named Allah over the North Sea. On 25th/26th October I flew my first Allah sortie as captain with the Squadron Commander as my 2nd pilot, followed by a night Allah sortie with the Flight Commander as 1st pilot. I was appointed as a Flight Commander in November.

What of the wives of those in the Service? Basically they put up with a lot, they have to be ready to up sticks and move at the drop of a hat, irrespective of their own personal lives or choices, to places they might not wish to go and in circumstances that are not always conducive to comfortable living. Mine is a good example; when I went to Rivenhall, not wanting any further parting, I found accommodation some ten miles away. We had no car so I cycled to and from the station but my wife was reliant on public transport. At least the hours were regular. Then I went to Langham. Arthur's wife Margaret and Marjorie were old friends and we were invited to share their house in Sheringham. Arthur, as a squadron commander, had a Service car which made travel to and from the airfield easy. Margaret had a private car which at least allowed the wives to go shopping relatively easily. This arrangement worked very happily for all of us but it was too good to last. The Squadron was moved to Brawdy in North Wales and the inevitable search for suitable accommodation faced us again. We achieved this by once again sharing, but before we had a chance to occupy the house we had found, the Squadron was moved to Chivenor in North Devon. I had moved from rented accommodation near Braintree while stationed at Rivenhall, then on to Sheringham while at Langham and then again to Brawdy and finally we moved to Barnstaple in Devon. There we once again shared a house with the quaint name of 'Pixie Dell': the boys in the Squadron called it the Squadron HQ. All this had taken place in the space of five months and my wife had had to make all the domestic arrangements.

I was promoted to Squadron Leader on 1st December 1945 and given Command of 517 Squadron, re-equipped with Halifax IIIs on Long Range met. sorties code named 'Epicure'. Arthur Southall continued as OC 521 flying 'Allah', both squadrons gathering met. information over the Western Approaches. The Halifax was more comfortable than the Fortress in which it was necessary to crawl through a narrow tunnel with petrol tanks on each side in order to get from the rear of the fuselage to the cockpit. The automatic pilot, George, in the Fortress was far superior to that in the Halifax and we missed it badly on our long, ten-hour, 'Epicure' sorties, which often took place in bad weather. Although the role remained the same, the flights were out to the west over the Atlantic rather than to the east over the North Sea.

A Long Range met. sortie was designed to obtain weather data at a number of height levels. The Squadron's task was to fly one sortie starting at ten a.m. and another at ten p.m. each covering the same route and each of approximately ten hours duration. The initial leg was flown at a millibar height of one thousand feet; along this leg descents were made to fifty feet by day and one hundred feet at night. Very often the weather conditions made visible sighting impossible, but the radio altimeter gave very accurate readings and no danger existed. The meteorological observer, an additional crew member for these flights, had a battery of instruments in his domain in the nose. He recorded readings that he observed himself, and obtained wind speed and direction from the navigator throughout the flight. This information was radioed back to the station and the weather maps prepared. This leg took us to the middle of the Atlantic at which point a sea level reading was taken, followed by a box climb, meteorological readings being taken at barometric levels up to five hundred millibars and at this level a second leg was flown for two hours. A couple of my younger pilots who flew together claimed that this leg, which was flown entirely on oxygen, had a very sexy effect on them. It didn't happen to me, just getting old, I guess. Incidentally these two, flying on a night 'Epicure', at about the furthest position from base, for some unknown reason had to ditch and a chance in a million put them down alongside a merchantman, who radioed news of their safety to base.

One of the Squadron pilots was a little man who had been a bus driver as a civilian. He was kidded by a number of crews because he always lay on a bunk for an hour on the final leg because he said he wanted to feel rested for a landing should anything go wrong. One day it did; he had to feather both engines on one side which requires a lot of strength to keep the aircraft not only straight but also in the air. He was diverted to St Mawgan, an airfield with long runways, where he made a perfect landing and the kidding about a rest being required died a death.

Chivenor had housed a Fighter affiliation unit flying Spitfire XVIs, but by the time we arrived all the pilots had been posted and the Spitfires remained on charge to the Squadron Leader Engineering, a terrific Welshman called 'Johnny' Johns. Now it so happened that he was an ex Brat, but from long before my time, who was an old friend going back to Tangmere days. I suggested that the servicing of four Spits, for which there was no allocation of staff, took up a lot of the time of his personnel whose real function was the servicing of the Halifaxes and that he should get rid of the aircraft.

'How do you suggest I do that, Tammy?'

'Well, I could get a bit of familiarisation and take them to the MU.'

(Maintenance Unit).

I had to agree when asked if I flown Spits that I had not, but that I had flown single engined Harts, Audaxes, and also a Fury, although how I could think that he could be persuaded that there was any similarity between these basic aircraft and the very sophisticated, for its time, Spitfire, I really do not know. In fact he was not persuaded at this stage, but I persisted and eventually he agreed. Whilst it was perfectly true that the Spitfires took up a lot of precious time, the real reason for the suggestion was to enable me to fly this superb aircraft as part of my lifetime desire to get my hands on any aeroplane that I could.

As part of 521 Squadron's met. duties at Langham, a Spitfire had been held to carry out a climb to obtain met. information. Arthur Southall was qualified to do this sortie. The point of all this is that I was able to quiz Arthur on the Spitfire and with the aid of pilot's notes felt confident enough to fly the thing. On 15th March I climbed into the Mark XVI, a five bladed prop version of the Spitfire, started and warmed up the engine and decided to test the magnetos. There are two spark plugs to each cylinder, one set of plugs supplied by one of the magnetos, the other set by the other. The engine was revved to a standard setting and each mag tested. The drop in revs on each must not exceed fifty, I think from memory. This done I gave the engine a further burst of power and nearly tipped the aircraft on its nose, much to the joy of the watching groundcrew. I taxied out and carried out the pre-flight checks, remembering that Arthur had told me to wind the rudder control fully to offset the considerable torque on take off. This done, I obtained clearance to take off, opened the throttle, gathered speed and found that once I reached flying speed I could not hold the aircraft straight, I quickly realised that I had wound the trimming tab the wrong way, so had to throttle back to hold my line and then, with difficulty, adjust the rudder trim until I was able to keep straight enough to climb. All very exciting, if rather stupid and overconfident. I gained sufficient height for aerobatics, which I always did on every possible occasion and although rusty on the slow roll, made a reasonable fist of it on the third attempt – Loops, barrel rolls and rolls off the top, no problem; rejoining the circuit, getting the 'Clear to Land' I came in and made a passable landing. I arrived back at dispersal to a grinning groundcrew who remarked, 'Now we've seen everything, sir.'

I took the last Spit to High Ercall, an MU in the Midlands, in April. It had flown under ten hours. When I climbed out of the aeroplane at the MU I was instructed to taxi to, I asked the civilian who was waiting for me, what was to happen to it. 'Put a hammer through it, scrap it,' he said. What a sad end to a beautiful aeroplane, I wonder how many met this fate? That Spit would be worth a great deal today and anyway it deserved a better end. And so I had had my bit of fun. Back to 'Epicures' and running the Squadron. I used to fly the night sorties to give me time to deal with the administration as well as the odd bit of flying, in Oxfords, Martinets, and Proctors during the day.

I had obviously tried to catch up too quickly and one night at the end of a long and arduous 'Epicure' I felt ill and went to see the MO who suggested rest and sent me to hospital. I think one of the nursing Sisters had an idea what was wrong with me, but nothing showed and I strained at the leash and returned to my Squadron. It was a pity I tried so hard for it was one step forward and two steps back which in the end might have made a difference to my career.

A couple of incidents worthy of mention occurred during my time on 517. An aircraft on take off was not accepted by one of the Captains, the same chap who had brought the aircraft back on two engines, who then took the stand-by aircraft. It was standard procedure that there was always a stand-by ready. On his return, an investigation was carried out and it transpired that when reaching about eighty knots a terrific vibration occurred. I decided to carry out an air test on the faulty aircraft, which confirmed his assessment that it appeared as though one wheel was oval. I took up the engineer officer who added his confirmation. The whole incident caused considerable confusion and a variety of tests were carried out. In the end it was discovered that a further inner tube, still folded, had also been fitted when a damaged one had been replaced. One would have thought this impossible, but there it was: the starboard wheel was completely unbalanced.

Collection of weather was of interest to the Press and a reporter from the *Western Morning News*, the Exeter based Devon newspaper that my wife had worked on as a reporter before our wedding, obtained permission to fly with us on an 'Epicure'. I decided to take him on a day flight to enable him to see more of what was taking place. Mr Twyford was middle aged and excited to learn that he was to go with us on a complete sortie. In fact it turned out to be rather more. He was kitted out with flying clothing, parachute and Mae West and instructed on the abandon aircraft and ditching procedures and then put in the care of the Met. Observer. He was positioned aft for take-off and on reaching our first leg height of a thousand feet, he came forward to the nose position where all the Met. Observer's instruments were situated; our passenger had been fitted with a helmet and I invited him to plug in so that he could listen to our jargon. Along the leg, a descent was made down to fifty feet to allow the barometric pressure to be read at sea level. The procedure was to make a steady descent every hour, the height being read off the radio altimeter and called out until fifty feet was reached, when this height was held until the Met. Observer had made his calculations, then back up to our operating height. Although I had told Mr Twyford that the radio altimeter gave a very precise reading above the sea, he admitted afterwards that he unplugged his helmet when he heard one hundred feet relayed; he said the sea looked very close from the nose position at that height.

On reaching the extent of the outward leg, somewhere near mid Atlantic, the sea level reading was followed by a box climb up to eighteen thousand feet with readings being taken at various levels during the climb; the navigator was also passing wind speeds and direction to the Met.Observer. As I have said the eighteen thousand feet leg required oxygen and the passenger was checked to see that he was properly connected. His only discomfort was that he got a bit cold at that height, but it was only just over an hour before we again made a box descent. The final leg was at a thousand feet with the usual sea level readings every hour. The final ones were at a hundred feet which was the laid down limit at night and it was by now dark, but I imagine Mr Twyford was no less apprehensive since it was not possible to see much in the dark.

About an hour out from base weather conditions were passed to us to the effect that Chivenor was under low cloud and heavy rain but it was considered possible to make a landing. In the event when we reached Chivenor the cloud base had lowered, our BABs (Blind Approach) and SBA (Standard Beam Approach) were on the blink and although a couple of passes were made we could not pick up the flare path lights so I requested a diversion. This was given as Bishops Court in Northern Ireland where I had never landed and a night landing in poor weather conditions at a strange airfield was going to be a challenge. The navigator was asked to give me a course to steer and an ETA which the Wireless Operator passed to Bishops Court and requested a weather report. This was as expected, heavy rain and a lowering cloud base. I also obtained a fuel state from the engineer since we had already been flying for eleven hours and the navigator's ETA gave us a further one hour and thirty minutes to Bishops Court. I thought that what had occurred and the prospect of battling through rain and low cloud might concern Mr Twyford, so I got him out of the nose with his minder, the Met. Observer, whose job was finished. He seemed not to be too worried, having been reassured by the crew that all was well and that a diversion was a routine procedure.

About fifteen minutes out from Bishops Court I contacted Air Traffic

Control who passed me landing instructions; rain persisted and the cloud base was reported as lowering to five hundred feet with a wind of fifteen knots. Fortunately I could make a straight-in approach and landing which I thought advisable in view of the deteriorating weather. I landed and taxied as instructed to a dispersal where we were collected and taken to the aircrew mess for a meal. It was after midnight and the accommodation for the night was in the huts used for diversion crews. I apologised to our passenger who claimed he was thrilled to have had this experience. I think he felt he was a youngster again, sharing with all these young men. I see from my Flying Logbook that I recorded three hours' actual instrument flying during the trip so our passenger must have been sitting and wondering what he had let himself in for. I suppose he was in blissful ignorance and I was the more worried of the two as I knew what the dangers were.

After a good night's rest and breakfast I ascertained that the weather at Chivenor was acceptable, filed a flight plan and took off to return to base. We arrived back some twenty hours after leaving. Quite an experience for the man from the *Western Morning News* but from which he had a very good article of his experiences published, which must have made it worthwhile. I said goodbye to Mr Twyford who sent me a very nice letter of thanks and a copy of a book he had written on the war-time blitz on his home town of Plymouth, *It came to our Door*, which he signed with a kind message to 'The Captain of J Jig for a memorable flight.' I see from my logbook that the day following my return from Bishops Court I flew a film unit exercise but gave no details and can only assume it was for camera shots from another aircraft for publicity purposes. We did a lot of PR work in those days.

The days of 'Epicure' were numbered, but before being disbanded I spent a few days training French Met. Observers flying from Bordeaux. A trained French Met. Observer flew with us and he did the training while we did the flying. I understand that the French continued Met. Sorties from Bordeaux. On 20th June 1946 I flew the last 'Epicure' and was posted to Headquarters Coastal Command, Northwood, as the Camp Commandant; effectively the Station Commander, but in a Headquarters with so many senior officers, a more appropriate term. Air Marshal Slatter, Commander in Chief Coastal Command, wanted a Cranwell trained officer to take over as Commandant of his headquarters. Apparently no such officer was available and in that event he insisted on an officer who was trained at Halton and as my squadron had been disbanded I was selected. I was interviewed by the C in C who told me what was expected of me and that I should report to the AOA (Air Officer Administration), Air Commodore Waring, to whom I would be responsible as Camp Commandant. He was First World War vintage, ex Royal Navy and therefore very Navy orientated. As a result he was very keen on giving airmen a piece of furniture that was an integral bunk cum wardrobe cum bedside table. He had one made and installed in his office but was not able to persuade the Air Ministry to adopt it. He was a bit of an eccentric, but very kind and supportive of me, as was the C in C on those occasions when I had to go to him.

The duties were to run the headquarters staff, in effect as a CO. The airmen and airwomen were housed in rather poor accommodation in dome shaped corrugated iron Nissen huts, which were cold in winter and very hot and oppressive in summer weather. It is a priority of a CO to ensure that the airmen and airwomen are made as comfortable as possible. I had a Flight Lieutenant to help me, but more importantly, a good Warrant Officer and a good disciplinary Sergeant, the two people who are the backbone of any station. The latter sometimes got carried away a bit and had to be curbed somewhat, but he was a good Senior NCO. As is always required when airwomen are part of station's personnel, a WAAF Flight Officer was also on my staff to deal with matters relating to the female service members. I found her most helpful since I had had little experience of dealing with airwomen, especially when it came to dealing with misdemeanours. Run of the mill charges were dealt with by the WAAF Officer, but when the offence was beyond her powers of punishment the offence had to be dealt with at my level. Nowadays I imagine, dealing with women would present no difficulty, but I was still old fashioned and felt a little diffident about treating a WAAF in the same manner as an airman especially when the old trick of weeping was applied. It was in these circumstances that the WAAF Officer was of great assistance and where I might have been too lenient she put me right.

The other difficulty I had was in dealing with the heads of the various sections. There were four group captains and one air commodore to keep happy. Each of them had run their own show and did not appreciate any interference from someone junior in rank and as a squadron leader I hadn't got much clout except through the AOA who gave me all the support I needed. I had to be very careful in my dealings with the personnel working for them and as diplomacy is not my strong point I did upset some of them occasionally.

It was after only a few months that I began to feel very tired and my wife begged me to see the MO. He sent me to hospital where I was diagnosed as having tuberculosis following the culture of a tubercle and I was destined to six months' bed rest, which was the normal treatment in those days. Not at first confirmed as having TB, I was admitted to Princess Mary's RAF Hospital, Halton, in a general ward. Some sixteen years previously I had been a patient in this hospital as an Aircraft Apprentice with a broken wrist. On that occasion I was in a ward with about twenty fellow apprentices; now I occupied a bed in an officers' ward, some of whom had been apprentices and some had also been PoWs. The doctor attending me determined after about seven days that I probably did have TB and decided I should be transferred to a part of the hospital reserved for long stay patients. This doctor was extremely kind and very sympathetic. He emphasised that I was being transferred to the TB unit only for investigation and he would be pleased to see me in London soon, as he was returning to his practice in civilian life having completed his time in the RAF as a wartime doctor. In fact after six months in hospital I decided that he would have forgotten his invitation and I did not take up the offer.

I received a typical RAF send off from the general ward bound for the TB part of the hospital. I was conveyed on one of those contraptions that were used to take patients to the operating theatre. My bed was in the centre of the ward and those in the ward who were not confined to bed collected flowers from the vases in the ward and placed them on my departing supine body to the accompaniment of the Dead March. Airmen have always joked about these things; they do not die, they 'buy it', or they have 'had their chips', a crash is a 'prang'. The actual words are never used; it is probably too close for comfort so has to be treated as a joke. Remember the comment between pilots going on a raid, 'Can I have your egg in the morning?'

I arrived at the TB unit and was put in a single room, as we all were, with a large window leading on to a ground level balcony which beds were pushed on to in the warmer weather. Two Princess Mary's nursing Sisters made me comfortable and aware of the routine. The doctor said I was to have complete bed-rest, but as a special concession I could get up for a daily bath and to use the lavatory. In the meantime various tests would be carried out. First came a pleural effusion in my left lung which gave some support to the TB diagnosis and it was decided to drain off the fluid, not a pleasant experience for me or the doctor as it transpired. A large needle was inserted into the pleura, care being taken not to go too deep which would be dangerous. Attended by a Sister, the doctor inserted the needle and drained the fluid, eventually tipping me up to extract as much as possible; he was certainly paler than the patient during the operation. A sample of the fluid was sent for laboratory testing and at the end of about six weeks I was told a tubercle had been cultured and I was to continue with complete bed-rest. For the first three months I took my blood sedimentation rate (BSR) and each morning had to swallow a rubber tube right down to the stomach to extract stomach juices. I was given a bottle of Guinness a day to promote my appetite which I had not lost anyway. I continued to feel very fit and had suffered no weight loss.

I was extremely lucky in having been diagnosed so early. Some of my friends were not so fortunate. One in particular – we had learnt to fly together and he had also been a PoW for over four years – had to have the affected lung removed. He and others in more advanced stages of the disease were transferred to a special ward away from the milder cases. The entrance to this ward bore the sign, 'Abandon hope all ye who enter here,' once again an example of black humour poking fun at a very serious situation. In fact, most of the patients recovered as it was known they would, otherwise the sign would not have been permitted and in fact would not have been made. During my stay two of the lovely devoted nursing Sisters contracted the disease and one ended up in the special ward even though all nurses had a regular monthly test in order to catch early contagion.

I held a Temporary Commission and had had good reason to believe that my services would be retained and that my Commission would be extended, or even that I would be granted a Permanent Commission in the General Duties branch. This now seemed to be in doubt and I felt that my life had reached rock bottom. My wife was having a baby and I was frightened that it might be affected by my illness. The doctor assured me that it was unlikely, but the fact that his reply was not positive left me with considerable concern. I did not realise how concerned I had been until I recently found a letter I had written to my wife at this time explaining how worried I was about my future in the RAF. Marjorie used to visit me every week, journeying from Northwood where we had bought a house. The train service was abominable, often breaking down, the heating poor or non-existent, which made every visit an endurance test. Having missed so much of our life together she insisted on making the journey, knowing how much I looked forward to seeing her and hearing about the progress of my daughter and how both were faring. The time taken to visit me was made worse since my daughter had to be taken to Majorie's sister in London and picked up again on her return: a full day of uncomfortable travel for a brief visit of about an hour.

The visits ceased in November, Marjorie went into the nursing home towards the middle of December and on the night of the 18th one of the nurses informed me of the birth of my son and that both he and his mother were doing well. By this time I had progressed to the extent that I was allowed to get up for an hour each day. This was increased fairly rapidly, and then began to include walks which again were increased in length.

Each excursion was followed by tests until I was considered fit enough to be allowed to visit Marjorie and my son for an afternoon. I was obviously delighted to see both looking well.

My progress continued and I was discharged from Halton on 2nd February 1947. After a period of leave I attended the Central Medical Board and was given the all clear, but was restricted to a flying height of three thousand feet. My appointment as Camp Commandant at Coastal Command HQ had been kept open for me and I went back to work, grateful to be with those I knew and who knew me. Having served my two and a half years as Camp Commandant at Coastal and having continued to badger the powers that be, at least I was in the right place to return to flying, I presented myself at the Central Medical Board as instructed and was delighted to be given a full medical category, 'Fit for full flying duties.' A posting to command No. 224 Squadron based at Aldergrove in Northern Ireland soon arrived and I took over on 5th October 1948. The Squadron had a detachment of half its Halifax aircraft at Gibraltar. I flew down to Gib to see the detachment, meet the personnel and get a view of things generally. It seemed to me that the squadron would operate more efficiently if the headquarters were moved to Gibraltar and all the Squadron aircraft were based there. I forwarded my recommendations to HQ Coastal Command under whom we were directly controlled and my request was granted, but with Aldergrove still undertaking the major servicing of the aircraft.

I moved the Squadron headquarters to Gibraltar on 20th October 1948. Married quarters were very scarce on the Rock and the RAF were 'arse end Charlies' in this respect; even the Air Officer Commanding had no official quarter and was loaned the Governor's Summer Residence since no other suitable accommodation could be found. The one Married Quarter allotted for RAF use, other than that of the Station Commander, was occupied by the Engineer Officer, one Johnny Johns, an old friend from my days at Tangmere and the same one that I had persuaded to let me fly the Spitfires at Chivenor. He was due to leave and I was to move into the Quarter when he left. Not wanting any further separation from Marjorie and the children, I arranged for them to fly out and be accommodated in a hotel. This unsatisfactory state of affairs relieved me of my entire pay which I handed over to the hotel each month. This lasted for six months, then Johnny Johns left and we occupied the quarter halfway up the Rock on the eastern end. A Security Post at which one had to show a pass was situated just below us. There were three quarters close together which had been Army Warrant Officers' quarters and were now occupied by a squadron leader and two army majors. We all became good friends and kept in touch for many years.

The AOC was at the same level but a few hundred yards towards the Europa end of the Rock.

As well as the eight Halifax aircraft of 224 Squadron, a couple of Martinets for drogue towing and a communication Anson, the airstrip was also used by BEA as a joint user, but under RAF control: RAF Air Traffic Controllers were responsible for all movements, both civil and military, and therefore I was designated OC Flying; later I was also given a staff job on the same HQ Staff headed by an Air Commodore. I was therefore fully occupied and loved it. The staff appointment involved very little until it was decided that a joint Services operation order was to be produced for the three Services on the Rock in the event of hostilities. I had the task of producing the RAF section. My initial thinking was to fly out my Squadron aircraft and personnel, as all aircrew and groundcrew could be evacuated in the eight Halifaxes. The airstrip could be put out of action fairly quickly in any case, making our aircraft useless, and we would be of far more use at another airfield, but of course it was necessary to co-operate with the other Services with whom it was obviously necessary to produce a joint plan and to this end a series of meetings had to be attended which absorbed a great deal of my time and became detrimental to my OC Flying and Squadron responsibilities. Any officer in the General Duties (Flying) Branch regards

*My Halifax during my command of 224 Squadron at Gibraltar*

being in command of a squadron as the most coveted of appointments and it was my intention not to be diverted from my command, if at all possible. I put this to the AOC (Air Officer Commanding), Air Commodore 'Cocky' Spencer, who agreed and said that there was an establishment for a Squadron leader Org. (organisation) on his staff and he would apply for the post to be filled. In due course it was and I was relieved of the job to concentrate on my real function.

It transpired that this was fortunate for it was decided that RAF Gibraltar was to be one of the RAF Stations 'Open' to the public. 'Open Days' were an annual event in the RAF with selected Stations being open to the public so that they could see how we worked. A lot of work was involved, each section providing displays and, of course, flying was one of the major attractions. As OC Flying it was my job to ensure that all aircraft movements were covered, but also that the civil air movements received no interference; visiting RAF aircraft for the display had to be adequately catered for which meant liaising with the OC Eng. (engineering) for the refuelling and dispersal arrangements of visitors. The available space at Gib is very limited and all the various precautions required for such an event have to be in place, with safety being of paramount importance not only for the flying displays, but especially for spectators. It was anticipated that young children would become bored and the armourers rigged up the bomb trolleys to form a train which took the children on a tour round the displays which might interest them. They loved it and it allowed their parents to spend time on the displays which interested them. I expect they would call it a mobile creche these days and require God knows what in terms of permission to cover the possibility, however remote, of one of the children getting injured. The whole thing would be more trouble than it was worth so would not happen and everyone would be the loser. We were not so sophisticated and both children and parents enjoyed themselves.

Air Commodore Spencer was meticulous in all aspects of his working life and was a stickler for detail. I thought I had covered everything when I was asked what arrangements had been made for lavatories. It had not occurred to me that the existing facilities would be insufficient and had to quickly work out the number of lavatories which would be required to cope with the anticipated numbers of people and the length of their stay. He was right, of course, there were too few on the airfield and the day could have been spoiled if ladies had had to queue. This was well before the days of the 'Portaloo' and meant arranging a considerable amount of digging and the provision of sacking windbreaks.

'Cocky' Spencer was an incredible man; he limped because he had a game leg, which was caused when he crashed whilst giving an aerobatics display. Having spent many months in hospital and still more in plaster, he crashed again as soon as he returned to flying. But on AOC's inspection, an annual event when the AOC reports on the efficiency of all stations under his command, in this case Gibraltar, he ran all of us off our feet and was still going strong when we had all wilted. He was somewhat older than any of us but insisted on flying the Halifax, difficult enough on a full size airfield when you have not flown a modern aircraft, but to fly at Gib with its one runway of reduced length was asking a lot. I sat alongside and became more and more apprehensive as we bumped and swung on various take offs and landings, sometimes taking three attempts to make a landing. He was a man with a slight impediment in his speech; he was also a man with a considerable flow of invective, which I was on the end of on a number of occasions.

That was one side of the AOC, the other was unrecognisable: a kind, loving, family man. The AOC, the senior ranking RAF officer at Gib, did not have a residence and as I have said the Governor made his summer residence available to him and during the time I was with 224 Squadron he lived there with his family. The Governor's summer residence in which Cocky, his delightful wife and young daughter lived was along a road about two hundred yards from my quarter and my daughter, then about ten years old, used to visit. On occasions when I came home after a hard day with the AOC and admitting it to my wife, my daughter would tell me how he would spend his time playing on the floor with the children. How this nice kind man could give anyone such a hard time, she could not believe. Similarly when we went on staff trips to the French at Port Lyautay and to Casablanca he was a different man. I was to serve him again when, as a Wing Commander, I was posted to Technical Training Command HQ on his staff as Org. I when he was Air Officer Administration (AOA) responsible for the administration of, at that time of National Service, about a third of the entire RAF strength. He was as irascible as ever, but at least it was shared by more officers reporting to him. Unfortunately this meant that there was no opportunity to see his lighter side.

I made reference earlier to the lack of accommodation for married personnel in Gibraltar and how I was forced to stay in a local hotel with my family for several months as a result. The RAF were not the only ones to suffer. In the same hotel were two Army families and we used to bet on which of us would obtain either a quarter or hired accommodation first. Houses to rent were also at a premium. I don't know who won, but my bank balance was almost completely depleted by the time I took over the ex warrant officer's quarter, positioned as I have said near the top of the Rock in a security area. My wife claimed that it was necessary for her to show her security pass in order to get back home after a visit to the town for shopping. Fresh water for bathing was only available from rainwater collected from the roof in water butts and this was in short supply. Salt-water washing was the order of the day using a special salt-water soap which left one feeling very sticky. One got used to it.

On the east side of Gibraltar huge catchment areas have been built for rainwater to be collected and stored inside the Rock. To enter this storage area is quite an experience. The temperature is a number of degrees cooler than the outside and on entering from the warm summer temperature, a very chill feeling is experienced. Another very different form of chill can be experienced by going to the top of the Rock where the radio station is situated. It is possible to look down on both sides and anyone uncomfortable with heights can find it very frightening. Visiting staff officers from Command Headquarters, Gibraltar came under the direct command of Coastal Command, and staff officers liked to visit since Gib was duty free and it was a nice jolly. They were taken up to the transmitter and many got down on their knees hugging the ground while being physically sick. The Barbary apes are a major feature of the Rock. There are, or were then, two colonies, one living halfway up the Rock, the other lower down near Alameda Gardens. They are both on the ration strength of the Army and it is claimed that if they ceased to exist on the Rock we would lose possession of it. As a result an Army Lieutenant looks after them very carefully. Very tame, they will sidle up to you and steal from your pockets if you are not aware of their habits. I did hear that they had been to 'Cocky' Spencer's house and stolen various things, but they had obviously not heard of his reputation or they would never have dared; or perhaps they had and knew that at home he was a different character.

The accommodation for the other ranks, certainly for the RAF, was sub standard and I felt very mean when inspecting and criticising my NCO and aircrew quarters, but insisted that some semblance of tidiness had to be maintained when I made my weekly inspection. For my part I made representations to a higher authority and at long last, a number of years later the RAF enjoyed excellent accommodation on North Front near the airstrip. I experienced this when I was invited to attend the presentation of the Standard to 224 Squadron at Gibraltar. I had retired from the RAF but was flown down in the C in C's aircraft and had a wonderful time. We were no longer the poor relations. A number of past COs were present, one from as far distant as Canada. Four days of reminiscing and celebrating. What a party!

The airstrip at the foot of the highest part of the Rock was not the easiest place to land and was almost impossible in some wind conditions. If the wind was from a westerly direction it met the Rock at its lowest point from where a steady rise in the surface terminated at about thirteen hundred feet. By this time various eddies had developed on the eastern side of the strip. On the approach to the eastern end of the runway, considerable air disturbance occurred, to such an extent that BEA aircraft were not permitted to land if the wind speed was in excess of 15 knots from the western sector and a diversion to adjacent Tangier was always available. Not wishing to have my aeroplanes diverted, I decided to test the danger in making a landing in these conditions and, feeling very confident in my ability to handle the Anson in any conditions after all the hours I had flown in them, took off when the eddies existed. Making the approach from the east was plain sailing until I was some eight hundred yards from touch down. The landing technique had changed from my training days and was now to make power assisted approaches. I encountered some turbulence which did not concern me, but between five and four hundred yards out and at about eight hundred feet, I started to drop like a stone. The airspeed dropped right back and there was little response from the controls, a very nasty feeling, and I began to think I would hit the sea and face an embarrassing interview with the AOC. Suddenly, the descent stopped, the aeroplane bounced upwards and responded to the controls, the airspeed increased to one hundred and twenty knots and I continued the approach normally. Fortunately the runway was sufficiently long to make a touchdown and stop, but in a larger aircraft it might have been more difficult. The lesson was learned and I decided to divert my Halifaxes when these conditions obtained.

The airstrip itself is interesting as it was constructed on the site of the old racecourse. When I was a small boy with my father stationed on the rock I attended a nearby school and at that time the racecourse was still in use. Stone had been excavated from the base of the Rock providing the best possible material for an airstrip, which also had the benefit of providing workshops and sheltered accommodation inside the Rock in the event of an attack. Initially, as I have said, the old racecourse was used, but when greater length was required later for the larger more modern aeroplanes, the extension went out into the sea between Gib and Spain. Incidentally, this had the added but unplanned advantage of allowing Sunderland Flying Boats to use this area of relatively calm sea. The strip was very close to a cemetery situated almost at the foot of the highest point of the Rock and on one occasion a Halifax ended up in the churchyard, but no one was hurt and thankfully no damage occurred to the graves. The Meteorological flights from Gibraltar, code named 'Nocturnal', were slightly different from those that I had flown from Chivenor, in that the first leg, straight out into the Atlantic, was at fifteen hundred feet rather than one thousand; the sea levels of course remained the same at fifty feet on the radio altimeter. A sea level reading at seven hundred miles was followed by a spiral climb, levelling off at step heights for the Met. Observer to take readings up to eighteen thousand feet at which altitude, on oxygen, the next leg was flown in an easterly direction for about four hundred miles. This was followed by a stepped descent to take a sea level reading, then back to fifteen hundred feet with periodic sea levels on the leg back to base. During the winter months conditions varied and the met. information we obtained was probably worthwhile, but during the summer the weather varied very little, if at all, from the briefing we had had eleven hours earlier and the crews' morale began to deteriorate. 'Was the little man on the bicycle still off Cape St Vincent?' was the standing joke I would hear from crews and I decided something should be done to relieve the monotony.

Gibraltar is small and has a very close community. My crews were not in the best of accommodation and fresh water was at a premium, in fact, the locals had to buy it. I put forward a proposal to Command that selected crews should be trained in the Transport Role and to this end I suggested a route to Malta and from there to airfields along the North African coast to Heliopolis, down the west coast of Africa and finally back to base which

*Mrs Spencer giving prizes at Gibraltar sports day. Author receiving a prize.*

would involve landing at different aerodromes. A modified scheme was accepted, which omitted the route down the west coast which had been a bit tongue in cheek on my part anyway. Landings at Luqa in Malta, Fahid Benina and Castle Benito were made under this programme, as were several of the airfields nearer to Gib. To the south were our diversion bases and Casablanca, Rabat, Port Lyautey and Tangier which were well known anyway. We soon felt that most airfields within our range were now known to most of the crews and short notice ferrying would cause no problems.

After only three months with the Squadron I received notice that I had been selected for the RAF Staff College, Bracknell in 1949. I had taken the Staff College qualifying examination while at Coastal Command Headquarters, basically an examination for promotion, but to include entry to Staff College if the pass was good enough. I did not anticipate this selection which could not have come at a worse time and the news shattered me.

Sir John Baker had recently taken over as C in C Coastal Command and was due to visit RAF Gibraltar; we came under the direct command of HQ Coastal Command and I submitted a request through Air Commodore Spencer for an interview with the C in C during his visit. Air Commodore Spencer supported my request and I was duly interviewed. Sir John was sympathetic, but could not promise more than that he would do what he could on my behalf. He supported my claim that it was not in the best interests of the Squadron that a change was to be made after only three months and in due course I was informed of my pre-selection for the staff course starting in January 1950. My relief was matched by that of my wife who had just moved into our married quarter on the Rock after months of uncomfortable and expensive stay in a Gibraltar hotel, apart from having sold our house near Northwood to join me at Gibraltar.

Sport in Gib was confined in the main to hockey and athletics. Rugby was impossible owing to the hard ground making it too dangerous; soccer was played but I found it very unsatisfactory as the hard ground and pronounced bounce made control of the ball extremely difficult. Hockey was not a game I had taken much interest in and had not played since I left my boarding school in India, but this and athletics were to be my main methods of keeping fit during my stay at Gibraltar. My stay included one sports day, a regular event on all RAF stations in those days, which was well organised and run by our PT officer. I managed to participate in my usual events, the hundred yards, two hundred and twenty yards and in the relay which I think we won. I also entered the shot put, an event I had started to experiment with at Calshot. Unusually, it was a team event for pairs; my ability was average but my partner was well ahead of the position and we hoped to beat the Rock record. In fact, neither of us came up to scratch as so often happens on these occasions and although we beat our opponents were nowhere near the record we had thought we would beat so easily.

A new sport for me was sailing. Air Commodore Spencer was keen on sailing and the RAF had some converted airborne lifeboats which could compete with other yachts in the sailing club. A crew of four handled these boats and I was persuaded to join a crew and soon became quite keen although not very proficient. We managed to turn the boat over on one occasion, much to the amusement of Cocky Spencer who dragged me out of the water. One of the crew managed to avoid a ducking by achieving a cat-like scramble round the boat as it turned over. He was one of my groundcrew so I asked him later if he didn't like getting wet and was amazed when he told me that he had had to do it because he couldn't swim. I had never thought to ask my crews if they could swim. I did in future.

These airborne lifeboats when used for their proper purpose were designed to be secured to the bomb bay of the aircraft and dropped on air-sea rescue operations to survivors from crashes in the sea who were in either dinghies or Mae Wests. The airborne boats contained water, rations and first-aid kits. A small sail could be erected and many lives were saved in this way. I don't think they complied with any recognised class for sailing events, so were allocated a special class in competitions. They were quite nippy and gave us a lot of fun and at about twenty-five feet in length and ten in the beam, they were capable of coping with quite heavy seas.

The Rock tends to become claustrophobic after a while and having acquired a car we used to venture into Spain for a break. At that time this was quite easy. La Linea, just across the border, needed only a local pass and to go further afield a short-term passport sufficed. Weekends to Torremolinos were a frequent occurrence and the occasional trip to Granada, if an extra day or two could be squeezed in, made a welcome change. My wife, who never lost the inquisitive nature of a journalist, particularly liked visiting the Alhambra Palace and the gypsy village. The other outings were to Tangier and Algeciras. Tangier was about forty minutes or so across the water, full of salesmen bartering like mad with great humour and very pleased to get half the asking price for their goods. I suppose they started at three times what they expected so had every right to look happy. The journey to Algeciras was by car through La Linea, then round the coast to a hotel noted for its food. These visits were made to relieve the claustrophobic effect of the Rock and just to sit enjoying an excellent lunch which occupied at least two hours and being able to look across the straits to Gibraltar relieved the tension for a while. Entertainment in Gibraltar consisted of frequent cocktail parties attended by the same people with the same conversation, until one knew who would be there and what the conversation would be; just like being back in the Bag. The summer and winter balls were much more enjoyable.

At that time Torremolinos was a very small fishing village with only one hotel suitable for us to stay at. It was delightful to sit out on the veranda of our room enjoying our breakfast with orange trees conveniently placed to enable us to pick the fruit while watching the fishermen hauling in their nets; these nets were dragged in from the sea onto the beach by a number of fishermen who, from what we could see, were poor. The explosion in tourism to Spain must have made the poor fishermen of our day very rich as a result. It was in this small hotel, where the food was excellent, that we would stay the night *en route* to Granada where, as I have said, the Alhambra was always a must. We would be provided with a Spanish omelette for our picnic on the way, which was very sustaining and never seemed to become dry as mine do. Perhaps they had more practice.

I paid a great deal less for the car that I bought in Gib, an old type Vauxhall, than I would have had to pay for a replacement in England, so I decided to take it home. At that time it was possible to get a space on a RN aircraft carrier if one called at Gib on its return to the UK, not as unlikely as it might seem since most called in at Gib when returning from Med. ports. The snag was that should the Carrier be ordered to a trouble spot the car would be pushed over the side with no comeback for loss. The alternative was to transport by shipping line, but on investigation this proved too expensive. The final choice seemed to be to sell in Gib and buy a replacement in England, but cars were difficult to get even if I could afford one. There was one final thought: drive it home. Decision taken. It could be fun, it would probably be interesting and I would have a car.

All too soon my time as 224 Squadron Commander came to an end, and as I had anticipated when I asked to stay on for another year. It was the last time I had the great pleasure of commanding a Squadron which I think the most satisfying appointment one can have as a pilot. With sadness I had handed over the Squadron to Squadron Leader Morley Mower, always referred to as 'M squared' with the feeling that it was the last time I would be lucky enough to have a Command. Incidentally, the last Halifax in service was a Mark 3 of 224 Squadron which flew the final met. sortie on 17th March 1952. After a week of farewell parties to say goodbye to the many friends we had made, both Army and civilian, as well as our own Service, we set off. The day prior to our departure we went down to say our final farewells to particular friends living at the bottom camp. My farewells were short lived as I discovered a water leak in the car which on investigation proved to be a carbon bush in the water pump: no problem, I'll get another and fit it. Easily said, but there were no spares in Gib, I could not even get a replacement water pump, and it would take at least two days to have one flown out from England. We had to leave the next day, the 1st December, to fulfil all my arrangements, so with the help of four engineer officers on the station we made another bush, fitted it and Hey Presto, no leak. We drove back up the Rock to our quarter to a cold dinner, tired children and a feeling of being cheated. The car had never let me down before.

Early next morning I made a quick check on the car with my fingers crossed. All was well and after a rapid breakfast I started to load the car while Marjorie dealt with the children and the food for the picnics *en route*. All done, we said goodbye to our two near Army neighbours, one of whom we kept in touch with until both he and his wife died recently. We said goodbye to our Spanish maid who would do the final clearing up and go to a friend who wanted her services.

During this time Marjorie had taken on the packing, as she always did, dividing everything into two piles. One for that which was to accompany us in the car which had to be kept to a minimum and the other, the bulk, to go by sea. My chore had been to make the necessary hotel bookings in Spain, get the petrol coupons as rationing was still in force, organise the Carnets, and complete the numerous forms that were required. We were also going to need traveller's cheques and road maps. We had decided not to waste time on hotel lunches as they tend to be lengthy affairs in Spain, so we bought a roof-rack, a picnic stove, a kettle and an assortment of plastic plates and mugs, so that we could picnic along the way. I also bought a couple of spare tyres and two cans of petrol for emergencies. I then decided to include a few small spares and my tools. All this left little room for clothing, especially as I had insisted on my uniform, including my greatcoat, being with us, just in case our baggage going by sea did not arrive before us as arranged.

We had decided it was not possible to carry a change of outer garments for the journey and Marjorie selected an old tweed coat and skirt while I went for a brown tweed sports jacket and fawn cords. The cords had faded into a near white and I asked if they could be dyed; after all Marjorie had plenty of time to spare. Ever willing, Marjorie purchased two packets of navy blue dye in which the cords were boiled. The result was not dark blue as planned, but a lurid peacock blue. Marjorie expected me to blow my top but was amazed at my reaction; they were perfectly all right and I felt rather proud to wear this unusual mixture. When you spend your life in uniform, occasionally a little flamboyance is a nice change. Overcoats were stowed in the back with the suitcases and although there was little room left for us, we just managed get in, albeit with little room to move and our small son sitting on the large picnic basket on the back seat. We had been told it was madness to attempt this journey in December, but we were always prepared for an adventure and enjoyed the challenge; I did however buy a set of chains in case of heavy snow which in fact were never used and so took up space unnecessarily. They continued to be stored in various garages as we moved around and to the best of my recollection never ever received an outing in anger.

# *CHAPTER 11*

## *Home to Staff roles*

And so we were off. Down the winding road, past the security post which was about half-way past the guns which had been dragged up the Rock when Gib was being defended against attack by Napoleon's navy, centuries earlier, and then through the British border post, across the airstrip where I took a last longing look at the Squadron Building on the right of the strip and so to the Aduana at the Spanish border. We had been expecting a long delay while the guards inspected our luggage, but were pleasantly surprised that we were dispatched remarkably quickly, largely I think because a small child always seems to fascinate the Spanish and on this occasion, seeing my small son, they spent most of their time talking to him and giving our belongings only a cursory inspection; incidentally, belongings were inspected only after the guard donned immaculate white gloves. Whether this was to protect him or his 'clients', I do not know, but it is a nice gesture.

We were assisted with the reloading of our baggage and then we were on our way through dusty La Linea and the even dustier Algeciras heading for Seville which was to be responsible for only our own problems. The picnic lunch on the way to Seville was not particularly enjoyable in the cold wind so it was a fairly rapid stop. We reached our hotel fairly easily and had communicating rooms which made it unnecessary for my daughter to have to call us if my small son needed help. At that time in Spain the electricity supply was somewhat unreliable and we were informed that it was frequently turned off. At the same time, the water shortage was such that we could only use the washing facilities in the mornings or evenings. It was unfortunate that our arrival at the hotel was just after the water had been turned off and the much looked forward to bath was denied us.

Our problems were not over, however, for the youngest member suddenly said, 'I'm going to be sick,' and was, just before his mother could get him to the lavatory. Getting the soiled clothing clean was a further problem since the water was off, as was the electricity which meant that even if they could be washed there was no drying facility. Jon was put to bed and soon went to sleep; after a while he seemed to be sleeping peacefully and we decided to go down to dinner. The remainder of the evening we spent in the room with Jon. At seven the next morning he charged into our room more full of beans than we were; the recuperative capacity of children is quite remarkable. Marjorie was keen on seeing the Cathedral and as this was the only bit of sight seeing we were going to be able to do, off we went. We returned to the hotel for lunch, before a visit to the shops ended our day in Seville.

When we got back to the hotel the receptionist told us that he had received a telephone message to inform us that the rooms at the Albergue at Manzanares were no longer available. These State run Spanish road houses are delightful places to stay and we were disappointed at having to make other arrangements at such short notice. The desk clerk hastened to reassure us by saying that he would book rooms at an hotel he knew in Valdepeñas which was not far from Manzanares. He gave us a brochure sent out by this establishment which spoke in glowing terms of the cuisine, promising central heating and hot and cold water in each room. It sounded in every way an ideal substitute for the Albergue, so we asked him to book two rooms for the following night. We set off in bright sunshine on Saturday morning for Valdepeñas and although the road was of poor quality and the car well down on its springs owing to our load, we made good time and foolishly I was pleased with the performance. Cordoba was behind us and half an hour later we stopped for our picnic of bacon and eggs, cooked on the primus stove, followed by oranges that we had bought in a village earlier. Having made good time we decided to have tea at about four thirty. The sun was still shining and it seemed better than sitting in an hotel; we must have been psychic.

Arriving at the hotel, 'La Paloma' – it means dove, a misnomer if ever I heard one – which was in darkness, Marjorie and I groped our way into a sort of hall and called for attention. After a very long delay, a woman, either the mother or the wife of the owner appeared. She seemed annoyed at being disturbed and had no idea that guests were expected. She told us we would have to wait until the man came back. After another lengthy delay, it was discovered that rooms had been reserved and she would lead us to the garage. We were directed to a narrow dirty lane, through a high stone wall onto a cobbled yard. A little further ahead loomed a dark barn, 'the garage'. Getting out of the car, we were welcomed by the squeals and grunts of a very large pig whose peace we had obviously invaded. Taking the clothes and other essential items that we would need, I locked the car with some doubts about it being there in the morning, but had no alternative other than to sleep in it which I am sure the pig would have resented and kept me awake all night. In any event I decided it was more important that I stayed with my family in that place. During my last days as a PoW I had occupied a pigsty with my colleagues quite contentedly, but this pig would have felt very out of place there.

We made our way to our rooms. There was still no electricity, but there was a wash basin; unfortunately both taps produced cold water. The radiators were also cold. Dinner would be in about half an hour, a chambermaid who produced an ancient oil lamp so that we could see to unpack, informed us. It was now well past Jon's bedtime and he was complaining about his lack of food. He was to have it with us, we were told. Eventually, summoned to a grubby dining room, bowls of a fish soup, a poor, very poor attempt at bouillabaisse with blobs of soggy bread floating on the surface was followed by fish and a tasteless meat course. Only one of us managed the garlic laden greasy soup, the one who could keep nothing down the previous night, my son, a whole bowlful of which he followed with the fish and meat. The rest of us could only manage the fish. I have never been more glad to leave a dining room. We went to bed leaving the door between the two rooms open. During the night we became aware that our door was being opened very quietly; it was obviously not one of our children, and at Marjorie's, *'¿Qué quiere?'* the intruder withdrew.

Early the next morning we paid our debts and left without breakfast, having decided not to stay a minute longer than was absolutely necessary. We could get the primus working and have an early picnic. We were on the road to Madrid at an early hour and making good progress to our next night stop at what we knew would be a clean, comfortable albergue at Aranda da Douro which would provide good food and above all a plentiful supply of hot and cold water, as well as central heating. Once again however, we were to suffer a problem; after about two hours, things started to get warm and when we stopped for lunch at about half past eleven, investigation, if it was really necessary, showed that the water pump had let us down again. I let the engine cool down while we had lunch, using the last of the water we carried to top up the radiator, and set off, driving as fast as conditions allowed. Eventually we reached a petrol station with a large garage attached. I had been warned about the Spanish mechanics, but needs must and taking off the water pump, I explained the problem. The mechanics quickly realised what had to be done and with considerable skill rectified the leak. The water pump was replaced, the radiator filled with water and we departed with the mechanics, who had given up their lunch break, waving goodbye and assuring us that we would reach Madrid and be able to watch the football there without trouble. These chaps were real mechanics, not the throw-away-the-faulty-bit-and-replace-it school, but able to effect repairs in the way in which it had to be done, the way in which I had been trained, by basic fitting practices. We were heading towards Madrid some two hours later, with no intention of watching Madrid play football.

Although Marjorie had been promised a few hours in the capital of Spain to visit some of the places of historic interest, the time we had lost made it necessary to press on to the comfort of the albergue at Aranda da Duoro. We were welcomed into the albergue, clean, warm and comfortable, with plenty of hot and cold water of which we all took full advantage. The youngest member of the family, after being bathed and changed, had a tray of food brought up to him and after he had been put to bed, the remaining three went down to the dining room to enjoy an excellent meal.

After an excellent restful night's sleep and a leisurely breakfast, I decided to visit the car to look at the self-starter which was performing intermittently. This I remedied quite quickly, but noticed a small drip from the cursed water pump. Knowing it needed one small adjustment and that the one tool that I required for this was the one tool I had not got, I decided to remove the pump, take it to the garage and fix it. I had intended to cash a cheque, but by this time the banks had closed and we were without money. The solution was to stay an extra night at the albergue and to cash a travellers cheque the next morning, but this would have delayed our schedule by over twenty-four hours which we could not afford to do. Marjorie, whose Spanish was far better than mine, asked to see the manager, a gentleman who had not deigned to be seen so far. The manager arrived and was informed of our predicament. Our appearance might have suggested that we were the type of people who would leave without paying the bill and we were relieved when he said, 'Do not concern yourself, Señora, settle the account when you return to Gibraltar.' He was informed that my tour of duty was over and I would not be returning. 'In that case, send the money from San Sebastian, it is not necessary for you to delay your departure for another day.'

With gratitude, Marjorie put the bill in her handbag and we started on our last leg in Spain at about one thirty. We crossed the lower Pyrenees in good time and the car at last behaved as she had always done, rather than the unreliable beast she had been recently; but the plan to cross the border into France that day had to be abandoned and San Sebastian was destined to accommodate the tramps that night. As it was known as the millionaires' playground, we were apprehensive and motored around looking for accommodation that might be within our means and suitable to our appearance. Millionaires seem not to play in December and all the places that appeared likely from the outside were closed. Eventually, stopping outside the most luxurious hotel overlooking the bay and casting caution to the winds, we walked in. Fortunately our shoes had been polished at the albergue, but I was still wearing the peacock blue cords and Marjorie her old tweeds. Sinking into the three inch thick carpet we enquired if we could have two rooms and dinner. Certainly, and did one wish a sea facing room? We asked the cost and were astounded to find it would be less than the awful Valdepeñas pigsty. Jonathan had an excellent meal brought to him in his room, was made much fuss of by the chambermaids and generally looked after, while the rest of us had dinner which was excellent, even though the variety offered at the albergue was absent.

Next morning I went into the Banco de España in the town and changed our traveller's cheques for sufficient pesetas to cover both the albergue and the present hotel bill. The money to cover the Albergue bill was sent and by about nine thirty we were heading for the border. At the Spanish Aduana customs officers gave the car a perfunctory inspection and did not bother about the luggage. On to the French border at Hendaye where once again we passed through without hindrance. Reflecting on the reasons for the generosity of the manager of the albergue we came to the conclusion that no RAF officer would travel in peacock blue cords and a 'ratting jacket', with his family similarly attired unless he was a man of some substance. How untrue, of course, but we were pleased that this view got us through Customs so easily and made the hotel so generous.

Arriving at Bordeaux I was able to obtain the necessary francs to cover our expenses across France. It was a strange thought, but the last time I had been here it was to drop bombs. We had completed a thousand miles since leaving Gibraltar and anticipated that the journey through France would present fewer problems. We had not made any bookings ahead for this part of the journey but had decided to adopt a different approach. Marjorie would ask me when we started each morning where I expected to reach that evening, and then consult her little guidebook for likely hotels.

The first turned out to be nothing grander than a small pub. The proprietor said he had rooms and would we like dinner in half an hour. The rooms were excellent and surpassed by the dinner. I have always fought shy of oysters which were on the menu, but my wife loved them and ordered a dozen. While I was waiting for my soup she noticed me watching her eating her oysters and offered me a couple which, feeling hungry, I took and immediately decided that I had been foolish in refusing to try them before, so ordered a dozen for myself. It became a standing joke in the family that my wife reminded me for years afterwards that I had failed to repay the two she had let me have from her dozen.

Our journey through France, continuing with our picnic lunches and using 'Les Auberges de France' as a guide for our night stops, was uneventful and very pleasant, but one night stop must be mentioned, at the Hostellerie Écu de la Bretagne in Beaugency; we were welcomed by the proprietor like royalty and at our very early departure next morning he waved goodbye with a flourish of his beret and with an overcoat over his pyjamas. Everything about this hostellerie was excellent, the rooms with *en suite* bathrooms which were a rarity in England in those days, central heating and above all the food. We vowed to return, but sadly never did. His appearance and enthusiasm, we discovered, were mainly due to his wife having presented him with a son in the early hours of the morning.

We reached Paris in drizzle and much as Marjorie wished to spend some time looking at the places of interest we decided that to drag the children round in this sort of weather was not on. So we continued on to Abbeville, which still bore the war scars of potholes in the road, where we stopped at an inn for lunch. The tickets for the car ferry had not arrived before we left Gib and the AA Agent had said that he would send instructions to his colleague at Boulogne to meet us at the quay with the tickets half an hour before sailing. I have always had difficulty in accepting on trust that something has been done and wanted to reassure myself in this case. I therefore decided to phone the AA office at Boulogne to make sure that the tickets were available. The availability having been confirmed, my anxiety was calmed and I relaxed to enjoy my lunch.

The car was duly put aboard and we followed. In spite of the very rough sea Marjorie ordered tea and we had a comfortable crossing, none of us being affected by the bucking and rolling ferry. The children wanted to make sure the car was safely secured and insisted on going to see for themselves; having checked and satisfied themselves, why children all think that adults are incapable of carrying out their jobs I'll never know, they returned and sat quietly until Dover came into sight. This kept them enthralled until we docked and disembarked.

Here my concern was renewed. Taking a car that has been purchased abroad into the UK has to comply with the regulations. The most important for me at this moment was the amount of tax that I would have to pay the

Customs and Excise before the car would be released. I had the necessary import licence and the amount of the purchase tax but the authorities at Dover seemed not to agree and only after lengthy perusal of papers and regulations was I allowed to present my cheque, collect the car and tell my tired family that we could now get on our way. This matter of import duty was levied on a car being brought into the UK by a person who had not owned the car for at least two years and the calculation of the amount seemed to differ depending on who, or where, the calculation was made. Having had to pay more than I had been told would be required, and therefore budgeted for, I was allowed to go. I wrote to the Board of Trade later and received by return a cheque for the amount I had overpaid, but that was of little help at the time.

The journey north to Burnley to stay with Marjorie's parents while we sorted things out was of no particular interest except for the fact that we had travelled some two thousand miles through Spain and France without any navigational problems, but as soon as we started motoring in England we soon lost our way. Signposting in this country is not very good at the present time and was certainly no better then. It is ideal for those who know the locality, but anyone new to the area will find themselves reaching a point at which the signs that they have been following suddenly disappear and they are left with a choice, left fork or right fork and even a compass is of no help; Murphy defined a law which says that if something can go wrong it will go wrong, so in keeping with this law inevitably the wrong choice will be made. It only happened once on this journey but it was frustrating. An amusing event occurred when we stopped for lunch at a small restaurant which was unlicensed and my small son when served with his food asked in a loud voice, 'Where's my wine?' He had been given watered down wine in France and thought he should have had it here. The two ladies who ran the restaurant gave looks of horror at this request from a three-year-old.

We settled in with our relations while I investigated renting accommodation for us while I was at Staff College. It was by now only about five weeks to the start of the course on 15th January. I contacted estate agents in the Bracknell area and without too much difficulty obtained a small cottage in the village of Windlesham, very close to Sunningdale golf course and some six miles from the College. Four cottages which had been those used by the workers on the adjoining estate had been taken over by Graham White, a well known aviator who had flown the first letters by air and had become something of a hero in the eyes of the ladies of my parents' generation. He lived close by and he came to see the inhabitants of his cottages from time to time. His two red setter dogs came more often; in fact, as soon as they realised that my daughter was an animal lover their visits became daily. These cottages had been modernised and furnished to a high standard and were ideal for us. Our neighbours were pleasant; I remember in particular, one Colonel and his family, a bit older than us but delightful company. School was not too far distant and we settled in fairly quickly; one has got to in the Services with the frequent moves and I suppose this was why we got on well with the Colonel so quickly.

On 15th January I reported to RAF Staff College, Bracknell and, after the usual preliminaries, a welcome lecture from the Commandant followed by coffee and meeting the directing Staff as a whole, we were allocated to the member of staff who was to look after us in groups of six for the duration of the course. Two Group Directors had overall responsibility for the students. Initially work and tuition were in the hands of one's DS who in turn was responsible to the Group Director. My DS was a New Zealander who had joined the RAF and, as all the directing staff had qualified earlier and had been recommended for DS duties at a later date. I am afraid I did not see eye to eye with my DS but got on fairly well with my Group Director and also with the DS who looked after us for a short period of time and who I found particularly helpful: a 'Penguin' but a good all round chap who used to go on tour with the Barbarians in a non playing capacity.

At the time there were two RAF Staff Colleges, Bracknell taking students who were not restricted on security matters and included Canadian, Australian, New Zealand and officers of the USAF. The other RAF Staff College students were restricted from certain classified information and students were from nations with whom we worked but who could not be given the sometimes delicate information available to us at Bracknell. RAF officers attended this other college and received the same psa qualification in the Air Force list.

Lectures and visits made socialising possible with most members on the course and I was soon friendly with a number of the Americans, whom I got to know initially through playing their game of softball, a mini form of baseball which I had learned as a PoW. There was also a Canadian and his wife with whom we became friendly in addition to many old and new colleagues in our own Air Force. Part of the idea of the college was to form friendships with people of similar ideas and this was certainly achieved.

Work at Staff College comprised a mixture of lectures covering a very extensive field, some of a very sensitive nature, exercises carried out by the group, some individually and visits to manufacturers, for example the Bristol Aircraft Establishment, now part of British Aerospace. A joint study with the students at the Army Staff College at Camberley and a trip to the 'Derby', were all designed to broaden the mind. Groups under the guidance of a Wing Commander Directing Staff (DS) included as large a variety of experience as possible. My group comprised a member of the RCAF, a member of the USAF and the remainder from the RAF, a Secretarial Squadron Leader and three General Duties Squadron Leaders like myself, all with flying experiences in different RAF Commands. Our DS was a Wing Commander in the RAF from the GD branch, but was a New Zealander. Our Group Director was a Group Captain, also from the GD branch. Other syndicates included members of all the services, not merely the RAF and from all Branches. The DSs were not all General Duties; one, a particular friend, who helped me more than my own DS, was an Equipment Officer, the rugby fan who accompanied the Barbarians on their Easter tour. A fair amount of time was spent in the syndicate with one's DS working on problems and appreciations and concentrating on brevity, reducing leaders in the *Telegraph* and *The Times* newspapers by a third, which I found good practice. I think the topic that I most enjoyed was 'Appreciations'. We were given a mass of facts and figures about an enemy and had to plan how best to deny him the means to continue the war.

Public speaking did not come easily to me and I found that when the first two-minute talk, which we all had to give, was played back, my voice sounded unrecognisable. I was not alone; most of those I spoke to felt the same way, but this did not help. In those days of course tape recorders were rare, answerphones non existent and video cameras too outrageous even to feature in science fiction, so the opportunity to hear your own voice was very much more limited than it is today. Also when it came to speaking for longer periods I found standing up in front of this select audience very frightening indeed and when the time came to deliver the thirty minute talk (I was allocated 'The beginning of democracy'), I found it necessary to refer to my written speech almost entirely although I had learnt it by heart. It was a difficult subject to put over and I felt ashamed of my effort but one or two of my friends gave me a 'Well done', giving me some comfort. In fact many of us had difficulty in addressing this august assembly in spite of being assured that there should be no difficulty since we were speaking among friends. My feelings were that I would prefer to make a fool of myself among people I did not know, rather than people with whom I had to be in daily contact for another nine months. However I did learn that public speaking was not something to take lightly and my preparation was always very thorough after this experience.

I was able to continue playing rugby, but soon discovered that the bruises and knocks which used to be recovered from after a shower and a few beers were not removed so quickly and it took a week, until the next match in fact, before they disappeared. Matches against RAF Station teams and the other staff colleges were played throughout the season, but I decided that at the age of thirty-six I would retire gracefully when I left Bracknell. A Proctor and an Anson based at White Waltham were available for us to keep our hand in and I managed to get in some twenty hours of flying in both aircraft. Flying may have been my profession, but it was also my pastime and greatest passion.

At the end of the course we were interviewed by either the Commandant or the Assistant Commandant and awarded psa if the course had been covered satisfactorily. In most cases the qualification was granted; only two failed at the end of the course and I think one was asked to leave half way through. The Assistant Commandant who had been an Apprentice at Halton and had gone on to Cranwell as a Cadet interviewed me. He was kind enough to say that he would have me on his staff.

# *CHAPTER 12*

## *Advanced Air HQ Malaya*

My posting came through as Squadron Leader Operations at Advanced Air Headquarters Malaya based in Kuala Lumpur at the Army HQ. As my Gib posting had been overseas I asked why I was posted overseas again after such a short interval and was told my posting had been to Aldergrove not Gibraltar; obviously it takes time for Air Ministry Postings to catch up. There was no point in arguing and in retrospect I was more than pleased, for it proved one of the most enjoyable times of my Service which is saying something, as there have been plenty.

My first consideration was whether to take my family to Kuala Lumpur. At that time the Communist Terrorists (CTs) were very active in Malaya and one or two friends at the College thought I would be ill advised to take my wife. I discussed it with Marjorie whose reaction was that we had been separated for too much of our married life already and if it was at all possible she would accompany me but thought it better that we left our daughter at home so as not to disrupt her education any further. While I was a PoW she had attended school with her two cousins, who now lived in London and attended a grammar school quite near to their home; my daughter had passed her eleven plus in Gibraltar, but had been refused entry to a grammar school in Berkshire while I was at Staff College as the local education authority would not accept the Gibraltar eleven plus. I was not able to persuade them to change their decision and it was therefore heartening to know that she could attend, with her cousins, the sort of school suited to her achievements. It was a difficult decision, particularly for my wife, but we both thought it best. It is a never ending problem which service personnel face, how best to cater for the education of their children when postings every two to three years mean that the children are changing schools at the same rate; Education Authorities are very unsympathetic to Service Children who do not fit in with their calculations, and the parents because they are moving around do not have the ear of the local authorities or of an MP that they know or who knows them and could make representations on their behalf. My own education had suffered and having seen my daughter's reaction to not being accepted although having achieved the necessary qualification, I put my son as a boarder as soon as we returned from Malaya. The children of service personnel now receive greater recognition, even to the extent of them being flown out to join their parents overseas if they are at boarding schools.

Having taken this difficult decision, the next step was to arrange for my wife and son, now aged four, to accompany me. This would only be possible if suitable accommodation could be guaranteed in KL. One of the DS at Bracknell told me of an Army Officer who had attended the college as a student a year previously and had been posted to KL, Major Huddleston who, he felt sure, would help. I wrote to Guy Huddleston and had an immediate reply that accommodation had been arranged. As a result of this I booked a passage on HMT (Her Majesty's Troopship) *Windrush.* As an aside, this was the ship used to bring the first immigrants to the UK from the West Indies after the war. If their trip was anything like ours they must have wondered what thcy had let themselves in for. The best decision ever made in my view was ceasing to use these antiquated vessels to convey service personnel to overseas stations. It took over six weeks of discomfort to reach Singapore. In my case this was not helped as going through Suez I was diagnosed as having mumps and was incarcerated in the sickbay in the bowels of the ship and told not to move. Each day the MO visited and asked anxiously if I had swellings anywhere else. I was quite ignorant of the danger of mumps if contracted after childhood. Fortunately, the swelling remained confined to my neck and I have suffered no after effects. The other wives, so Marjorie told me when I returned to civilisation, looked at her in a sorrowful manner with the bolder ones asking if I had any swellings lower down. When I did return to the fold in the last few days of the voyage I was eyed rather keenly and knowing by this time what they were thinking could have happened, said loudly, 'No need for concern, ladies, I am sound in wind and limb and everywhere else.'

On arrival in Singapore we disembarked and were accommodated in Raffles Hotel which was sheer luxury after that voyage. It is an excellent hotel in all respects and our short stay there was the best recuperation we could have had after the ordeal of the troopship. Many years later, my daughter, who had married into the RAF, returned from Singapore by

Transport Command, the journey taking about twenty-four hours. With two young children she was shattered on arrival at RAF Brize Norton, but her discomfort was limited to twenty-four hours, not nearly six weeks. There is no doubt that the use of Transport Command to convey personnel and their families saves manpower and cost. Our short stay in the Raffles Hotel ended when we were told that our journey to Kuala Lumpur had been arranged. We were to travel on the armed train leaving Singapore in the morning. CTs were reported as being very active on various parts of this journey and instructions were given as to the action we were to take should an attack, or sabotage on the line, occur. All service personnel were armed against this event and troops specially trained to protect the trains were with us. There was, of course, some apprehension from everybody about this journey, mine being for my family. However, all was well and no incidents prevented the train reaching Kuala Lumpur on time. I had been in touch with Guy Huddleston who met us at the station and told us that we had been booked into the Station Hotel until more permanent accommodation could be found and we settled in after a party in the hotel. As I have said, accommodation had to be arranged before one could set out for KL, but I did not expect once again to be installed in an hotel. In fact, it proved to be an arrangement which was worse than that at Gibraltar because accommodation was only possible at the hotel for a limited period, a fortnight I think from memory. Nothing suitable had become available in this time and Guy Huddleston, saying the fault was his, invited us to stay with him and his wife Gill. Guy was GSO2 at Advanced Air HQ and a firm friendship between the two families was established.

There was no alternative, Kuala Lumpur had few suitable hotels in the early 1950s, and we accepted the Huddlestons' generosity gratefully. In fact, their house was fairly spacious and at that time servants in Malaya accepted extra work as a matter of course. In one respect our presence was useful; Gill became ill and Marjorie was able to keep the house running during her absence in hospital. It was not long afterwards that we found a house in Klang Road and moved in when Gill came out of hospital. The Advanced Air Headquarters occupied a large room as part of the Army Headquarters Malaya; the establishment was one group captain, three squadron leaders, three Intelligence Officers and a flight lieutenant Adjutant. Of the three squadron leader Ops on the establishment one was provided by the RAAF and all the remaining posts were RAF including one of the Intelligence Officers who was a squadron leader.

Patrols in the deep jungle were most uncomfortable. It was wet and humid, insects and particularly leeches caused great discomfort and the ever present fear of an ambush made life for the patrols almost unbearable with little to show for it. The SAS went for deep penetration patrols, often taking weeks before coming back to civilisation. The SAS Camp was not too far from KL and I accepted an invitation to dinner in the officers' mess which gave me some insight into this elite unit. The officers' mess was a Malayan *basha*; the dinner was excellent, and followed by the usual games, which seem to be substantially the same at mess nights in all the services. One in particular was to climb on to a rafter and circle the roof without touching the ground. I am sure they were being kind to me in not insisting that I had a go and I was very grateful for it would have cost me 'drinks all round' if I could not have done it. I stayed overnight at the Camp and was wakened at about three thirty in the morning by noise and movement. It transpired that a deep jungle patrol was setting out in an hour's time. There had not been a sign of this either at the Camp or at KL HQ. The first we would have heard about it would have been a request for a supply drop.

Nearly four fifths of Malaya is covered by a variety of closely packed trees reaching to a height of two hundred feet to get to the sunlight, forming an almost impenetrable canopy below which lies a damp, humid undergrowth, the classic tropical rain forest. To penetrate this jungle it is

*With the Army in Malaya, but not too deep in the jungle. Author third from left.*

necessary to hack your way through with a *parang*, the path produced becoming overgrown so quickly that it will have disappeared completely if you try to retrace your steps as little as a week later. There are multitudes of mosquitoes capable of biting through thick jungle clothing and big black leeches which cling to clothing that is brushed against the undergrowth and which in no time at all are deep into all parts of the body, blood-sucking at an alarming rate. The only way to get them out of their attachment is by touching them with a lighted cigarette as any other method tends to leave their heads *in situ* with the prospect of infection. Many types of snake inhabit the jungle, as well as many screeching animals which make life unpleasant. Altogether it is not an attractive place to have to fight a war against a well-armed and organised enemy with considerable experience of the conditions. This was what our troops were up against.

It was termed an 'Emergency' out of regard for the Malayan economy, in particular the tin mines and rubber plantations which were largely British owned and which relied for cover on the London Insurance market. The term 'War' would have destroyed this, so 'Emergency' it always was. To those of us who were there it felt just like a war. It would appear that the forces opposing the CTs had superiority since there were ten thousand police and eleven battalions of troops against five thousand CTs. In fact the police had no arms at this stage and there were only four thousand armed fighting men, giving the CTs a numeric superiority. The CTs had originated as a force to fight the Japanese, 'The Malayan People's anti Japanese Army'. It became 'The Malaya People's anti British Army' with its declared aim to take over the whole of Malaya to establish a Communist State. The British formed this Army from Force 136 as a expedient during the war and had supplied arms and rations from the air. Much of this had been stored in caches to be available when required and much of it still remained in caches and now was when it was required. The CTs therefore were not short of arms and it is ironic that we had supplied them. In the first six months, four hundred and eighty-two police, troops and civilians, including British planters and tin miners, were killed and four hundred and four were wounded against four hundred and six CTs killed and two hundred and sixty-eight captured; how many who were wounded of course is not known. They were not getting the upper hand and we were getting stronger.

I had been involved in Malaya even before I took up my posting to Kuala Lumpur. In 1947/48 I was Camp Commandant (CO) at Coastal Command Headquarters, Northwood, at the time of the air disaster in which Sir Edward Gent, the High Commissioner for Malaya, was killed with all crew and passengers coming in to land at Northolt. The nearest RAF Station to a crash is responsible for the initial enquiry and this was how I became involved. Fortunately the matter was taken over by higher authority and I took no further part. The High Commissioner who followed was Sir Henry Gurney who was killed in an ambush when going to Frasers Hill during my time at Advanced Air Headquarters, KL. In fact, the ambush in which Sir Edward Gurney was killed was not established for that purpose, but merely to get arms for the CT platoon who set up the ambush.

In the early days of the emergency it was a simple matter for the CTs who were well organised in regiments and quite ruthless in obtaining their needs to carry on the fight. Arms they had in plenty, but food and money were not always available. However it was not difficult to terrorise the large population of Chinese 'squatters' into providing both. Squatters lived on the jungle fringe and either willingly or with some persuasion gave the CTs what they wanted. Sir Henry Gurney decided to deny, or make more difficult, this supply of CT needs. He arranged for the move of some six hundred thousand Chinese squatters from the jungle fringes into prepared villages under guard and thus deprived the CTs of their easy pickings without which it would become more and more difficult to continue the fight. The greater protection of these villages made it difficult for the CTs and gave confidence to the people in the villages to resist the demands. As a result the CTs started to cultivate clearings in the jungle for food. Very soon these were located and helicopters spraying chemicals reduced the yield or killed the crops entirely; as a result the CTs were being deprived of the means to continue the fight and although it did not happen while I served in Malaya the 'Emergency' was eventually brought to an end.

Sir Gerald Templer, appointed following the untimely death of Sir Henry Gurney, was created a 'Supremo', with far greater powers than any of his predecessors had had. He continued with the policy of restricting the help being obtained from the Chinese squatters by relocating them in villages under guard and giving them grants of land and thus a stake in the country which they had not had when living on the jungle fringes where no such entitlement existed. The intention was to weld together the various nationalities and to make them feel that it was Malayan Independence that they were going to achieve together against the threat which now faced them. He was untiring in his efforts, visiting rubber plantations and letting the tappers see what he was doing for their country and for them when independence was achieved; he visited hospitals and schools with his wife, who played a large part in persuading the women of the need to discard racial difficulties and to pull together for the good of Malaya. On one occasion, I do not recall why, I was at King's House, the Governor General's residence, when Templer arrived from a visit hot and tired, in a helicopter. He jumped out, went straight into the house, took a shower and was off on another visit in fifteen minutes flat. Remarkable.

The tin miners and rubber planters were not forgotten; as long as they looked after their staff they had his support, but if they erred in this respect they received the rough side of his tongue, and that could be very rough indeed. Rubber planters and tin miners lived in isolated places and travelled in heavily armoured vehicles, usually large American models or Jaguars with heavy armour plate for a windscreen with a narrow slit for the driver to see through. It was the rubber planters and tin miners who, living in remote and isolated houses, were the first casualties at the beginning of the Emergency. Quite unsuspecting, a number were simply massacred in their houses simply because they were British. Precautions followed, of course, but those living in isolated estates were always at risk. Indeed, anyone away from the large towns or travelling by road or rail could be ambushed at any time.

As we were acting in support of the Army, we worked with a major, initially Guy Huddleston with whom I got on extremely well, as I did with the other major and a captain. The major on duty would receive requests for an attack to be carried out on specific targets and our job was to advise how best a particular target could be dealt with and to issue operation orders to the squadrons. The captain received requests for supply drops to the jungle patrols and operation orders were made to the Dakota supply drop aircraft based on the airfield at RAF Kuala Lumpur some three miles distant from the HQ. When the establishment was filled we three Squadron Leader Ops. worked eight hour shifts, but the RAAF were not always able to meet their commitment and we often worked twelve hours on and twelve hours off and since targets came in throughout the twenty-four hours we were kept very busy.

The Ops. room was friendly and we worked well with the Army. Targets which the troops on the ground wanted attacked were either pinpoint requiring rocket attack or larger targets on which stick bombing was applied. I went out with the patrols on one or two occasions and thought that a short burst of fear occasioned by either of these two methods was soon forgotten by those under attack. I held the view that if it was possible to keep an area under attack for a sustained period it was more likely to lower the morale of the CTs and cause them to surrender. To this end I submitted a paper to the AOC in Singapore suggesting the use of Sunderland Flying Boats to cover a fairly large area dropping anti personnel bombs. If memory serves, over a hundred of these small bombs could be carried and released in a continuous stick as the Sunderland flew up and down the target area. The chances of the target being accurately marked by the Army and accurately hit from the air in jungle which all looks the same I thought a very hit or miss affair whereas the sustained bombing of a comparatively large area would be more likely to get close to those being attacked. Whether or not my paper made any impact I am not aware, but I did lay on Sunderland attacks and did not hear of any criticism from Air HQ Malaya. The AOC made visits to the Advanced Air HQ and on one occasion Air Marshal Mills made reference to the paper but with no comment good or bad. It is an interesting thought that ten years or so later in Vietnam the USAF used B 52s for carpet bombing in a very similar way to the one I was recommending.

During my time at Advanced Air HQ, I served three AOCs, Air Vice Marshal Blucke for a very short spell, but we saw little of him at KL. He was very concerned about the Brigand losses and the number of crews killed in them. AVM Scherger, RAAF, succeeded him and he visited frequently, taking considerable interest in both our work and our play. He enjoyed golf and would bring his golf clubs and come to the Royal Selangor Club for a game with me. He was kind to me on the occasion that I brought our Auster back from RAF KL after servicing and put it on its nose when I landed. He was in the Ops. room on a visit when I came in and told him that I had bent one of his aeroplanes.

The small airstrip, Noble Field, was used by the AOP (Air Observation Post) Flights. The Ops. Staff had an Auster at their disposal housed there and serviced by RAF personnel. Our Auster was a dual control version and the dual seat backrest folded forward when the seat was not occupied. Landing on the shorter strips it was necessary to motor in with a lot of engine and to cut the engine when just over the end of the strip, bring the control column right back smoothly and the Auster would sit down with a very short landing run. Well, it only failed once, Murphy's Law ensuring that it was when the AOC was watching. In my case the dual control stick was fitted and the back of the second seat, which was down, prevented the full rearward movement of the control column and over on her nose she went. The watching ground crew were most amused and said I was out while the Auster was still in motion. I suggested the inclusion of a note when flying dual control Austers when the dual seat was not occupied that the second control column should be removed. My accident report went to Air HQ but nothing further was heard, thanks, I suspect, to the intervention of AVM Sherger.

We also had an Anson which was kept at RAF Kuala Lumpur some five miles away where there was air traffic control and runways capable of taking the Dakotas which were based there and the Lancasters which were used for bombing sorties against the CTs, but based in Singapore. I only saw Lancs once at KL when one of the Australian Squadrons landed there. The Dakotas were employed in dropping supplies to the jungle patrols on requests made to the Ops. Room, which were vetted by the Army Captain responsible and passed to us to issue the Ops. Order. In fact the Captain seldom had to refer to us, except for us to sign the Order, as he knew the job backwards and no danger of overloading was likely. Incidentally, he had been a PoW of the Japanese which had left him with a nervous twitch, but he was sound in his judgement and a likeable man.

I made full use of the Auster to visit the various units in Malaya, all of which had a landing strip alongside their HQ. These strips were about two hundred yards in length and twelve to fifteen yards wide, sometimes less, a little like trying to land on a par three golf hole. Winds in Malaya are normally very light and it was seldom necessary to land crosswind. The take-off presented little difficulty: rev up on brakes, brakes off and the Auster would be airborne in between one hundred and one hundred and twenty yards from brake release. On one occasion it was necessary to test this; a period of heavy rain at between three and four o'clock every afternoon occurred almost without fail. The strip at which I had landed five hours earlier was

*A tiny outpost in the middle of nowhere. I could get the Auster into the smallest strip. This one is about 150 yards.*

flooded; I had to return to the Ops. Room to take over duty that evening and I kept watching the water receding until I decided that darkness would prevent me from getting back unless I took a decision soon. Fortunately, now only one end of the strip was flooded and the water was still receding. I paced the distance from the end of the strip to the water, one hundred and ten yards. I was on my own so at least the Auster was light. I held the Auster on the brakes with full revs. Off brakes and a little prayer and I was airborne within five yards of the water.

The Anson I flew as much as, if not more than, any of the pilots on the Ops. Staff. I flew General Urquhart, the Army Commander, on visits to RAF Butterworth, Taiping and Ipoh, the GOC and Police Commissioner on two visits to units and on many occasions I took Army Staff to visit units either in the Anson or in the Auster when only the landing strips were available. By flying these senior officers I was able not only to get more flying than would have otherwise been possible but to get the opportunity of visiting many more of the units fighting the terrorists in Malaya and therefore getting to know the Commanders. I think I liked the trips to the small strips in the Auster best. I recall particularly the occasion when a captured terrorist claimed that he could pinpoint the location of a terrorist

*Waiting for an attack by Lancasters on the bomb line. Author in the middle of the trio.*

hideout from the air. I had some doubts, firstly that he could identify a spot in the jungle, all of which looks much the same, and secondly that it was safe to carry a terrorist. I accepted the risk provided an extra man came with us to keep the CT under control and to act as an interpreter. In fact, as I had suspected, the CT had very little idea where he was in the air.

I went on a number of supply drops in the Dakotas from KL airfield. Drops were normally made in the early morning; the patrol making the request for supplies would give a grid reference and state the time they wished to receive the drop. In the early mornings in Malaya the jungle is covered in heavy mist and the sighting of dropping zones could be very difficult, but the Dakota chaps became very proficient in finding the patrol and the dispatchers in getting the supplies on to the DZ accurately. Obviously a Dakota would carry sufficient supplies for a number of patrols and it was impressive to see how efficiently the work was done of dropping to a number of DZs on the same sortie when flying over a canopy of jungle that all looked the same. We had come a long way with our navigation in what was really a few short years.

Even more impressive was the evacuation of casualties from the dense jungle. Trees, striving for light, grow to some two hundred feet and it is necessary to clear an area of sufficient size to allow a helicopter to descend and pick up the casualty. Blasting trees to provide sufficient space for the pick-up is done by the patrol and it seemed to me as an onlooker that the rotor blades barely missed the trees on the perimeter of the clearing. I flew with Flight Lieutenant Dowling who was an expert with his Dragonfly helicopter. Helicopters were used to a much greater extent when Sir Gerald Templar took over and decided to starve the CTs into submission. The decision to deprive the CTs of food which was rigidly pursued by Sir Gerald Templar eventually resulted in the end of the Emergency. Attacks on the ground and from the air in support of the troops on the ground caused discomfort but was never likely to bring about a decision, but by depriving the CT of his food his will to continue ceased.

With the approval of the Group Captain in charge of the Ops Room, I decided to visit as many of the ground forces headquarters as possible in order to discuss with them how best we could provide our support. I usually took one of our Intelligence Staff or one of my opposite numbers in the Army with whom we worked, with me. These visits were made in the Auster from Noble Field. When visiting units with or near an airfield it was possible to take up to four passengers, as I did in the case of Major General Urquhart when he was accompanied by his ADC and the Police Commissioner which I have mentioned. The ground forces were not all from the Army; some were isolated police posts. I visited one in particular with a very small strip which was manned by two British and four Chinese police. The two British chaps apparently remained in this isolated spot for about a month at a time, a deadly dull existence anyway, and I was amazed to learn that one of them read Edgar Allan Poe while he was there. These trips were not entirely for the benefit of acquiring knowledge, of course, for it will have been gathered that my love of flying made a big contribution to my willingness to spend much of my off-duty time in this way.

In addition to the supply drops in the Dakota, I went with Flight Lieutenant Wadhams on a Brigand strike, and also flew as a passenger in a Meteor flown from Tengah to Kluang and back to Tengah in order to get some idea of flying over the jungle at the speed of these aircraft. Although I submitted a paper on the use of Sunderlands to keep an area under control for longer periods than other attacks I did not go on any of these nor in the Lancaster

By the QUEEN'S Order the name of
Squadron Leader J.A.B. Tams,
Royal Air Force,
was published in the London Gazette on
6. March, 1953.
as mentioned in a Despatch for distinguished service.
I am charged to record
Her Majesty's high appreciation.

Secretary of State for Air

*Mention in Dispatches*

attacks, but I did go with an Army unit on the bomb line during a Lancaster attack. I enjoyed my work immensely and it came as some surprise when I received a 'Mention in Despatches' for my work. Visits to Singapore airfields, Butterworth, Tengah, Changi or Seletar, the Sunderland base, to discuss targets with people on the spot or to take Army personnel to visit their Headquarters were numerous and helped me to appreciate the problems from the other man's point of view and therefore lead to greater efficiency and less confusion.

On one occasion, returning from Changi with a group of Army Officers that I had taken to Singapore, one of the Anson's engines started to overheat rather badly and I was forced to shut it down. The normal procedure for reporting was taken and since I was more than halfway to KL I decided to continue on the one engine although there was a danger that this too would overheat. I was not on the distress frequency at this stage and my call was picked up by the AOC, AVM Mills, who was on his way back to Singapore in his Devon. He saw us and kindly turned round and accompanied us back to KL. We were losing height but not dangerously and had no trouble in making a single engine landing, which, after all, is practised monthly to ensure that it is a matter of course should the necessity arise. Obviously the passengers were aware of our problem, but I assured them that the Anson was well able to fly on one engine but that as a precaution seat belts should be fastened and there should be no smoking. An Army captain was obviously very frightened and I told my navigator, Flight Lieutenant Godwin, who was on our staff as an Intelligence Officer and who had flown with me quite a lot, to pacify the frightened officer, but it was not until the AOC's Devon joined us that he calmed down. I thanked the AOC after I landed and he resumed his journey to Changi. When we got out of the aircraft the Army Captain very dramatically assured me that I had saved his life and that he did not know how to thank me. He was a member of the headquarters amateur dramatic society and played a good part. I said rather pompously that the RAF were trained to cope with these minor emergencies and that there had never been any danger.

I had little opportunity for sport, but managed to play the occasional round of golf, especially when AVM Scherger, the AOC prior to AVM Mills, came to Advanced Air HQ to visit the Ops Room. He liked the friendly atmosphere at the Selangor Country Club. He returned to Australia where he became the RAAF CAS (Chief of the Air Staff), a very friendly man with whom I got on well. I have been extremely fortunate in the senior officers I have served: in fact I have always found them accessible and ready to listen. My experience can be summed up as, 'Do your job and you will get all the support you need.' Having re-read the last part of this narrative, it seems likely that I could be accused of name dropping, but my intention was merely to indicate the kindness and understanding I received from the senior officers I served under. I was, of course, privileged in serving in a small headquarters which was under direct scrutiny by the AOCs who would normally not come into direct contact with a Squadron Leader.

Social life was centred round the Arakan Mess which was under the control of the Army Headquarters at Kuala Lumpur. All officers' messes are run in much the same way and the few RAF officers who were members fitted in easily and happily. The Sunday lunches were particularly enjoyable as we were joined by wives on these occasions. Outside the Headquarters the Selangor Country Club provided golf, swimming, gymnasium facilities and of course a restaurant and bar. It was handy for the wives with small children who could spend their time in the pool or sitting on the patio. Marjorie, who was not keen on constant coffee parties, used the Club quite a lot until our small son started school when to fill her spare time she worked for Police Intelligence at their Headquarters in Kuala Lumpur; it saved her from coffee-housing and provided the means of keeping her mind active. The work was enjoyable and as I spent so much time away was a useful pastime as well as providing pin money. The school which my son attended was run by the Army and gave the very young a good educational foundation. On our return to England I decided to put him as a boarder to avoid the constant school changes inherent in service life and it was here that the headmaster confirmed that the early schooling had given him a good grounding.

At the end of my time at Advanced Air Headquarters Malaya, I received an award, which, like the Mention in Dispatches, I felt was undeserved

CENTRAL CHANCERY OF THE ORDERS OF KNIGHTHOOD.

*St. James's Palace, S.W.1.*

*1st June,* 1953.

The QUEEN has been graciously pleased, on the occasion of Her Majesty's Coronation, to give orders for the following appointment to the Most Excellent Order of the British Empire in recognition of distinguished service in Malaya:—

*To be an Additional Officer of the Military Division of the said Most Excellent Order:—*

Squadron Leader Francis Adrian Burdett TAMS (43076), Royal Air Force.

*Supplement to the* London Gazette *1 June 1953*

since I had enjoyed my time there so much and did not think I had done anything special. The *Supplement to the London Gazette* for 1st June 1953 gives the appointment as an Officer of the Most Excellent Order of the British Empire to Squadron Leader F.A.B. Tams in recognition of distinguished service in Malaya. Because I was leaving Malaya before the award could be given I had the additional privilege of attending an Investiture at Buckingham Palace and receiving it from Her Majesty. I was particularly pleased by this decision since it made it possible to take my daughter with us to the presentation ceremony at Buckingham Palace. Two periods in her young life had been without my presence and the decision to leave her when we went to Malaya had been quite a wrench. She was now at an age when attending an Investiture with us would be meaningful to her. It gave us great pleasure and I think she enjoyed it.

But I have got ahead of myself. The humidity, rather than the heat, in Malaya saps one's strength and holidays to either the Cameron Highlands or Frasers Hill were used to recharge our batteries. It had been while on his way to Frasers, as we always called it, that Sir Henry Gurney was ambushed by CTs and killed and as such it was somewhat risky to make the journey. An armoured convoy was arranged at set intervals to escort those visiting either of these holiday resorts. In fact, any journey by road or rail in Malaya held dangers from CT ambushes which restricted the movement of civilians and it made it such a claustrophobic existence for most people. I soon realised how fortunate I was in being able to fly almost anywhere. The rubber planters had to get about, of course, which is why they had their makeshift armoured cars. Rubber planters living on their plantations were very vulnerable and had to have armed protection; but it was not a pleasant existence.

This then made it important for occasional breaks and the Camerons and Frasers were well patronised. A bungalow was booked, complete with servants, and one was able to enjoy a real FIRE, not that it was absolutely necessary for warmth, but it gave a feeling of Home. The climate never changes in Malaya; it is the same all the year round. Those wonderful little soldiers from Nepal guarded Frasers. I would follow a Gurkha anywhere! I had told my young son what good soldiers the Gurkhas were and, rather foolishly had said that if they drew their kookri it had to be used. When entering Frasers Hill a Gurkha on guard was keen to show the young man his kookri, which they always carried, and forgetting what I had told my son I told the soldier to go ahead at which my son screamed in apprehension. It took a long time for me to get round the comment by saying it was only against someone bad.

Another incident occurred when the film of *The Wooden Horse* was to be shown at the local cinema in Kuala Lumpur. Somehow the cinema proprietor discovered that I had been in the camp involved and had assisted in this escape. In fact, when I was interviewed by a journalist from the local paper I made it perfectly clear that although I had made a contribution, as had many others, I had not necessarily been tunnelling. By the time the article had been hacked about to make a better story, I appeared as the great hero of the piece. A newspaper will resort to almost anything to make a normal story special. To deny these stories merely marks one as being modest and the stories become more embellished and embarrassing. Anyway, my wife and I went to the cocktail party prior to the opening, enjoyed the best seats and had royal treatment throughout. 'Hey Ho', what it's like to be famous however undeserved! On another occasion, either a film or television company decided to make a film about the Emergency and I was involved in some scenes purporting to be planning an operation, I think with the SAS; certainly their CO was at the meeting which lasted a whole morning. By the time the cuts were made it would have been missed if one blinked. What a waste of time.

The return to England was still by HM Troopship. The choice available to us was the *Windrush* which had brought us to Singapore or the *Trooper*. Since our trip out had been so uncomfortable I settled for the latter. How wrong I was: it took eight weeks and we were passed by *Windrush*. Air Marshal Mills said I could fly the family down to Changi, but the Anson was U/S and we were flown by his pilot in the Devon. We stayed the night at the transit camp and embarked the following morning. We embarked on the *Trooper* on 24th July 1953. I shared a cabin with two other senior officers and our wives shared cabins in the bowels of this antiquated ship. It was bad enough for me, but ghastly for Marjorie and my son, sharing what was little more than a boxroom with another air force wife and her children. This was to be endured for eight weeks of battling through stormy weather in which it was all the ship could do to keep moving forward. Fortunately, we are all good sailors and the bucking gyrating ship did not afflict us with seasickness so most of our time was spent on deck trying to keep our balance and fighting the wind which always seemed to be heading us. I forget exactly where it occurred, but the last straw was watching the *Windrush* pass us, I think it was just after Ceylon, now of course Sri Lanka. We called at Colombo which I had known as a clean, well kept city, but which on this visit seemed uncared for and dismally dirty. We went ashore and even though it was disappointing, it gave us the opportunity to walk on a stable platform and enjoy a little space. Marjorie had known Pondicherry as a young girl when her father was the manager of a cotton mill and she also noticed the reduction in standards from the days of the Raj, although Pondicherry was in fact French. The remainder of this journey is best forgotten. We reached Southampton after eight weeks, got through customs without much difficulty and headed north yet again to Marjorie's parents in Burnley.

While there on leave I received my posting to Bomber Command Headquarters at High Wycombe, as Org. 2. This is a branch which deals with postings and establishments within the Command. Before leaving Malaya I had intimated to Air Marshal Mills who was taking over as C in C of Bomber Command, that I would like to join the 'V' Bomber Force. Soon after my arrival at Bomber Command he interviewed me in this connection but decided that my age would be a barrier and I heard no more. I was forty and shortly afterwards my promotion to Wing Commander and a posting to Headquarters Technical Training Command as Org. 1 came through. I suppose in retrospect that it may well have been my promotion rather than my age that precluded the move as it would not have been possible to take over a squadron without any experience either on the aircraft or in the command and my rank would have restricted me from any other appointment.

On first reporting to Bomber Command we moved into accommodation in the town, as married quarters were not available. This was the normal practice in those days and a special wife was necessary to accept the frequent moves and having to live in places which were far from the standards one would expect. Progress has been made over the years and these days there is a much more civilised system of 'hirings' and, of course, since the size of the Service has reduced so dramatically, married quarters are available to many more, if not all, personnel. In fact, after about six weeks of temporary accommodation a married quarter at Bomber Command was available and we moved in. Moving into and out of married quarters involves a 'Marching in' and a 'Marching out'. This involves every item being inspected and signed for; any damage or discrepancies are noted and ultimately paid for. This is quite an experience, especially if a new quarter is involved, because all the cooking pots and pans are covered in a thick preservative paste which has to be removed and this was what confronted us when moving into the quarter at Bomber. A further frustration is that most of the utensils are extremely heavy and unlikely to be used by present day wives, but had to be cleaned nevertheless. We did all this only to be told a week or two later of my promotion and posting to Technical Training Command at Brampton. We were 'Marched out' and 'Marched in' to another quarter at RAF Brampton which fortunately had already been occupied.

On 14th January 1954, I reported at Headquarters Technical Training Command after only just over four months at Bomber Command. It seemed unlikely that a flying appointment would be given to me and it was sensible to make the best of it; after all I was a wing commander on a permanent commission and although I was destined for desk jobs I was able to keep myself in flying practice using the station Anson based at Wyton and occasionally scrounging trips from friends in the hope that in the future a flying appointment might materialise. At that time Tech. Training Command comprised about a third of the total Royal Air Force manpower, principally because of the large numbers of National Service personnel being recruited at stations in the Command who were specifically engaged in training the tradesmen for the RAF. Group HQ was responsible for a number of these stations and one group in particular for those stations engaged in the major repair of engines and airframes. A group captain was responsible for the Organisation Section of the HQ and he in turn was responsible to the AOA (Air Officer i/c Administration). As Org.1 I had the responsibility for the organisation of working conditions within the HQs and in general for the stations within the command. Org. 2 was responsible for the manning levels and Org. 3 for accommodation, both living and working.

Each of these sections had a wing commander in charge, with a squadron leader and a junior officer to assist him. I had a squadron leader (GD) and a warrant officer who had recently been commissioned and promoted to flying officer, with considerable administrative experience, who was a great help to the section. Org. 2 and Org. 3 had Admin wing commanders with GD (flying) subordinates. A pretty fair balance. Our group captain was from the Secretarial Branch and the AOA was Air Vice Marshal 'Cocky' Spencer who had been my AOC in Gibraltar.

The Group Captain, 'Tiny' White, a large man as the name indicates, was keen on getting into the air and as I was the only wing commander who flew, he used to get me to fly him to various stations on official visits. It became customary for me to fly a number of command staff officers on visits and in the course of this I managed to visit my friend Arthur Southall who commanded a Canberra Squadron at Marham. It was there that I took the high altitude decompression test prior to getting dual instruction in a Meteor and a Canberra. I was allowed to attend the Tech. Training Command Instrument Rating Flight at Debden and obtained a Master Green Instrument Rating which I renewed at the same Flight a year later; the first rating was in Oxfords and the later one in Varsitys. I retained this highest instrument rating until my retirement, taking the six monthly tests in various aircraft.

I had expected a very dull time at HQ Tech. Training, which was known as 'the elephants' graveyard' since so many people retired from there, but found it far from dull. I managed forty-five hours on the Prentice, twenty-seven on Chipmunk, fifty-two on the ubiquitous Anson, twenty-three in the Oxford on the Instrument Rating Flight and fifteen hours and thirty minutes renewing my instrument rating on the Varsity. I also managed to have dual on Meteors and Canberras. I flew to all manner of new airfields and had a great time. 'Tiny' White took me for the odd game of golf, which was my only sport during this time. I was persuaded to take on responsibility for Command athletics as well as boxing. As a result of National Service, talent naturally existed in large numbers and we had good representation in both sports. I remember in particular Derek Ibbotson as an excellent middle distance runner who later held the world record for the mile, but more particularly as a first class team member, always prepared to drop back during a race to encourage a colleague who was lagging. Brian London was naturally one of our star boxers who would sit on his stool and glower at his opponent and frighten him into submission. Both went on to make their names in civilian life. The most stylish boxer in the team was Dick McTaggart who won the lightweight gold medal at the 1956 Olympics.

I suppose the most important and taxing job we had in Org. 1 was in planning for the support of the civil power. This was a time of strikes and it was necessary to have plans ready to provide the necessary support in an attempt to prevent a complete disruption of one or more services in the country. The RAF has to continue to operate, to train and to be ready as always for any emergency. Front line units are always loath to part with people and it fell to our command to provide the bulk of the personnel, but inevitably certain trained people had to be provided from other units and small battles did occur.

I had had some misgivings about my posting to Tech. Training Command. However, it transpired to be far from the boring time I had anticipated; more flying than I had thought possible and the bonus of flying the Canberra, a most gentlemanly aeroplane, and the Meteor which rushed round the circuit so fast when I was doing my circuit and bumps dual that I had barely got thc undercarriage up before I was selecting 'Down'. After the aircraft I had been flying I found little time to think, but it soon became more natural and I was able to cope with the rapid response required and enjoyed it. My superiors were very kind in allowing me to have the time for these activities; after all I was in a non-flying Command.

The Commander in Chief during my first eighteen months was Sir Victor Groom who had a reputation for insisting on the minutest detail being observed and for being quite peppery when it was not. Fools were not suffered gladly and it was easy to be classed as a fool in his eyes. This was at the Command HQ. I did not come into contact with him to any great extent, except through running the Command athletics and boxing teams, and found him understanding and not at all difficult to work for. The AOA, Air Vice Marshal Spencer, had a bark far worse than his bite as I had discovered when I served directly under him in Gibraltar where his Quarter was fairly close to mine and my daughter, then aged eleven, used to go to play with his daughter by his second marriage and 'Cocky' would join in. My wife was also friendly with Mrs Spencer and could not understand why I thought him a hard taskmaster. He certainly had his lighter moments, as I mentioned earlier. The only change in the top ranks during my stay was that of the C in C, Air Marshal George Beamish, taking over from Air Marshal Sir Victor Groom. AVM Spencer and Group Captain White left at the same time as me.

# *CHAPTER 13*

## *Back to St Eval*

My attempt to get a flying job proved to be impossible; they were few and far between anyway and my age did not help. I considered that it would be to my best advantage to try to return to my old Command, Coastal. I asked to go back to St Eval which 217 Squadron had opened in 1939. St Eval was now the base for four maritime squadrons flying Shackletons and I would be close to flying even though not in it. The request was met since there was a wing commander vacancy at the station. My hope that it was the wing commander Flying was soon dashed when I was informed that it would be as wing commander Administration.

I arranged to visit St Eval and flew down in an RAF Wyton Anson. I was met by a Wing Commander Murray who, having welcomed me, asked if I had come to stay and looked very disappointed when I answered in the negative adding that my posting had not been confirmed, but that it seemed more than likely to be within the next week or two. Murray was one of the Squadron Commanders and had been put in charge of administration until the post was filled. He wanted to get back to running his Squadron and felt it a waste of his time to be 'pushing paper' around. The Station Commander also wanted the post filled as soon as possible and wished to see me. Group Captain Charles Inness interviewed me in his office and confirmed that he wanted the appointment filled as quickly as possible. Two incumbents in a short time had been disposed of and with two thousand personnel and some two hundred and fifty married quarters to administer it was essential that a qualified wing commander filled the post. I had been selected and he wanted me now. It was out of my hands of course, but it seemed that St Eval needed someone more than Org. 1 at Tech Training Command. I felt somewhat apprehensive, however, since having got rid of two wing commanders it appeared that I was to work for a real martinet. However, I had asked for the posting and would have to make the best of it.

My posting date duly arrived and I flew down to St Eval, but my family were to remain at Brampton until the married quarter reserved for the wing commander Admin. post was available. It was occupied by a previous wing commander Admin., which made life a little embarrassing when pressing for a 'marching in' date. Charles Inness applied a little pressure and after a week or two we 'marched out' of the Brampton Quarter and 'marched in' at St Eval. The quarters were arranged with the Station Commander in the centre of the senior Wing Commanders, Flying on one side and Admin., me, on the other.

The CO had a small dachshund and I had a Labrador cross boxer, named 'Crackers'; he was such a soft soppy dog, but a real character. While we were busy moving in, taking over the inventory and so on, Crackers wandered across the grass in front of the CO's house and the little dachs, protecting his property, attacked Crackers who although soft and soppy would have none of it and bit the dachs's ear which resulted in a great display of yelping. The Squadron Commander's Quarters were immediately opposite and Murray, who had met me and was so anxious for me to stay, shouted across the narrow road, 'I shouldn't bother to unpack, Frank.' But I was not the third wing commander Admin to be posted and in fact a firm friendship was established between the two families which still exists and although Charles died a year or two past, his wife Margaret and I exchange Christmas cards and news every year.

The Wing Commander Admin. job was enormous and time consuming. The CO was a stickler for getting things done correctly and thought nothing of holding a conference at seven thirty in the evening or at weekends. Social life was excellent and parties were numerous and inevitably Charles and Margaret would either be at their quarter or ours. The young officers frequented our house and Charles and I were often left with the washing up after a dinner party. The young officers came, of course, to see my daughter, now an attractive seventeen year old. My son was in boarding school at Kimbolton, so we only saw him during holidays. Charles had two sons and they too were boarders, so were infrequent visitors. When they were on holidays the two families got on well as the two boys were of similar age to my daughter.

So much for the social side which seemed never ending. The work side, too, was very time consuming; for me it was like running a small town; in fact the previous chap who did my job would answer calls by announcing himself, 'The Mayor of St Eval'. Married quarters, marchings in and out, maintenance, complaints, welfare: it is quite amazing how much help is necessary for young families when the man is away, sometimes for months at a time. This is a major job if families are to be kept happy and the men who are away know that they have someone to turn to for help so that their morale does not suffer. As a result a Families Officer responsible to the Wing Commander Admin. keeps this most important aspect of a station running smoothly. Other functions, all with specialist officers reporting to me, were the various Churches, the medical requirements, accounts, buildings, catering and discipline. I have never shirked delegating responsibility once I have assessed the person to whom I am going to delegate and have always given my complete backing in times of controversy. I have always believed that those working for you give better service if they know they are trusted. Stations in those days ran on the three-prong system, the Admin. Wing, the Flying Wing and the Technical Wing, each with a wing commander responsible to the Commanding Officer. The CO trusted my judgement and let me get on with the job, as I did with my subordinates. The three senior wing commanders worked well together and the overall result was a happy, well run station, always busy, sometimes overworked, but always efficient.

In 1939, on my previous visit, St Eval was still in the process of construction. Accommodation was primitive for both ground and aircrew; we married types were lucky in being able to live with our families in the many houses which had been provided as holiday accommodation on the Cornish coast and which we were soon able to rent. The St Eval I went to in 1956 was a very different station from the one I had gone to in 1939. Four Shackleton Squadrons were based there with the complete backing of Tech. Wing, run extremely efficiently by Wing Commander Roger Whipp, an ex 'ranker' commissioned from Warrant Officer rank. Planned flying, planned maintenance was enforced rigidly by Roger and the results were outstanding, the squadrons attaining full flying hours with maximum aircraft serviceability. Shortly after my arrival the Flying Wing was handed over to Wing Commander John Holgate who had joined 217 Squadron at St Eval in 1940 after having his training at Cranwell reduced owing to the outbreak of the Second World War. I was responsible for the Admin. Wing, providing for the well being of some two thousand airmen and airwomen and in addition some two hundred and fifty married quarters, some housing personnel from St Mawgan, our sister station just across the valley. Ironically, St Mawgan was retained when St Eval was closed in 1959. I was not quite in at the death, but much of the closing down was done in the last few months of my RAF service.

The airfield was very different. Two concrete runways had been provided instead of the wire mesh on grass of 1941 and I was pleased to see that my suggestions, made to Wing Commander Revington when he had said, 'Come alongside, Tams, I would like your opinion,' during one of his walks on the original airfield, had been accepted. Not a difficult recommendation, of course, since the strong prevailing wind at St Eval made the choice of direction fairly obvious, but never the less gratifying. No longer were night landings made using goose-neck flares to provide the flare path, and dispersal areas for the Squadron's aircraft were now hard standings, no more mud; in addition, protection was provided for the ground crew working on the aircraft. Major servicing in Tech. Wing was of course, carried out in the hangars. All very different, much more efficient and particularly conscious of the need to give those hard working ground crews good conditions in which to work.

I had a very able Equipment Officer who ran a very efficient section and gave me little or nothing to worry about. His family and mine got on well together and visits to his house were as frequent as their visits to ours. The Families Officer was a hard working flight lieutenant who had come up through the ranks and therefore was well aware of the needs of families whose husbands are away on courses and detachments; it is remarkable how some wives seemed unable to cope when their husband was away for any length of time and relied on the Families Officer as a shoulder to lean on. I can recall few cases when he required my help. The RAF Regiment officer reported to me, as did the Physical Training Officer, but again, both gave me very few headaches. The Padre looking after the C of Es and the Father for the RCs were extremely good, in particular the RC Father who was able to solve a number of problems which he dealt with and informed me of afterwards, saving me from having to become involved in disciplinary action. Lastly, discipline: a very good Station Warrant Officer kept the airmen under control in the best way possible, since St Eval was a very busy station and the men were required to work long hours which he took into consideration when dress or behaviour was not quite up to scratch. This was an attitude of which I approved and supported, only interfering when I considered that he had been unfair. I have always said that the success of a station is more down to the Station Warrant Officer than any other individual, and this one was no exception.

I had a squadron leader in charge of the accounts section: no more lining up for that time wasting pay parade, this was done by each section in very short time, the payments being sent to each section from my accounts section.

The squadron leader doctor became a firm friend and the only assistance required from me was in administrative matters, usually concerned with families in Married Quarters or inspections in the kitchens. This brings me to that gem of catering officers, Flight Officer 'Tommy' Thomas, who was a WRAF who managed to provide menus for the airmen far superior to that provided in either the sergeants' or the officers' messes, both of which received extra money for messing from each member of the mess. Tommy noticed that breakfast was not attended by all airmen entitled to it and realised that at weekends similar savings could be made in the ration allowance. In this way she made available money which she used to provide at least three main course choices and two or three choices of puddings. She won the Command Catering prize for the two years I was there and I was proud to be included in the photograph of the catering staff after one of these successes. Tommy had an Alsation called 'Tiger'. I have already mentioned my dog Crackers, who was in trouble on his first day in Married Quarters. Crackers was in the habit of visiting the cookhouse where Tommy, quite wrongly, used to give him a bone. This took place at about 1100 hrs, each day. One day, Crackers and Tiger arrived at the same time. Not unnaturally, Tiger resented the intrusion and attacked Crackers, the inevitable result being a good scrap. Poor Tommy was distraught; she telephoned me to tell me what had happened. Although she had not been present, she had seen the state of Tiger, who terrorised the other dogs on the station and, thinking Crackers must have been badly mutilated, was extremely worried. I told her not to be concerned, Crackers should not have been there anyway, but in any event he was not hurt, he was with me with only a slight wound. Apparently Tiger had fared less well. The two dogs then became the best of friends and terrorised the rest of the camp dogs with impunity.

So there it was, I was lucky with my CO and with my staff in whom I had complete confidence, allowing them to get on with their jobs as the experts they were. I held a weekly meeting in my office of the officers responsible for the main sections, to iron out any problems and to keep us all informed of what was happening. Once a fortnight the Station Commander held a meeting of the three Wing Commanders for the same purpose; he would also call impromptu meetings to discuss special projects. All in all a full life.

It was my intention to get as much flying as possible with the Shackleton Squadrons and in particular to renew my Master Green Instrument rating. I started this in August when I was able to arrange dual instruction in a Shackleton and achieved co-pilot standard by the end of that month. Thereafter I took every available opportunity to fly with one or other of the squadrons on their normal Coastal Command Training. Believing that I could not become proficient enough on the Shackleton to renew my instrument rating in that aircraft I kept my hand in on the faithful 'Annie'. I was completely at home in the Anson having flown some twelve hundred and fifty hours in the various marks over the years. Wherever I had been there had always been an Anson to fly. I took my renewal test in this aircraft in December 1956 and renewed my Master Green. This Instrument Rating has to be renewed every six months and I achieved this again in July 1957, again in an Anson, and in January 1958, I took the test in a Shackleton and obtained the much sought after renewal. In fact, in spite of my original trepidation, I found the test easier in the Shackleton. My final Instrument

*A Shackleton over Buckingham Palace*

Rating Test was achieved in a Shackleton in September 1958. I retired from the Royal Air Force in January 1959 and managed to fly an Anson for thirty-five minutes on my last day.

During my time as Wing Commander Admin. at St Eval I took part as a crew member on all the exercises necessary for Coastal Command crews. In March 1958 the Air Cadets came for their summer camp and I spent a lot of time giving joy rides in the Chipmunk and getting in one of my favourite flying pastimes, aerobatics, not with a Cadet I may say. I certainly achieved my aim on the flying front: I flew with the squadrons on their normal training exercises, and I acted as a co-pilot when a SAR (Search & Rescue) was called in aid of a missing USA Liftmaster. I was involved in a standby SAR on Purple airways, the flight path restricted to Royal flights, on HM the Queen's visit to Portugal and one other of similar pattern as the Royal Escort standby, at the Rockall weather ship *Juliet*.

The sudden requirement to take troops to Nicosia involved using all available aircraft and we embarked thirty-three passengers at Abingdon bound for Luqa (Malta) and on to Nicosia where they were disembarked. We returned to Luqa the same night and back to St Eval the next day. A very satisfying experience for me, but it must have been very uncomfortable for the troops being airlifted, as we had no proper seating for them. Another nice trip was to Malta with the Wing Commander Flying, Wing Commander Holgate, to get in circuits and landings away from base in good weather conditions. From Malta we flew to Idris for more circuits and bumps where we met some opposition from the Station Commander who opposed our landing. We landed anyway and were made very welcome when we discovered that we had been PoWs together. He gave the reason for objecting to us landing: they had been inundated with aircraft putting into Idris merely to collect the duty free spirits available there. However, all was well when two old Kriegies got together. I recall the discomfort of the return journey from Luqa as a result of the failure of the heating system which necessitated a pilot change every hour because of the freezing conditions in the cockpit.

At one point Charles Inness made up his mind to have a unique piece of silver for display on Mess dining-in nights and we went to great lengths to get it to his liking. A silver buzzard was obtained and to have it mounted on a base approved by Charles occupied many hours of conference in the Mess in the evenings. Eventually it was to his liking, a silver plate inscribed with the names of the officers at St Eval was attached and the piece known as the St Eval Buzzard became the centre piece on dining-in nights. I wonder where it is now? I believe it went over to St Mawgan when we closed and that Station assumed all the responsibilities which had been held by us.

Charles Inness was posted to Malta in mid 1958, and was replaced by Group Captain Whelan, a Canadian who had joined the RAF. Our working relations were good but socially did not reach the level of those between Charles' family and ourselves. Charles asked me if I wished to join him on the staff in Malta but I did not think this to be a good move for me.

Towards the middle of 1958, nearing my time for posting, I began to put out feelers as to my future. It seemed likely that I would not get a posting in Coastal and that it would be in some staff job. I was not looking forward to this and since I was nearing the retirement age of forty-seven for a Wing Commander GD officer, I was approaching forty-five, I began to consider my options. I was feeling frustrated with dealing with National Service Entrants, some of whom resented being made to serve and complained about the smallest detail and either wrote to, or got their mothers to write to, their MP. On one occasion this triggered off a PQ (Parliamentary Question) which was referred back to the station at which the chap was serving and everything had to be dropped to give priority to the PQ. I used to interview all airmen leaving the station before I signed their final 'clearance chit'. In the case of National Servicemen I used to ask if they thought that the experience had been beneficial or a waste of time. It was interesting how the opinions varied: most tended to feel that it had been beneficial, a few, generally those who had tried to fight the system, didn't.

At this time the RAF was over manned in some commissioned ranks and the 'Golden Bowler' was available as an inducement to get volunteers to resign. I think Charles Inness would have persuaded me not to apply but he was no longer my CO and I duly applied. The reply from Air Ministry was fairly prompt: 'Services still required.' So I soldiered on, still spending more time dealing with the whingers to the detriment of those good airmen who genuinely needed help. A visit to the station by a friend working in an Air Ministry postings department prompted me to ask that if I requested early retirement would it be granted. He said he couldn't envisage a problem even though my 'Golden Bowler' request had been turned down. I made the application and it was granted, to be effective on my forty-fifth birthday. It was permissible to take early retirement, on a reduced pension, two years prior to the normal retiring age for the branch and rank of the applicant. The Treasury saved three hundred pounds on the 'Golden Bowler' and additional savings on a Wing Commander's pension. I could not understand the logic of accepting my early retirement having turned me down for the 'Golden Bowler' a few months earlier. However, it was my choice and it was more likely that I would get a job at forty-five, rather than at forty-seven, or maybe fifty had I been promoted to Group Captain. In fact I was employed by a wine company within weeks of leaving the RAF, although it must be admitted that a visit by a Kriegie friend who was the sales manager in the firm, helped.

I learnt just before I retired that had I not done so my posting was to have been to RAF Duxford, a Fighter Command Station which was to close down. In retrospect, my decision to retire early was obviously a wise one, for it is bad enough closing a station in a Command where one is known and respected, but quite another matter closing a station in another Command in which one is totally unknown. Running down and closing any station is painful. St Eval, which 217 Squadron opened in 1939, was particularly poignant for me and although I had had no close association with Duxford, I knew it for the historic part it had played in the Battle of Britain. I am pleased that I made the decision I did. Another factor was that I had managed to keep in flying practice at St Eval; I see from my flying logbook that I managed a total of two hundred and thirteen hours and twenty-five minutes, broken down as one hundred and thirteen hours and ten minutes on Shackletons, fifty-three hours and twenty-five minutes on the good old Anson, twenty hours and thirty-five minutes Chipmunk and five hours and twenty minutes Varsity. I cannot imagine that I would have been so fortunate

*My last dining-in night.*
*OC Flying, Wing Cdr. Holgate; OC Tech. Wing, Wing Cdr. Whipp;*
*Station Commander Group Capt. Whelan; AOC 19 Group AVM Gil Saye;*
*Wing Cdr. Tams, Admin., the author.*

in Fighter Command.

And so, on 16th January 1959, I left St Eval and retired from the Royal Air Force after almost twenty-nine marvellous years, ever thankful that I became a Trenchard Brat. There is no point in recording my career in the wine trade. I started selling in the Midlands, meeting many wine merchants with whom I got on well. I soon became a Regional Manager and retired at the age of sixty-two in 1976 in the Cotswolds, took up golf, and have been both Captain and President of my Club which was followed by the honour of being County President in 1984.

A lot has happened, but as far as I am concerned I am still a Trenchard Brat. Once a Brat always a Brat.

# *Appendix A*

## *A BRIEF HISTORY OF ROYAL AIR FORCE HALTON*

Halton has been associated with the Armed Forces since 1912 when manoeuvres were held to exercise the defence of London against an attack from the North. Alfred Rothschild offered assistance and hospitality to the defending forces, whose resources included three aircraft and an airship. This link between Halton and aviation has continued ever since.

During the Great War, the estate was used as an overflow for the Aldershot Garrison, and later became a Demobilisation Centre. The increasing use of air power on the Western Front led to the training of 'Boy Mechanics'; the demand was so great that, in 1917 alone, 14,000 were trained at Halton. Shortly after Rothschild's death in 1918, the estate was sold to the Army, and was soon passed over to the fledgling Royal Air Force. The far-sighted Lord Trenchard, realising the fundamental importance of highly-skilled aircraft engineers to his vision of a professional Air Force, decided to establish a centre of excellence. The vision became reality when, in 1920, No 1 School of Technical Training was founded at Halton. The Aircraft Apprentice Training Scheme, begun at Cranwell in the same year, was transferred to Halton in 1922.

The Second Word War brought an enormous increase in the scale of training at Halton, with up to 5,000 trainees being accommodated at any one time. In spite of its proximity to London, the Station remained undamaged throughout, with only two bombs falling on the estate, neither of which exploded. Peace brought an inevitable reduction in the pace of training in the Royal Air Force; however, the three-year apprenticeship remained at the core of technical training throughout the Cold War.

Halton's relationship with the Royal Family dates back to the first visit by a Sovereign when His Majesty King George VI visited the School in 1939. Later in the same year, His Majesty approved the official badge of No 1 School of Technical Training. The School hosted several further visits from members of the Royal Family, culminating in 1952 when the School was honoured with the award of a Sovereign's Colour from Her Majesty Queen Elizabeth II, in the first year of her reign.

Replacement Colours were presented by Her Royal Highness The Princess Margaret in 1968, and again by His Royal Highness The Duke of Kent in 1990. When No 1 School of Technical Training moved to Royal Air Force Cosford in 1994, the Colour accompanied it. Earlier this year, Her Majesty graciously accepted the Air Force Board's submission that Halton's unique position as 'Gateway to the Service' merited the recognition of our own Colour. Today's Graduating Course have the signal honour of forming the first Escort Squadron to the first Queen's Colour ever awarded to a Royal Air Force Station. Although the Apprentice Scheme ended in 1993, Halton's strong and continuing links with its past are emphasised by the presence here today of so many ex-Apprentices, including Sergeant Apprentice (later Wing Commander) F.M.A. Hines, who received the Colour from Her Majesty in 1952.

The recent reviews of the Armed Forces have led to major changes in the organisation of the Royal Air Force's ground training. However, the demise of the Apprentice Scheme, and the move to Cosford of the School, have not detracted from Halton's pivotal role in moulding and developing the Service's airmen and airwomen. Many of the young men and women graduating today, specifically those going into non-technical trades, will receive their trade training here. Later, all of those selected to become non-commissioned officers will receive command and management training here to fit them for their increasing supervisory responsibilities.

# *Appendix B*

## *NOTE ON THE RAF APPRENTICESHIP SCHEME*

Marshal of the RAF Lord Trenchard's aim in setting up the Apprenticeship scheme in the early 1920s was to produce an elite corps of highly skilled engineers who would provide the backbone of the newly formed Royal Air Force.

When Apprentice training in the RAF ceased in 1993, more than 50,000 had graduated, mostly from Halton. Over 20 per cent were commissioned, many achieving the highest ranks with several serving on the Air Force Board. One became the Chief of the Air Staff. During the Second World War, in which several thousands of ex-Apprentices gave their lives, one former Apprentice was awarded the VC, three the GC, thirty four the DSO, three the MC. Awards for bravery to ex-Apprentices currently total over 900, and 2,500 have been mentioned in dispatches. Over 1,200 have been honoured with State awards.

Ex-Apprentices have made their mark in later life with many becoming leaders of industry and commerce. One became a Bishop, another was head of the Metropolitan Police, one sits in the House of Lords and another is a well-known radio and TV presenter. Numerous ex-Apprentices have established international reputations in sport and athletics none more prominent than Group Captain Don Finlay who was captain of the British Olympic Team in 1936. Probably the most famous ex-Apprentice was Air Commodore Sir Frank Whittle, who gave the world the jet engine.

As Halton was acknowledged globally as the premier military aeronautical engineering college, many foreign and Commonwealth air forces sent young men to be trained there. Several of these subsequently reached the highest ranks in their respective Services and had distinguished careers afterwards. Air Marshal Yunis, for example, became President of Pakistan Airlines.

The vast majority of ex-Apprentices, however, became Senior NCOs and highly skilled engineers as Trenchard had originally intended. After the war, many thousands found their way into industry and the aerospace industry in particular. Today ex-Apprentices are to be found in every corner of the globe, in all walks of life. Several thousands are still serving in the RAF of course, and continue to attain the highest ranks.

# *Appendix C*

## *THE TRIBUTE: A SCULPTURE TO COMMEMORATE THE RAF HALTON APPRENTICE SCHEME*

To celebrate the 75th anniversary of the creation of the RAF Halton Apprentice Scheme, a sculpture was unveiled on the Station on 31 October 1997. The sculpture, designed by an ex-Apprentice, is a representation of the first workshop task undertaken by most Apprentices in their basic fitting phase. This exercise introduced Apprentices to the use of hand tools and developed their ability to work accurately to tight specifications. It involved

*The Tribute*

chipping the scale from a block of cast iron and filing it to precise dimensions before cutting an accurate inch square hole in the centre. A brass cube had then to be filed to fit precisely into the hole. The exercise remains an abiding memory for all ex-Apprentices, and makes a wryly appropriate commemoration!

The cast iron block is represented in Welsh slate. The brass cube is constructed in gilded York stone and is bolted on the front of the main structure. The Apprentices' arm badge, a four bladed propeller encircled by a brass ring (known colloquially as the 'wheel'), shown inscribed on the front of the sculpture, is also gilded. Etched on the sides of the main structure is an inscription explaining the reason for the sculpture and what it represents. The whole structure, set in a submerged concrete base, is erected in front of Kermode Hall, which was the Apprentices' school.

# Appendix D

## RECORD OF SERVICE

| UNIT | FROM | TO | COMMENTS |
|---|---|---|---|
| Halton | 09/09/30 | 18/08/33 | Aircraft Apprentice |
| Calshot | 19/08/33 | 12/06/36 | Engine Repair Shop |
| Brough | 12/07/36 | 05/09/36 | Basic Flying Training |
| Netheravon | 29/09/36 | 27/05/37 | Advanced Flying Training |
| Boscombe Down | 28/05/37 | 08/06/37 | 217 Squadron Anson |
| Tangmere | 09/06/37 | 04/12/37 | 217 Squadron Anson |
| Manston | 07/12/37 | 04/04/38 | Navigation Reconnaissance Course |
| Tangmere | 05/04/38 | 18/02/39 | 217 Squadron Anson |
| Leuchars | 19/02/39 | 03/03/39 | 217 Squadron Anson |
| Tangmere | 04/03/39 | 05/04/39 | 217 Squadron Anson |
| Thorney Island | 05/04/39 | 07/05/39 | Blenheim conversion. Blenheim Delivery Merignan Malta, Mersa Matruh Ishmalia, Hubbanyia |
| Tangmere | 08/05/99 | 25/08/39 | 217 Squadron Anson |
| Warmwell | 26/08/39 | 01/10/39 | 217 Squadron Anson |
| Tangmere | 02/10/39 | 07/10/39 | 217 Squadron Anson |
| St Eval | 08/10/39 | 25/05/40 | 217 Squadron Anson |
| Silloth | 27/05/40 | 24/06/40 | Beaufort Instructors' Course |
| St Eval | 26/06/40 | 15/02/41 | 217 Squadron Beaufort. Shot down over Brest |
| Germany | 15/02/41 | 08/05/45 | PoW Stalag Luft 1, Stalag Luft 3 |
| Rivenhall | 19/07/45 | 24/09/45 | Station Adjutant |
| Langham | 25/09/45 | 03/11/45 | 521 Squadron Long Range Met. - B17s |
| Chivenor | 03/11/45 | 21/06/46 | OC 517 Squadron Long Range Met. - Halifax |

| | | | |
|---|---|---|---|
| Northwood | 24/06/46 | 24/07/46 | Camp Commandant HQ Coastal Command |
| Halton | 25/07/46 | 02/02/47 | Princess Mary's RAF Hospital |
| Northwood | 03/03/47 | 05/10/48 | Camp Commandant HQ Coastal Command |
| Aldergrove | 05/10/48 | 20/10/48 | OC 224 Squadron |
| Gibraltar | 21/10/48 | 15/01/50 | OC 224 Squadron |
| Bracknell | 15/01/50 | 15/01/51 | RAF Staff College |
| Kuala Lumpur | 23/02/51 | 23/07/53 | Advanced HQ Malaya |
| Naphill | 28/09/53 | 14/01/54 | Org. 2 HQ Bomber Command |
| Brampton | 14/01/54 | 01/06/56 | Org. 1 HQ Tech Training Command Promoted to Wing Commander |
| St Eval | 02/06/56 | 19/02/59 | Wing Commander Admin. Retired from RAF |

# Appendix E

## Forms 540

| Aircraft Type and No. | Crew. | Duty. | Time Up. | Time Down. | Details of Sortie or Flight. |
|---|---|---|---|---|---|
| Beauforts. | | | | | |
| L 4907 | P/O F.A.B. TAMS 43076 | STRIKE | 16.20 | | Day strike against the [illegible] in BREST. |
| | F/O A.H. STRATFORD 70593 | | | | None of the machines returned. |
| | Sgt C. CRANNON, 550474 | | | | |
| | Sgt W.F. SHERIDAN [illegible] | | | | |
| L 9794 | P/O WILLIAMS C. J. L. | " | 16.35 | | |
| | Sgt A. RUSBY [illegible] | | | | |
| | Sgt R. COLLINS [illegible] | | | | |
| | Sgt J. THOMSON [illegible] | | | | |
| W.6493 | F/O R.W. GAIR [illegible] | | 16.40 | | |
| | Sgt J. WEBSTER [illegible] | | | | |
| | Sgt A. BRIDSON [illegible] | | | | |
| | Sgt W. ABBOTT [illegible] | | | | |

R.A.F. Form 540

See instructions for use of this form in K.R. and A.C.I., para. 2349, and War Manual, Pt. II., chapter XX., and notes in R.A.F. Pocket Book.

**OPERATIONS RECORD BOOK**

of (Unit or Formation) 217 Squadron.

Page No. 76.15

No. of pages used for day

| Place | Date | Time | Summary of Events | References to Appendices |
|---|---|---|---|---|
| St. Eval | 15/2/41. | 0605 | from 12,500' toward the S.W. The target was partly obscured by cloud, but 4 - 250 lb. A.P. bombs + 12 - 25 lb. incendiaries were dropped through a gap from 8000'.<br>Four bursts were seen on the North bank of the Loire and near the railway line. Few searchlights were seen when approaching the target, but these were in the distance.<br>Eleven Hampdens of No 50 Squadron arrived and 'gardened' on the 15/2. (see 540 for 14/2)<br>Photographs taken during the morning showed that the HIPPER was in Brest again. Judging by reports which may or may not be accurate, she had slipped out of Brest, scattered one of our convoys and sunk six ships, thus causing much grief in high quarters. Three aircraft of 217 were ordered out as soon as possible to make a daylight raid, and took off about 1630.<br>In the opinion of those best qualified to judge on the station, this was not a justifiable war risk. The damage which three machines armed with 500 lb. S.A.P. bombs at the target could inflict on the Hipper did not justify the very serious risk to the three machines and the small chance of making more than one direct hit at the most increased rather than decreased the inadvisability of the action.<br>The Photographic Reconnaissance Unit had reported that Brest was protected constantly by a fighter patrol, probably armed with cannon. The protective armament of the Brestfort consists of one [illegible] gun, one [illegible] gun, [illegible] [illegible] | |

# Appendix E

| Place | Date | Time | Summary of Events | References to Appendices |
|---|---|---|---|---|
| St. Eval. | 15/2/41 | | Cloud cover over the target would give protection from fighters, but low cloud base (on the particular occasion it was reported to be 1500') would mean that the attacking aircraft would have to go through flak from the ground worked on sound location, and flak from the HIPPER probably worked on sight. So the aircraft would have nearly 20 miles of flak to avoid in all, on the sound location work through cloud.<br>The Squadron C.O. Wing Cmdr. BOLLAND, represented that the risk was not justified both to Wing Cmdr. REVINGTON, Station C.O. & to Group Captain IKTIS, S.A.S.O. at 19 Group.<br>The three machines failed to return.<br>A change in the Establishment was notified to the Squadron about two months ago. It was decided to have one pilot, one observer & two wireless operator air gunners in each crew, in place of the old method of two pilots, one air gunner and one wireless operator. This has been done, and the Squadron has been busily engaged in training the new observers.<br>At first the feeling was against observers, in that their standard of navigation was not up to that of the pilots (all the observers posted to 217 were inexperienced in operational flying, and as a general rule, newly trained) but the observers have shown themselves to be keen and well up to their job, and are settling down well after the necessary training. The feeling now seems to be that if the Squadron is kept on bombing, the pilots would prefer observers; if the Squadron returns to general reconnaissance work, pilots would be better, because trained in G.R. work, while the observers are trained only in navigation & bombing.<br>Sqdn. Leader GRIEVE of H.Q.C.C. visited the Squadron to find out the feeling towards observers. | |

# *Appendix F*

## *AIRCRAFT AND HOURS FLOWN*

| TYPE | ENGINE | SINGLE ENG. DAY | SINGLE ENG. NIGHT | MULTI ENG. DAY | MULTI ENG. NIGHT |
|---|---|---|---|---|---|
| Blackburn B2 | de Havilland Gipsy | 51 40 | | | |
| Hawker Hart (TRS) | Rolls Royce Kestrel | 61 05 | | | |
| Hawker Audax | Rolls Royce Kestrel | 34 35 | 10 05 | | |
| Avro Tutor | Armstrong Siddeley Lynx | 8 55 | 7 05 | | |
| Avro Anson | Armstrong Siddeley Cheetah | | | 1366 35 | 149 50 |
| Bristol Blenheim | Bristol Mercury VIII | | | 28 10 | |
| Hawker Fury | Rolls Royce Kestrel | 0 25 | | | |
| Miles Magister | de Havilland Gipsy | 9 40 | | | |
| Lockheed Hudson | Wright Cyclone | | | 4 00 | |
| Bristol Beaufort | Bristol Taurus IIa | | | 127 55 | 66 55 |
| Handley Page Halifax | Bristol Hercules | | | 501 45 | 93 15 |
| Miles Martinet | Bristol Mercury | 14 35 | | | |
| Boeing B17 | Wright Cyclone | | | 39 00 | 63 05 |
| Percival Proctor | de Havilland Gipsy Queen | 30 30 | | | |
| Airspeed Oxford | Armstrong Siddeley Cheetah | | | 26 10 | 2 30 |
| Supermarine Spitfire | Rolls Royce Merlin 266 | 3 05 | | | |
| Douglas DC 3 Dakota | Wright Cyclone | | | 6 30 | |
| British Taylorcraft Auster | de Havilland Gipsy Major | 59 25 | 1 20 | | |
| de Havilland Chipmunk | de Havilland Gipsy Major | 27 15 | | | |
| Percival Prentice | de Havilland Gipsy Queen | 59 00 | 2 05 | | |
| Gloster Meteor VIII | Rolls Royce Derwent 8 | | | 6 25 | |
| English Electric Canberra | Rolls Royce Avon RA3 | | | 2 25 | |
| Vickers Varsity | Bristol Hercules 264 | | | 19 20 | |
| Avro Shackleton | Rolls Royce Griffon | | | 140 40 | 10 00 |
| TOTALS | | 360 10 | 20 35 | 2268 55 | 385 35 |

# *Appendix G*

I received a letter some years ago from Mr G. Haworth who had discovered my name and address from Roy Nesbit who is chairman of the Beaufort Aircrew Association and in it he says that he often wondered about the Beaufort which took the place of the Hampden originally briefed for the mission. With his permission I include extracts from his letter which gives some indication of the importance of this attack.

> When the Hampden crew was briefed it was stated, 'The Government are very worried by the serious losses being inflicted on our vital Atlantic convoys by surface raiders of the German Navy particularly the *Admiral Hipper*, a cruiser which recently sank seven out of a convoy of nineteen ships. This cruiser operates from Brest, tends to slip out to wreak havoc on a convoy approaching Britain, returns to Brest for supplies before again sailing to wreak more havoc on approaching convoys.

The letter goes on to say that Churchill is personally demanding action against this threat.

> A Hampden of 50 Sqn. was to carry a bomb load of two 2000 lb. and two 500 lb bombs, the heaviest bomb load ever carried by a Hampden. The plan was to dive bomb the *Hipper* which was known to be in Brest Harbour. A daylight attack was essential to sight the target, thus night attack was not considered. It was essential that the cloud base was above 4,500 feet as, even in the proposed dive, the velocity of the bombs would be insufficient if released above that height. The Hampden proceeded to St Eval, the nearest base to Brest, the day before and all was ready for the attack next morning. At Met. briefing cloud level was too low and the Hampden attack was cancelled.

And so it was that 3 Beauforts of 217 Sqn. were detailed for the attack just before dusk on the same day carrying armour-piercing bombs and I was to lead this small formation. Forms 540 tell the rest of the story at 'Appendix E'.

# *Appendix H*

Dept.Q.J.

P.357344/41/P.4.Casualties.

19 February, 1941.

Madam

I am commanded by the Air Council to express to you their great regret on learning that your husband, Pilot Officer Francis Adrian Burdett Tams, Royal Air Force, is missing as the result of air operations on 15th February, 1941.

I am to explain that this does not necessarily mean that he is killed or wounded, and if he is a prisoner of war he should be able to communicate with you in due course. Meanwhile enquiries will be made through the International Red Cross Society, and as soon as any definite news is received, you will be immediately informed.

In the event of any information regarding your husband being received by you from any source it would be appreciated if you would kindly communicate it immediately to the Air Ministry.

The Air Council desire me to express their sincere sympathy with you in your present anxiety.

I am, Madam,

Your obedient Servant,

Charles Evans.

Mrs M Tams,
Sunnyside,
Trenance Estate,
Mawganporth,
Cornwall.

No.217 Squadron
Royal Air Force
St Eval,
Nr. Wadebridge,
Cornwall.

Reference: 217S/2430/46/P2

16th February 1941

Dear Mrs Tams

I am writing to offer you the deepest sympathy of the Commanding Officer and all air crews in the sad news concerning your husband. I would first say that Wing Commander Bolland would apologise for not calling to see you since Saturday evening, but he has been called away on duty this morning, and I am sure he will call as soon as he possibly can.

I feel there is little I can put on paper that will express the loss we all feel now that your husband is not here. Wing Commander Bolland held him in great esteem as I hope and expect you know. His courage, ability and willingness for any job in the air were exemplary, and he was regarded by us all as an absolute stalwart.

I am sure you will realise that there is distinct hope that he will have been taken prisoner of war. In certain previous circumstances we have been told through the International Red Cross at Geneva that our airmen have been held as prisoners, and I sincerely hope that this is the case on this occasion. You may rest assured that wherever you are the Wing Commander or his staff will be quick to inform you of any news that may be received.

I feel, and hope that you do also, that you have friends about you, but I would be pleased if you would write to one of us - the C.O. or any officer in the Squadron - if there is any way in which we can help you. Please do not hesitate.

Please accept the sincerest sympathy of all members of this Squadron, of which your husband was, without doubt, a popular member.

Yours sincerely

R. B. King
Squadron Leader, for Wing Commander,
Commanding No. 217 Squadron, St. Eval.

Mrs Tams,
Sunnyside,
Mawgan Porth,
Newquay, Cornwall.

No.217 Squadron,
Royal Air Force,
St Eval,
Nr. Wadebridge,
Cornwall.

Reference: 217S/2430/46/P2

22nd February, 1941

Dear Lt Tams

I was very pleased to receive your letter of the 18th February.

I am sorry indeed to confirm the news that your son has been reported as missing. You will, being a Service man, appreciate that I cannot give complete details but I will say what I can.

Pilot Officer Tams was the Captain of an aircraft, and in fact the leader of a small flight which left this aerodrome at 16.30 hours on Saturday, the 15th instant, to carry out a day-light bombing raid on enemy occupied territory. As W/T communication is necessary at certain stages of the Flight, and no communication of any description was received from any of the aircraft, the assumption is that they were forced to land either by anti aircraft fire or engine failure. The anti-aircraft fire supposition is probably correct, particularly as a German communique stated that two aircraft had been shot down. I am reluctant to give you any place names, but I would affirm, as I have already told your son's wife, that there is distinct hope that they will have been taken prisoners of war.

No doubt you are aware that the Air Ministry is eventually informed of the particulars of prisoners of war, and I would add that the Unit is informed almost as quickly. As you have now contacted me I can assure you that I will inform you of any information I receive as soon as I can.

I would like you to know how much we miss your son. I have no hesitation in telling you that he was fearless, unhesitating and a first class pilot in our particular line. He was a stalwart in this Squadron, and I as his Commanding Officer particularly grieve to lose such a pilot, and his brother pilots to lose a popular comrade.

His wife is bearing up admirably, and was yesterday travelling back to Barnham. If there is any way in which I can be of service to either of you please do not hesitate to write.

Yours sincerely
(G. A. Bolland) Wing Commander, Commanding
No. 217 Squadron, St. Eval.

Royal Air Force Station
St Eval
Nr. Wadebridge,
Cornwall.

27th February, 1941

Dear Mrs Tams

I was delighted to be able to send you a telegram last night informing you that your husband was a prisoner of war. The signal which we received, a copy of which I enclose with this letter, states, as you will see, that Flying Officer Stratford and Sergeant Cannon are also safe although, unfortunately, both your husband and Flying Officer Stratford have been wounded. I feel sure though that Pilot Officer Tams, with his excellent constitution, will make a quick recovery, and I look forward to hearing more of him and meeting you both again in happier times.

I would repeat that if there is anything I can do for you at any time I will be only too pleased to do so.

Best of luck,

Yours

A. P. Revington

Mrs Tams
The Cot
Down View Road
Barnham
Bognor Regis
Sussex

# *Appendix I*

From: Air Vice-Marshal F.R.W. Scherger, CBE, DSC, AFC
Air Headquarters,
Malaya.
R.A.F. Changi,
Singapore 17.

June 1953

My dear Frank,

I was pleased to see that your excellent work at Advanced Air Headquarters has been rewarded. You have done much to promote cooperation and goodwill between our Service, the Army and the Civil Forces. Congratulations and my best wishes for the future.

Yours sincerely,

F. R. W. Scherger

Sqn.Ldr. F.A.B. Tams, OBE,
Advanced A.H.Q. Malaya,
KUALA LUMPUR

From: Air Chief Marshal Sir John W. Baker, KCB, MC, DFC, ADC
Ministry of Supply

St. Giles Court,
1-13 St. Giles High Street,
London W.C.2

Museum 3644
Ext.1046

C.A./1/6

2nd January 1954

My dear Tams

I was delighted to see your promotion in the New Year list. My warmest congratulations and every good wish for the future.

Please don't bother to answer this.

Yours sincerely,

John W. Baker

Wing Commander F.A.B. Tams,
Headquarters, Technical Training Command,
Royal Air Force,
Brampton Grange,
Brampton, Hunts.

## *Appendix I*

From: Air Marshal G. H. Mills, CB, DFC

Headquarters
Bomber Command
RAF High Wycombe
Bucks

Telephone: High Wycombe 2000

BC/903/CinC: 1st June, 1953:

My dear Tams

I was extremely pleased to see your name in today's Honours List. It was awfully good to see your extremely hard and devoted work recognised.

Yours sincerely

Squadron Leader F.A.B. Tams, OBE
Advanced Air Headquarters,
Royal Air Force,
Kuala Lumpur,
MALAYA:

P.S. Hope to see you home before long.

G.

# *Appendix J*

Summary of Anson flights as Squadron Leader Ops at Advanced Air HQ Malaya.

- Recce in the Kluang area in support of 2/6 Gurkhas with the Commissioner of police and three police officers
- Taiping – Butterworth – Kuala Lumpur
- Recce with Major Huddleston in Kluang area for 2/6 Gurkhas
- Recce with GOC in Kluang area for 2/6 Gurkhas
- Recce with GOC, Commissioner of police, Chief of Staff and GSO1 Headquarters Malaya in Kluang area
- Various flights to Ipoh, Taiping, Kluang, Tengah, Khota Bahru, Seletar, Changi and Bayan Lipis
- Taking Major-General Urquart to Ipoh, Butterworth, Taiping and Kuala Lumpur

Flights in the Advanced Air HQ Auster from the AOP Base at Noble Field

- Bentong – Raub – Benta – Segamat – Seremban – Malacca – Kluang – Muar

As an observer on

- Supply drops in KL based Dakotas
- A Brigand air strike
- A Meteor air strike
- Dragonfly rescues
- Dragonfly spraying of CT jungle gardens

All of which provided me with experience to aid me in my Operations role.

*Appendix J*

During the posting I made visits to:

- The King's African Rifles (I believe Idi Amin was there as RSM)
- The Maori Regiment
- 40 and 42 Commandos
- A number of Gurkha units
- Various Police units

Total flying time as Squadron Leader Ops:
Anson 74 hours 55 minutes (45 minutes at night)
Dakota as 2nd Pilot 6 hours 30 minutes
Auster 59 hours 25 minutes